Aconcagua

Aconcagua

The Invention of Mountaineering on America's Highest Peak

Joy Logan

The University of Arizona Press • Tucson

The University of Arizona Press

www.uapress.arizona.edu

Library of Congress Cataloging-in-Publication Data

Logan, Joy.
Aconcagua : the invention of mountaineering on America's highest peak / Joy Logan.
p. cm.
Includes bibliographical references and index.
ISBN 978-0-8165-2950-6 (pbk. : alk. paper) 1. Mountaineering—Argentina—Aconcagua, Mount. 2. Aconcagua, Mount (Argentina)—Discovery and exploration. 3. Aconcagua, Mount (Argentina)—Description and travel. I. Title.
GV199.44.A72A2647 2011
796.52209826'4—dc23 2011025184

Publication of this book is made possible in part by the proceeds of a permanent endowment created with the assistance of a Challenge Grant from the National Endowment for the Humanities, a federal agency.

Manufactured in the United States of America on acid-free, archival-quality paper containing a minimum of 30% post-consumer waste and processed chlorine free.

16 15 14 13 12 11 6 5 4 3 2 1

Contents

Illustrations

Unless otherwise noted, all photographs are by the author.

Acknowledgments

First and foremost I am especially grateful to all the *andinistas* of Mendoza, the Aconcagua *guardaparques*, the doctors, guides, base-camp workers, *arrieros* (muleteers), the Hotel Refugio staff, and the international expeditionary members who generously offered their time and cooperation during this study. While I dare not name them all here, I offer each and every one of them my heartfelt thanks and appreciation. Without them there would have been no project. In particular, though, I would like to thank María Rosa Zucchelli, Armando Párraga, and the Mendoza Patrulla de Rescate de Alta Montaña for making my first visit to Plaza de Mulas a most remarkable experience for any high-altitude novice.

Although this project built from my previous work on gender, transculturation, and nationalisms, it clearly marked a new direction for my research. I am most appreciative of the University of Hawaiʻi Research Relations Fund and the University of Hawaiʻi Humanities Endowment Fund for having faith in the merit of this project and for partially funding my initial fieldwork. I would also like to offer my most sincere gratitude to the Andean scholar Marcia Stephenson, whose own work has inspired me to think outside the academic box of my discipline, so to speak. Marcia's professional encouragement and advice have been invaluable in helping me conceptualize the framing and completion of this project. I also thank the University of Arizona Press and the UAP editors for their help and guidance as I finalized the manuscript for publication.

To my colleagues and friends across the globe I would like to express my affectionate appreciation for their enduring support throughout the varying stages of this project. Paul Chandler has been steadfast and patient in assisting with the practical exigencies of the preparation for fieldwork and the completion of a manuscript. María del Mar Torreblanca López has consistently offered first-rate technical and editorial advice, all tempered with an exuberant sense of humor. Bill and Melodee Metzger, whose friendship I can only describe as priceless, have always been the first to offer encouragement. I thank them for their thoughtful reflections and insightful feedback shared over many evenings on the lanai in Mānoa, and I am eternally grateful for their careful and detailed reading of the final manuscript. My warmest thanks go to my mother, Evy, in San Diego, for letting me cloister myself away in her house to write during the summer and for providing a West Coast staging area for my many trips to Argentina. And in Mendoza, I have always been able to count on Greta Verstraete, Lissi Entre Ríos, Daniel Contreras, and Ana Laura Fernández, who have my deepest thanks for their inventive and resourceful assistance and for their stalwart encouragement and support.

Finally, my greatest debt lies with the Mendocino mountain guides, and my wonderful friends, Juan Araya and Pablo Gurrieri. Theirs were the stories that first inspired me to envision this project and they have walked with me, literally, every step of the way to get here. I am grateful to them beyond words for their unyielding assistance on and off the mountain, for their unwavering friendship, which I will always treasure, and most importantly, for introducing me to el Aconcagua.

Introduction

Recuperating Bodies, Recovering Texts

When you speak of Aconcagua, you also speak of death.
—FERNANDO SORIANO (2009)[1]

"Where are they?" was the question I felt compelled to ask my guide, Pablo, when I finally stood before the 3,000-meter vertical wall of the majestic South Face of Mount Aconcagua. I had heard the story many times before and had been moved by the memorial in the Andinista Cemetery, located near the trailhead to the Aconcagua Provincial Park. Whether out of respect, a sense of compassion, morbid curiosity, or a combination of all three, I asked where the frozen, lifeless bodies of the three young Brazilians were hanging on Aconcagua's icy wall. Pablo indicated a general area on the mountain, although I already knew not to expect to see anything but snow and white. The bodies of Mozart Catão, Alexandre Oliveira, and Othon Leonardos cannot be seen from the vantage point of El Mirador, the lookout for Plaza Francia and the South Face. This viewpoint is where mountaineering expeditions for the Northern Route on Aconcagua stop to rest and eat lunch during their first day of acclimatization and this is where Pablo and I sat with our sandwiches as he detailed the history of the south summit. In response to my question, Pablo retold the story of how in 1998 three of Brazil's top climbers were hit by an avalanche as they attempted to reach Aconcagua's pinnacle by following one of the most technical and difficult routes on the mountain. Othon Leonardos, who suffered two broken legs, radioed back to base camp to report the logistics of the fall as he and his unconscious teammates lay trapped on the side of the mountain. He spoke to his base-camp team for several hours as he waited to die. The bodies of the hapless Brazilians have not been recovered and probably never will be.[2]

Figure I.1. Argentina. (Map by World Sites Atlas [sitesatlas.com]).

It is not gratuitous that I have decided to introduce my examination of the social and cultural history of Aconcagua in Argentina's central Andes with this well-known tale of frozen death on the mountain's treacherous South Face. It is that threat of death, that lure of high-stakes adventure where life itself is wagered, that has most vividly created mountaineering's mystique. And it was my query of this mystique, which has come to give definition to Aconcagua in the twenty-first century and to produce both material and representational consequences for Mendoza, Argentina, that provided the impetus for my research on the evolution of the social, cultural, and economic meanings and uses of the highest peak in the Americas.

I first began to imagine the contours of this study while spending a summer evening under the stars, drinking mate with local mountain guides, at Puente del Inca, the staging area for the Northern Route of Aconcagua. The guides' yarns and anecdotes of camaraderie, spirituality, adventure, risk, poignancy, and heroism on the mountain piqued my interest, not only with respect to their reasons for choosing this profession but also with regards to the everyday practices of their way of life. However, it was especially their suggestion that I visit the nearby Andinista Cemetery and their insistence that I had to learn about death on the mountain in order to better understand the local life of Aconcagua mountaineering that led me to muse about what other kinds of stories such mountain tales as theirs might hold.

In my first visit to the Cementerio de los Andinistas I became fascinated with trying to piece together the mountain's history from those other storylines that, from the start, interested me more than the actual year count of individual life spans documented on the tombstones. It was those barely audible accounts whispered by the gravemarkers of Aconcagua's fallen, those that spoke to me of the local community's changing, and sometimes conflicting, relationships with the mountain, that I was moved to hear more clearly. The traces, echoes, and memories of those stories were what led me to begin the research for this book.

So starting this introduction with one of the most sensationalist and lurid aspects of the history of Aconcagua mountaineering, the death of the Brazilians on the South Face, is a natural point of departure for several reasons; first it was one of the tales that initially sent me to visit the Andinista Cemetery and envision this study. Moreover, I could also rationalize the need to first characterize mountaineering's mystique in order to question how Aconcagua figures into it. Nonetheless, this initial curiosity about Aconcagua does not accurately depict the way that my study subsequently developed or the guiding rationale of this book. Beginning with this tale

Figure I.2. A memorial in the Cementerio de los Andinistas to one of Brazil's most renowned climbers, Mozart Catão, who died in 1998 on Aconcagua's South Face.

of death not only allows me to humanize the mountain's sports history, but it also provides a point of departure for considering the ways in which Aconcagua mountaineering intersects, reflects, disrupts, and constructs concepts of nation, gender, ethnicity, adventure, modernity, and tourism.

Despite my cogent personal justifications, or at least they seem so to me, of starting a mountaineering-themed book with references to death, I know that it is actually a well-worn trope, already exploited by Sherry B. Ortner's (1999) invocation of death in the title and the introduction of her seminal study *Life and Death on Mt. Everest: Sherpas and Himalayan Mountaineering*. It is an undeniable fact that the notoriety of tragic death has characterized the idea of mountain climbing ever since its rise to popularity in Europe in the mid-nineteenth century. When the British explorer Edward Whymper made the first summit of the Matterhorn in July 1865, it was not just his accomplishment of reaching the top of the Swiss peak, but also the horrible toll that the endeavor took when four of Whymper's companions slipped during the descent and fell to their deaths that made the moment such a memorable and pivotal one in mountaineering's origins. In fact, much of the literature that chronicled the European first ascents of the mid-nineteenth century included just such tales of frightening accidents that created a public stir and drew attention to mountaineering (Johnston and Edwards 1994, 461–462; Nunn 1987, 136). The celebrity of the Matterhorn summit and the resulting tragedy were also magnified by the story of the long-standing competition between Whymper and John Tyndall, a race that Whymper finally won on his successful but disastrous ninth attempt to climb the mountain, chronicled in his *Scrambles amongst the Alps* (1893).[3] The context of how success and tragedy played out in the aftermath of that first Matterhorn summit points to issues, tensions, and forces that would come to imbue mountaineering with a modernist set of social and cultural associations. This meant a far-reaching acclaim that would serve to embolden a sense of national pride (in this case, British), sketch the contours of adventure, and tout modern manly virtues as gallant effort, selfless sacrifice, and heroic valor in the face of peril.

In the late twentieth century other issues also became salient in the context and process of mountaineering. While effects of globalization, change in expedition sponsorship, and the commercialization of mountaineering brought about differences in the way celebrity, nation, identity, gender, and adventure came to be understood in association with the sport, the salacious highlighting of death and stories of survival have remained a constant in its characterization. The tragic loss of eight lives on Everest on May 10, 1996, is a case in point. The events of that day have spawned a long list of best-selling books (most notably Jon Krakauer's *Into Thin Air: A Personal Account of the Everest Disaster*), journal articles, a TV movie, and even the introduction for Ortner's (1999) anthropological study.[4] In many ways all these narratives served to reposit the same kinds of considerations that spurred the earliest stories of mountaineering. They reflect several common social and psychological reactions to mountaineering: a fascination with those individuals who seemingly flaunt death by choosing to climb a mountain, a curiosity about how the men and women who survived the unsurvivable fought for life against all odds, and a hunger for imagining both the acts of heroism and scenes of dying. But these narratives of the Everest disaster also do much more. They engage in a contest to lay blame wherever they suspect it: on competitive personal and agency tensions that may have caused guides to make mistakes out of pride and arrogance, on the commercialization of adventure that may have allowed physically unprepared, but paying, customers to slow down and jeopardize the entire expedition, and on the need for cost-effectiveness that may have overridden prudent judgment based on good mountaineering sense. These narratives also allow concerns to glean through about the mountaineering industry's possibly exploitative relationships with local peoples and its damage to ecological systems.

All of these kinds of charges and speculations were more recently brought to the fore in Mendoza itself in Aconcagua's 2009 summer climbing season when the Mendocino mountain saw a loss of five lives within the first two months, as compared to only one during the entire 2008 season. Two of the deaths occurred during a horrific snowstorm, when a Mendocino-born guide living in the United States, with minimal experience on Aconcagua, continued to lead his group of Italian climbers, who had employed him via the Internet, up the nontechnical Normal, or North, Route toward the summit of Aconcagua later in the day than park rangers, the rescue squad, and experienced guides would recommend. Once at the summit the weather changed drastically and in the sudden whiteout the group became disoriented and began to descend down across the treacherous and technical route of the Polish Glacier rather than to return in the direction from which they had come. The guide eventually radioed for help and thus began the largest rescue operation that Aconcagua has seen. The rescue squad and park rangers, and also private support agencies and guides, risked their lives in the blizzard, having to first summit the peak braving furious winds and paralyzing cold in order to cross over the mountain's top to descend nearly 600 meters to where the wayward expedition had wandered. By the time the group was reached, one of them had already fallen to her death and the guide later died of pulmonary and cerebral edema during the rescue attempt.

The Mendocino news reports at first recounted and praised the heroics of the rescue team that brought three of the five stranded mountaineers back alive. A month later, however, the media vociferously questioned the rescuers' actions when a three-minute video of the nearly thirty-hour operation was unofficially released and created a very contentious public and international uproar. The video, which shows a failed attempt by five rescuers to bring the guide to his feet, concludes with their attempts at pushing and pulling the stricken man by a rope as he attempts to crawl up the slope. It was played repeatedly on national news and made its way to other television stations around the globe, as well as to YouTube and numerous Internet news and blog sites. Heated arguments began about whether or not the rescue squad had acted appropriately and ethically in assisting the agonizing guide and if they had or had not left him behind to die on the mountain. Claims by mountaineering experts of the valor, selflessness, and strength of spirit of the rescue squad and volunteers countered the allegations by others of selfish, apathetic, and immoral actions on the rescuers' part and of the folly of mountaineering in general. What became clear in the February 2009 media scandal was that Mendoza itself now clearly recognized the cleavage between local social and practical understandings of what the mountain and mountaineering mean to the region. The arguments that followed in the media-driven tumult not only refuted the accusations that the rescuers "stood around as if they were in a café on the corner" by explaining that at nearly 7,000 meters of altitude in blizzard conditions no one is physically able to perform optimally and that anyone who would assume so "doesn't know anything about the mountain."[5] Mendocino-based sources also especially debated the cost to the provincial budget of having to provide regular and emergency rescue services, including air support, for international mountaineers, and argued about whether the role of the government should increase or diminish in terms of administering services for the mountaineering industry in general. Out of these debates other nagging concerns also arose again in the media coverage about the image of Argentina and Mendoza conveyed by the mountaineering industry, worries about the cost to the ecology of the provincial park exacted by mountaineering, and strident reiterations of the importance of Aconcagua mountaineering to the province's summer tourism economy.

From Whymper's summit in 1865 to the 1996 Everest tragedy and the disaster-ridden summer of 2009 on Aconcagua, all of those concerns, worries, speculations, fascinations, accusations, and dreams that inform the social and cultural interpretations of the mountain spew forth from mountaineering tales of death. Such tales also speak of the meanings of adventure, the cult of the hero, the dynamics of global-local relationships, and the rise of the tourism industry. It is the innate multiplicity of these tales that justify, at least to me, my introduction of this study by eliciting memories of the disastrous expedition of the Brazilians in 1998.

While the tragic, icy bodies of the three Brazilians remain hidden and ghostly on Aconcagua, the understandings of adventure and sacrifice that they represent are very much present in the history, practices, and cultural valuing of the mountain and mountaineering in Mendoza, Argentina. But more explicitly, the specific tale of the Brazilians' heroic and doomed attempt to scale one of the most difficult walls in the Andes is actually recounted nearly every day during climbing season at El Mirador, with the South Face as backdrop. It is there at nearly 4,200 meters of altitude that guides of commercial mountaineering and trekking expeditions, especially those from Mendoza, in an effort to entertain, inform, and motivate their clients, play off romantic notions of the connections between individual self-realization, spiritual transcendence, perilous physical challenge, and national prestige by invoking the horrific and poignant story of the Brazilians on the mountain wall. Those unseen bodies generate powerful narratives of danger, risk, and sacrifice that heighten the expectation of adventure for climbers setting off to summit the highest peak in the Americas, albeit via the much less technical, more accessible, and much safer Northern Route. The Mendocino guides, in their telling and re-telling of the story of the Brazilians' climb to death, enact an autoethnographic performance that also re-scripts the mountain, whose first summit was claimed by a British expedition and its Swiss guide in 1897, as both South American and Mendocino. In defining autoethnography, Mary Louise Pratt refers to those instances when "colonized subjects undertake to represent themselves in ways that *engage with* the colonizer's terms," or in other words, autoethnographic texts are those constructed by subaltern subjectivities in response to or in dialogue with metropolitan representations (2008, 9). This is how I interpret the storytelling performances of the Mendocino guides as they position themselves and narratives of local and South American participations on the South Face in direct dialogue with the nineteenth- and twentieth-century feats of Europeans who took Aconcagua as their own and in which early local Mendocino cooperation was absent or unacknowledged. The Mendocino guides, standing on their personal authority of experience, knowledge, and their physical presence on the rocky, barren ground of El Mirador, tell the history of the South Face by including the tale of the Brazilians and highlighting stories of summits and routes made by local mountaineers to complement the stories of the French and Italian initial, most notorious claims to the South Face. Thus, these local guides insert themselves, Mendocino tradition, and South America back into the long-standing record of Anglo-European dominance on Aconcagua.

By characterizing the most dramatic and biggest sacrifice on Aconcagua as South American and telling little-known (outside of Argentina) stories to their international clientele about Mendoza's most successful climbers, the Generation of the 80s, the Mendocino guides reterritorialize the mountain as South American and Argentine. This narrative reterritorialization is a fluid and nonlimiting overlay that does not belie the hybridity of the mountain's identity or the multiple transnational locations of Aconcagua in global collective memory. As part of the autoethnographic text that the Mendocino guides weave, this re-telling and re-taking of the mountain is illustrative of the transculturative mergings of history and culture that construct Aconcagua as South American, Argentine, and Mendocino while

Figure I.3. Aconcagua's South Face as seen from El Mirador. The first Mendocinos to summit via this nearly 3,000-meter wall were Danielón Rodríguez, Lito Sánchez, Alejandro Randis, and Domingo Alvarez in 1986. Along with the Colombian Manuel Barrios, they followed the route set by the French expedition in 1954.

also acknowledging it as a site of European (principally, British, French, Italian, Swiss and German) and, most recently, North American traditions.

Locating Aconcagua

What exactly is Aconcagua, then? And where is it located? Mount Aconcagua, geographic coordinate on the map of Incan and Spanish empire building, of General José de San Martín's heroic advance to continental independence, and of Charles Darwin's youthful scientific exploration of South America, is most recognized across the globe today as a location for international mountaineering and adventure tourism. As the highest peak in the Western hemisphere (6,962 meters), Aconcagua, in the central Andes of Mendoza, Argentina, forms part of the circuit of the Seven Summits, a mountaineering route that contains the highest peak on each of the continents. The peaks of the Seven Summits serve as magnets that annually attract thousands of mountaineers and trekkers from all over the world. As part of an itinerary of international mountain adventure, Aconcagua, together with the nearby Uspallata Valley, has become one of the most important destinations for Mendoza's travel industry and is considered a top attraction for international travelers during the austral summer season, which is November through March.

Conquest, revolution, and exploration have forged the variable relationships that Mendoza has held with its high mountain region, and the momentous forces of these three movements have provided Mendocino mountaineering with the origin stories that have come to fashion its own self-definition. The Incas conquered the area, which marked the southernmost boundary in Argentine territory of the Tahuantinsuyo, or Incan Empire, during the reign of Tupac Inca (1471–1493). Although Incan domination of the region was brief, approximately from 1475 to 1532 (Schobinger 2001d, Bárcena 2001), the empire successfully incorporated the native peoples of Cuyo into its southernmost extension, the Collasuyo, and left behind material signs of its presence there in the vestiges of *tambos* (way stations), roads, and spiritual beliefs. Aconcagua's importance for the empire has been a special point of conjecture since the discovery of an Incan mummy there in 1985 by mountaineers, which also has served to posit an Americanist and indigenous connection to Aconcagua mountaineering.

Patriotic zeal has also colored Mendoza's valuing of the Aconcagua region as a symbol of the heights to which the nation would rise to secure Latin American independence. General José de San Martín, known as the Liberator, led his Army of the Andes in 1817 in its historic and monumental crossing of the Cordillera, a multipronged attack through the Andes of San Juan and Mendoza (skirting Aconcagua), to defeat the Spanish in Chile and to clear his way to Lima and the combining of forces with Simón Bolívar. San Martín's feat is routinely referenced within Mendocino mountaineering circles, not only as a symbol of the sacrifice and valor necessary to conquer the Andes, but also as a modern and local origin of mountaineering that predates the first European mountaineer-explorers.

The most noted nineteenth-century European explorer of the Aconcagua zone and the one most proudly heralded by Mendocinos was Charles Darwin, who visited both the city and province of Mendoza in 1835. Darwin traveled from the Pacific coast of Chile across the Andes through the southern Portillo pass to the capital city of Mendoza and returned to Chile via the northern provincial pass that borders Aconcagua. He chronicled his journey in *The Voyage of the Beagle* (1839). Darwin's exploration of the area, conjoined with the magnitude of Darwin's reputation in Western science and thought, has held great significance for local mountaineers. Exploration of Aconcagua became a clear marker of Western modernity and Mendocino mountaineers have come to see themselves as Darwin's heirs in this respect. In addition, the invocation of Darwin as a precursor of Aconcagua mountaineering has served the mountaineering industry to foment that dream of experiencing adventure and exploring the unknown that has motivated the development of mountaineering across the globe.

The first expeditions to the Aconcagua zone for specific mountaineering purposes were made by late nineteenth-century European explorers nearly fifty years after Darwin, and except for guiding and portering assistance by local muleteers, or *arrieros*, they actually registered little effect on Mendoza's lifestyle. Today that story has changed for a twenty-first-century Mendoza that has refashioned its sociocultural fabric to benefit its ambitious promotion of mountaineering, now a primary component of its tourism industry. Reminders of mountaineering's prominence lace the capital city center in the form of mountaineering agencies and gear shops. In terms of touristic intake, the business of providing support, transportation, and lodging for mountaineering clientele, especially since the 1980s, has become an extremely profitable one for local entrepreneurs and hostelry. Mountain guiding has become a very viable, if not lucrative, career choice in Mendoza and has become institutionalized within the provincial educational system. The Provincial Department of Natural and Renewable Resources, as the recipient of Aconcagua revenue, also reaps the benefits of the Aconcagua climbing industry. Even the Mendoza police force has its hand in Aconcagua mountaineering as it staffs Aconcagua's specialized High Altitude Rescue Squad. From university students and rural workers seeking summer employment, to doctors seeking a bit of summer adventure, Mendocinos from all walks of life intervene in the Aconcagua mountaineering project. In sum, mountaineering in Mendoza has become a social, cultural, and economic institution with far-reaching consequences for education, law enforcement, the tourism industry, employment options, and natural resources within the province. The social cross-section of Mendoza that mountaineering embodies also eloquently serves as a medium in which complex issues of identity politics play out across negotiations between the local and the global.

Argentina: High Expectations

In 1878 the historian Alfred Joseph Deberle wrote that "Argentina seemed to be called to rival the United States of the North, not only for the richness of its territory, but also for the activity of its inhabitants and for the development of its industry and the importance of its commerce" (1878, 231). It was into such an Argentina of great developmental expectations that Aconcagua mountaineering made its debut. During the following decades, heavy European immigration, increased foreign capital investment, and incipient industrialization projected a modern and progressive Argentina, but one that also came to be racked by social strife, labor conflicts, and civil and political unrest throughout most of the early twentieth century. By midcentury the populist leader Juan Perón, who nationalized many of the industries and projects that foreign, especially British, capital had underwritten earlier, spearheaded another big wave of collective pride and belief in Argentine potential, modernity, and westernization. Deposed by a military coup in 1955, Perón returned from exile to the presidency in 1973 and to an Argentina being pulled apart by militant factions on both the left and the right. His death in 1974 left Argentina in the ineffectual hands of his third wife, María Estela (Isabelita), and led to the eventual overthrow by the Argentine armed forces. This period of military rule (1976–1983), the Process of National Reorganization (el Proceso), is also commonly known as the Dirty War, in which the military kidnapped, tortured, and murdered approximately 30,000 of its own citizens in an effort to expunge what it considered to be subversive (socialist, communist, populist) elements of society. The 1982 war with Great Britain over the Falkland Islands that ended in Argentine defeat spelled the end of the military's rule. The return to democracy in 1983 again brought anticipation of peace and prosperity, but by the end of the decade hyperinflation and an exorbitant foreign debt brought Argentina to its knees. The restoration of the Peronist party to power in 1989 seemed to herald a new direction of economic stability for Argentina that halted dramatically at the end of 2001 with the devaluation of the peso, a revolving door of five presidents in three months, the closing of banks, the governmental issuing of scrip to pay federal employees, and a disillusioned and desperate populace decrying where the bright and future Argentina was that had once been so confidently heralded. Mountaineering's development from the nineteenth century to the twenty-first century has negotiated and reflected all these historical and contemporary forces that have transformed Argentina from a potential modern rival of the United States to a "third-tier" country struggling to avoid being labeled a "risk nation" for globalized capital.

Originally, Mendocino mountaineering emerged as an outgrowth of the development of Western modernity, generally defined as the rise and consolidation of industrialization, capitalism, urbanization, the nation-state, and the West's identification with the concept of modernity itself (Hall 2000, 45). Belief in modernity assumed that history would progress linearly, with the help of advancements in the social and natural sciences, toward a better future (Castro-Gómez 2002, 28). An outgrowth of modernity's project was its "naturalized" drive to accumulate knowledge (and capital) in order to subject nature and space to human will (Castro-Gómez 2002, 26–27; Bayers 2003, 4–5), which is what both spurred and justified Anglo-European imperialist expansion and early Mendocino mountaineering.

A closer look at how mountaineering developed from exuberant expectations of modernity through unsettling postmodern distress illustrates how neocolonialism has framed the construction of both the image and the materiality of Argentina. Neocolonialism, in the broadest sense, refers to the limitations of an independent state's ability to develop itself due to economic and political pressures and machinations from dominant or imperialistic external powers. According to Pratt (2008), the neocolonial state, in taking on the values of the metropole and seeking to fulfill them, "is unable to do so, yet unable to exit the system . . . norms generated elsewhere cannot be implemented where one is, but cannot be refused either. One is forced to be a second-class member of a club in which membership is not optional" (226). Mendoza's move to embrace mountaineering on Aconcagua exemplifies this dynamic; it emerged from within a modern system of values that symbolically emblazoned beliefs of European natural and national superiority in mountaineering endeavors in the Andes and in which Mendocinos decidedly figured as second-class citizens, if they figured at all.

Mountaineering Zones of Contact

Through the lens of mountaineering this book intends to bring into focus the histories and modes of European imperial expansion that transformed and codified the Southern Cone in the late nineteenth century and to direct attention to how constructions of gender, race, ethnicity, and regional and national identities have depended upon Mendoza's dialoguing with, integrating, and amending European conventions as it has modified its own self-conceptualizations. In other words, examining the development of the mountaineering industry in this way provides a stage on which to lay bare the workings of transculturation and to illustrate the socioeconomic and cultural dynamics of neocoloniality, globalization, and international tourism.

In thinking about the usefulness of transculturation for cultural critique I have been most influenced by Pratt's definition and usage of the concept, a process that takes place in the contact zones, "social spaces where disparate cultures meet, clash, and grapple with each other, often in highly asymmetrical relations of domination and subordination," and in which marginalized groups do not just assimilate hegemonic meanings and practices, but rather, as part of the transculturative process, "select and invent from materials transmitted to them by a dominant or metropolitan culture" (2008, 7). Pratt's understanding of transculturation suggests the urgency in examining culture and narrative from more than just the dominant perspective, which serves to explain this book's multiple foci and diversity of subject matter in the consideration of how mountaineering developed on Aconcagua. However, by employing the concept of transculturation as a theoretical frame in the manner of Pratt, I cannot ignore other considerations of the dynamics of the model and the problematics that it may evoke, especially in terms of indigenous identity politics. Transculturation, first coined by Fernando Ortiz (2003) in 1947 in his study of the sociocultural repercussions of the tobacco and sugar industries on Cuban society, was taken up and retooled by Angel Rama (1982) as an instrument for literary analysis. Its usefulness for cultural critique has been challenged by cultural critics like John Beverley (1999), who argues that transculturation promotes integration and acculturation of difference into the national body politic, and ultimately is at the service of the consolidation of the nation-state and modernity (1999, 43–47). In fact, mestizaje—the racial and cultural blending that is the result of transculturation—has been understood to be an identity category of the modern assimilationist politics of nationhood in countries like Bolivia and Peru that served to erase indigenous identities and concomitantly weaken indigenous claims to traditional lands, self-governance, and cultural autonomy (Canessa 2005, 14–15; Larson 2004, 6–8). Conversely, in the Aconcagua zone, it is mestizaje itself and the process of transculturation that are being invoked as the basis from which a claim to indigeneity is being staked. In looking at the process of re-ethnification in the mountain zone in chapter 3, the question of how mestizaje could inform and "authenticate" indigeneity and serve to create an identity category for grounding legal and land-tenure claims becomes a focal point of my analysis.

Charting the Text

I have structured this book according to the framework of a mountaineering experience. The first part of the book deals most specifically with preparatory efforts that might inform a contemporary Aconcagua expedition: researching history about previous expeditions, garnering information and inspiration from mountaineering stories, and examining gear and expectations. The last chapters focus on mountaineering practices that move from an expedition's meeting place in the capital city of Mendoza, to the staging area of Puente del Inca, and successively on up the mountain to the base camp of Plaza de Mulas. I conclude each chapter with a "debriefing" section, which traditionally has been an essential component of the mountaineering process (Mitchell 1983, 1).

The first five chapters of the book provide a context for interpreting the multiple origins and meanings of Aconcagua mountaineering. Chapter 1 treats the arrival of the first European scientist-explorers, cited as the founders of Aconcagua mountaineering, through a study of nineteenth-century travel literature and other narratives of modernity. Chapter 2 deals with the patriotic Argentine origin of mountaineering, as symbolized by the feats of General José de San Martín, and the creation of heritage industries, tourism, and memory. Chapter 3 characterizes the indigenous nature of Aconcagua and the process of contemporary re-ethnification in Argentina. Chapter 4 considers notions of affect and capital that have fashioned the international popularity of Aconcagua, and looks at their role in creating a transnational tourism market. Chapter 5 examines the changes that globalization and Argentine redemocratization have had on Aconcagua and the resultant sociocultural institutionalization of mountaineering in Mendoza.

The second half of the book is more ethnographic in nature as it characterizes the practices, performances, and meanings of contemporary mountaineering in Mendoza. Chapter 6 considers the roles and functions of mountain guides living and working in Mendoza and deals with issues of regional and national identity. Chapter 7 follows an expedition up the Northern Route to base camp and scrutinizes the performativity of adventure, gender, and modernity. Chapter 8 offers an ethnographic analysis of the base camp by focusing on the tensions between the national, the global, and memory.

Ultimately, the spirit of this academic endeavor has been grounded in my effort of reciprocity toward Mendoza itself. As I conducted research, interviews, and ethnographic fieldwork in Mendoza and on Aconcagua I always saw the project as a collaborative venture, and indeed it was. I am by no means the expert on Aconcagua. What I have learned has been generously shared with me by the real experts living and climbing in Mendoza. My intention has always been that my interpretations in this book might provide another, be it somewhat unorthodox, history of Argentine mountaineering and the relatively untold account of the Aconcagua industry in Mendoza that might find resonance with those people actively engaged in mountaineering there.

So, where are they? Where are the bodies of the Brazilians? This book never gives a detailed, geographical pinpointing of where the Brazilian climbers are located in degrees of latitude, longitude, and altitude. I know that they remain hanging somewhere on the South Face, but their exact location is not the only or best answer to the question that started this introduction. Where are they? They are in the stories, in their own tale of challenge and tragedy, and in the narratives of nation and identity, adventure, modernity, tourism, and globalization that mountaineering on Aconcagua tells. While the ill-fated bodies of the Brazilian climbers can never be recovered, Aconcagua's stories give insight into the circumstances of why they are there on the frozen wall in the first place, and it is these stories that this book attempts to recuperate.

CHAPTER ONE

"They All Want to Be Indiana Jones"

Travel Literature and Modernity

No other and loftier peak rose before me. Everything was beneath my feet.

—STUART VINES, SPEAKING OF THE FIRST ASCENT OF MENDOZA'S TUPUNGATO THAT HE MADE WITH MATTHIAS ZÜRBRIGGEN IN 1897 (1950, 311)

Argentina's central Andes Mountains of Mendoza province have formed part of a corridor long associated with heroic adventure. In European travel writing of the early nineteenth century, according to Mary Louise Pratt (2008), the crossing of the Argentine Andes figured into a "canonical heroic paradigm for the Englishman's South American journey," a journey charted by an arrival in Buenos Aires, a traverse of the Argentine pampas, and the crossing of the Andean Cordillera in order to reach Santiago or Lima from where the voyage home by sea would be initiated (145). Such travel narratives of heroic adventure provided the template for the first European scientist-explorers on Aconcagua who are considered by local mountaineering circles to be the forefathers of Mendocino mountaineering.

Today's international mountain enthusiasts who come to the Americas' highest peak to search for adventure equip themselves differently from adventurers of the nineteenth century. Insulated by Capilene underwear, protected by Gore-Tex shells, armed with chemical hand warmers, and fashioned by The North Face's Aconcagua down vests, today's adventurers stand in stark contrast to those early European explorers who were dependent only on wool, leather, and the heat of their own personal ambition. Yet the mind set of those first explorers, with regard to adventure, Mendoza, and modernity, still echoes in the stories and practices of mountaineering today. This chapter sketches how local mountaineering has interpreted the significance and legacy of those first European adventurer-explorers and European modernity to invent contemporary Aconcagua mountaineering and to redefine Mendoza's relationship to its mountains.

The Sleeping Giant

Mount Aconcagua . . . there it was, waiting for someone to dare to climb it. Until at the end of the 19th century, European scientists, with a longing for knowledge and adventure, arrived in these distant lands of South America, more specifically in Mendoza, to conquer the Andean colossus.

—CARLOS CAMPANA AND JORGE OMAR CAMPANA (2004)

Although Charles Darwin had written of the high mountain region of west central Argentina earlier, it was not until the end of the nineteenth century that mountaineering tales of Mount Aconcagua began to circulate. Aspirations to climb Aconcagua, and to write about it, were foreign to the Argentine province at that time, and so, according to local common knowledge, as the Mendocino journalists report above, Aconcagua was destined to lay in wait, much like Sleeping Beauty, for a daring and adventurous soul to brave its slopes. Aconcagua's fairy-tale awakening eventually occurred when European scientist-explorers, drawn by dreams of "conquering" the mountain, first made their appearance in 1882 to mark the advent of mountaineering.

The presence and activities of these men on the Argentine mountain, as a consequence of Western modernity, chronologically paralleled the arrival to the region of the train, the telegraph, electric lights, the city's first indoor plumbing system, and a new wave of European immigration. Beyond simply offering up mountaineering as a complement to a list of material signs of technological and economic advancement, the stories produced by and about these first mountaineers provoke other readings of the workings of modernity in Mendoza. They pointedly serve to address the positioning of the area within a modern world order, as well as to bring up questions about how travel, adventure, and tourism have engaged the construction of regional identity.

Today Aconcagua no longer slumbers and is very much awake to the mountain-climbing fantasies of thousands of individuals who come to Mendoza from over sixty different countries every year with the hopes of reaching the highest summit in the Americas. In marked contrast, the city of Mendoza, founded in 1561, traditionally envisioned Aconcagua and the Andes in a very different and more negative manner.[1] The early Spanish settlers of Mendoza did not consider the height of its mountains an attractive or desirable challenge. Rather, the Andes were seen as a barrier to communication and an estrangement from a Mendocino sense of self and place. Pablo Lacoste (2002), a Mendocino historian, claims that the idea of the mountains traditionally held by the Mendocinos until the early twentieth century harkens back to colonial times and evokes telluric images of death, physical suffering, severe cold, and fear, which left an imprint on Mendocinos of the mountains as being desolate and deserted.

Mendoza province developed, primarily, as a farm and agricultural center (now especially known for its wine production) in opposition to the mountain range located on its western fringe, which separated it geographically, but not politically, from Chile. By 1776 the province severed its administrative ties to the Governorship of Chile and was incorporated into the Viceroyalty of Río de la Plata. This facilitated the relegation of the mountain area to a territorial, and later a national, limit against which the capital city of Mendoza and the province would find definition, and hindered the inclusion of the Cordillera into the project of Mendocino development. Although the 1,000 kilometers to Buenos Aires was nearly three times the distance to Santiago, the Mendocino Andes made travel and access to the Chilean capital, especially during the winter months, hazardous and highly undependable. This meant that Mendoza, from the eighteenth century onward, found its connection to the world, and later to the nation, via the pampas and Buenos Aires.

Counter to Mendoza's long-standing aversion to and lack of interest in its mountains, German and British adventurers, traveling in the name of scientific exploration as they began to compete to make first ascents of high Andean peaks toward the end of the nineteenth century (Domicelj 2003, 46), became intrigued by the Mendocino range. Mendoza's Aconcagua became an enticing destination for those early European mountaineers to play out national, individual, and scientific competition.

Mountaineering Today

Güssfeldt is considered the pioneer of Aconcagua and a glacier carries his name.

—NICOLÁS GARCÍA (2003B), *LOS ANDES* JOURNALIST

Nowadays, the memory of the arrival of those first scientist-explorers in Mendoza is especially heralded not only in the local press, but by current-day Aconcagua mountaineering enthusiasts in guidebooks, journal articles, and contemporary expedition accounts, and on official, commercial, and personal websites. Today's Mendoza mountaineering community, via a varied and globalized media, memorializes its past by pointing to Paul Güssfeldt (1883), Edward A. FitzGerald (1897), Stuart Vines (1897), and Sir Martin Conway (1898) as the founding fathers, and they trace a line back to the area's heritage of science and exploration as first established for Western audiences by Charles Darwin (1835).[2]

The first expeditions to the Aconcagua mountain zone by these nineteenth-century European explorers, who all left written accounts of their journeys, were made almost exclusively outside Mendoza's socioeconomic circuits, with the exception of guiding and portering assistance by local and Chilean arrieros, familiar with transportation work in the high-altitude zone, and went unnoticed by most Mendocinos. Such is definitely not the case today. More than 125 years after the German geologist Paul Güssfeldt's first ascent attempt in 1883, which garnered him the title of "Pioneer of Aconcagua Mountaineering," but not the summit, Mendoza has aggressively commandeered mountaineering for its own.[3]

The institutionalization and professionalization of mountaineering in Mendoza especially reads as a congratulatory sign of the region's modernity when its oft-noted origin story, the coming of the scientists-explorers, is referenced. The epigraph above, taken from Mendoza's most popular daily newspaper, exemplifies this, not only in the laudatory register used to describe those European scientists who dared to climb and conquer, but also in what is only evoked or alluded to: that message of the region's modernity that Mendocinos, familiar with the presence of the local mountaineering industry, can easily read between the lines. It insinuates that Mendoza has followed along the trajectory laid out by the modern tenets of science, knowledge, and adventure that drove the first Europeans to seek out Aconcagua and subsequently Mendocino climbers have become the rightful heirs to their legacy. Moreover, emphasis on these founding moments not only draws focus to a continuity with the past, but it also highlights the current distance from those originary acts of scientific exploration and reinforces a narrative of the progress of modernity in Mendoza that has culminated in its current status as an active player in the globalized industry of international mountaineering.

Although local mountaineering lore singles out the first scientist-explorers as initiating this story of modernity, it is not their voices, nor the functions and meanings that they constructed of Mendoza and mountaineering, nor the manner in which they incorporated their understandings of the area into a modern worldview that drive this narrative. Rather, it is a Mendocino interpretation, the popular collective meaning and cultural value ascribed to those first European mountain adventurers, not what they actually wrote, that serves as the cue for Mendoza's self-construction as modern. Nonetheless, those first mountaineering tales of Aconcagua, written by European explorers, provide a window to the subtexts of Mendoza's Cinderella story of the modern. The tales reveal the region's evolving engagement with Western modernity to be much more complex than the stories narrated by official histories, popular beliefs, and marketing propaganda. These late nineteenth-century mountaineering narratives construct Aconcagua as a destination of promising opportunities for science and adventure, one dependent on a European center–South American periphery model of the world. While the model that the mountaineering tales depict complements the power dynamics inherent, but not as explicitly visible, in all other congratulatory versions of Mendocino progress, it also highlights to a much greater degree the supposed fixity of these relationships and the racialized, classist, and gendered suppositions that underwrite them. Moreover, it is the entrenched nature of the geopolitics of this model that continues to problematize the roles, functions, and practices of contemporary mountaineering within the sociocultural and economic relationships that Mendoza has evolved with its high mountain region.

Masculine Fantasies

Maps, sketches, samples, and collections are their trophies of conquest.

—"LA GRAN AVENTURA" (2005)

I remember the first occasion we beheld it we all stood gazing at it in silence until one of the porters broke the spell by ejaculating "What's that?"

—STUART VINES (1950, 315), MEMBER OF THE EDWARD A. FITZGERALD EXPEDITION OF 1896–97, SPEAKING OF ACONCAGUA

The first mountaineering narratives of Aconcagua, dating from the 1880s, were clearly an outgrowth of earlier nineteenth-century travel writing that "contributed in different ways to [the] enterprise of inscribing Spanish America into the territory of European knowledge" (Salvatore 1999, 199).[4] The most acclaimed model of scientific travel narrative dealing with the Mendoza-Aconcagua zone, and the one most frequently cited by the first mountaineers, was penned by Charles Darwin in his visit to the area.

In 1835 Darwin made a circuit from Valparaiso, Chile, across the Andes through the Portillo pass into what he called the "republic" of Mendoza (2004, 288). He journeyed through the capital city of Mendoza to return to Chile via the northern provincial pass that skirts Aconcagua. He recounts his 24-day journey in chapter 15, "Passage of the Cordillera," in *The Voyage of the Beagle*, generally recognized as "a superb travel journal, filled with vivid narrative, well-sketched characters, exotic locales, . . . as well as a record of his geological and biological observations" (Quammen 2004, xix). Darwin's reading and writing about the Mendoza area exemplify the ways that nineteenth-century travel narratives mapped Latin America onto an imagined worldscape that served to construct and justify the cultural and economic hegemony and modernity of the North in juxtaposition to the socioeconomic paucity and backwardness of the South. In this way, Darwin set the narrative frame for the writings of future mountaineer writers like Güssfeldt, FitzGerald, Vines, and Conway, as he depicted exotic sites and characters alongside scientific observations, and in so doing, established and maintained national and hemispheric hierarchies.

In the story of Darwin's two crossings of the Mendocino Andes his narrative informs and speculates about the mules, beetles, locusts, guanacos, cattle, geology, and geography of the region. Darwin's descriptions of Mendoza's populace are akin to his narrative treatment of the flora, fauna, and landscape of the area; they serve as objects of observation and analysis. In his consideration of the zone, Darwin's scientific gaze especially focuses on racial and social differences with respect to European sensibilities. He writes of a "very fat negress," with an enormous goiter, "a poor and miserable object of a degraded race" to voice his surprise at the Chilean officials who offer the kind of courteous greeting he is sure would never be found for her in Europe (2004, 280). At the border post, Darwin, ever alert to racial and social variations, finds his attention drawn to only one of the four men in attendance, "a thoroughbred Pampas Indian: [. . .] kept much for the same purpose as a bloodhound" (192). The rest of the Mendocino population is basically ignored by Darwin, except for what might be considered its most exotic element: "the lower orders [who] have the lounging, reckless manners of the Gauchos of the Pampas" (295). In essence, Mendoza, in terms of its social makeup, is very negatively sketched by the author as racially exotic, lower class, diseased, lazy, and dimwitted. Darwin concludes that "the town had a stupid, forlorn aspect . . . the happy doom of the Mendozinos is to eat, sleep, and be idle" (295).

D. Graham Burnett, in his study of scientific expeditions to British Guiana that were undertaken around the same time as Darwin's forays into Mendoza, states that during this period in general, "geographical exploration alloyed science and colonialism in a project to extend metropolitan territory and enmesh foreign people in metropolitan commerce" (2002, 33). This ultimately meant creating the desire and rationalizing the need for European intervention. Darwin's description of the Mendocino Andes region accomplishes both objectives in justifying his and future European interest. It sets up Mendoza as needing an influx of British efficiency, morals, standards, and work ethic. At the same time it heightens the attractiveness of the mountains, first as a wellspring for the study of natural and geological sciences, and second as a site rife with transcendental possibilities. Indeed, Darwin's unenthusiastic appraisal of the capital and citizenry of Mendoza and the little textual space he dedicates to the cultivated countryside greatly contrast with his narrative zeal and pleasure in recording his experiences in the high mountain zone.

Darwin finds much to pique his interest in the Andes. His gusto for observing and collecting runs so high that the effects of the puna, or high-altitude sickness, he claims, are overcome by his delight in finding and describing fossil shells (287). Darwin's enthusiasm for the scientific opulence and the aesthetic splendor of the mountains contrasts with the desultory aspect that he draws of the capital city. At the top of the Portillo pass, Darwin writes of the "glorious view" that "produced a scene no one could have imagined. Neither plant nor bird, excepting a few condors wheeling around the higher pinnacles, distracted my attention from the inanimate mass. I felt glad that I was alone: it was like watching a thunderstorm, or hearing in full orchestra a chorus of the Messiah" (287).

It is not really surprising that Darwin, the discerning scientific observer, would invoke the romantic notion of the sublime. The sublime, as elicited by views of or from the mountains, was a common element in romantic literature and thought during the period, and the juxtaposition of romantic aspects with documentary exposition has been a common duality in travel writing (Salvatore 1999, 205). It is significant, however, that Darwin's ability to combine a scientific eye with the transcendence of spirit lays the foundation for characterizing the mountaineer explorer as an exceptional modern individual and national subject. Peter L. Bayers has found in his study of mountaineering narratives of Denali and Everest at the end of the nineteenth century that this invoking of romantic convention alongside the more generalized descriptive and rational discourse contained in most mountaineering accounts created an image of "mountaineers, [who] by ascending mountains, are somehow literally able to bridge the gap between the material world and a sublime, powerful ideal" (2003, 7), which justified both logically and metaphysically the nationalist imperialism of their endeavors.

Bayers's study further argues that in the late nineteenth century, mountains "offered white men particularly unique symbolic spaces on which to enact their masculine fantasies, figuratively elevating their supposed masculine virtues to 'new' heights . . . 'elevating' the supposed virility of the imperial male body to dominate the natural environment, or the rational, masculine imperial mind that coolly and systematically manages the challenges of the natural environment or the indigenous people encountered and used on the expeditions" (2003, 5). Darwin's judgmental critique of Mendoza and his self-professed prowess in the mountain area construct his textual persona as being superior in both mind and body, prefiguring the mountaineering psyche that Bayers describes. As further demonstration of the strength that his intellectual and corporeal equilibrium exhibited in being nonplussed by the altitude, Darwin bolsters his image of authority in his sojourn back to Chile via the Aconcagua route by mocking the local reputation of the difficulty of the passage. Although the area was known for the "worst passes in the Cordillera" and the "worst stream in the Cordillera to pass," Darwin concludes that "the real danger is nothing" (2004, 297), putting into doubt both the rational and physical capabilities of the locals (already inscribed as inferior in terms of class, race, and morality) who had issued such warnings, and effectively feminizing them.[5]

This propensity for local knowledge to be shown as faulty, deficient, or false is a common thread of these narratives, exemplified by Stuart Vines, the surveyor for the FitzGerald expedition in 1897, in his chapter "Tupungato Ascended" in *The Highest Andes*. Vines's text describes Darwin's hypothesis of volcanic activity on Tupungato, the peak on which Vines had just claimed a first summit. Vines reveals that Darwin wrote that he thought that he could "make out the form of a large crater" on Tupungato and supported his supposition with information he had gleaned from an arriero who claimed to have seen smoke at one time in the vicinity (1950, 317). Vines corrects Darwin by stating that the latter must have been speaking of a different formation of peaks and adds that "[a]s to the arriero's remark, it only shows that the mule-drivers of the Cordillera played with the truth sixty-two years ago as badly as they do today" (317).[6] With his new vantage point and additional information, Vines rationalizes that Darwin's conclusion was incorrect yet truthful. However, the arriero, who might have indeed seen smoke from a mudslide or rock avalanche, which is not uncommon (I myself have seen such occurrences in this area), is not assumed to have made an honest mistake in his syllogism, as Darwin might have. For Vines, the arriero is simply lying. Vines's passage demonstrates the maxim running throughout these narratives that European logic, knowledge, and truth progressively improve and advance and always trump local experience and understanding. This passage also

Figure 1.1. Matthias Zürbriggen was the first to summit Aconcagua in 1897. He did so via the North, or Normal, Route, seen here from above Camp Canada (center left). Conway's Rocks are lower center right, and Plaza de Mulas is at the lower center.

illustrates how the representation of Mendocinos in these mountaineering texts owes as much to literary traditions and archetypes created by earlier nineteenth-century travel literature as it does to the observational discernments and reasonings (themselves never neutral as they are always already preconditioned by earlier literary formulae and the ideological stances of Western modernity) of the mountaineering writers.

It is within these same traditions that Edward A. FitzGerald profiles Mendoza and Mendocinos in *The Highest Andes* (1899), his chronicle of the expedition he organized to Aconcagua (1896–97), which resulted in the first summit.[7] FitzGerald, who summarizes in his own narrative Darwin's *Beagle* accounts of his passage through the Mendocino Andes, glosses over the new Mendoza constructed after the 1861 earthquake to concentrate on what he finds exotic, different, and deficient. FitzGerald focuses on the ruins and devastation of the earthquake, the danger of the region's severe weather, the area's uncomfortable and substandard rail travel, the unhurried attitude toward work of the locals that makes his efforts there "troublesome," and the appearance of the arrieros whose "general get-up and demeanor are exceedingly picturesque" (1899, 17). FitzGerald extends Darwin's negative portrayal of the inhabitants of the zone beyond lazy and idle to cast them, particularly the arrieros, as being deceitful, threatening, and criminal. This in turn serves to highlight the Englishman's higher degree of bravery, morals, and wits. A review in *Quarterly Review* ("Recent Mountaineering" 1901) of FitzGerald's book concluded that "[i]t can hardly be said that the merits of man make up for any shortcomings in the scenery of the Andes. The half-caste muleteers are a vile race, and the prudent traveler eats with his revolver on the table and barricades his bedroom door. Mr. FitzGerald even suggests that it may be judicious for him on occasion to sleep under his bed in order to avoid being shot at through the roof" (145).

This scene, invoking images straight out of the American Wild West, depicts the arrieros as "vile, half-caste, thieving, murderous muleteers" and illustrates how the journal's readers are conditioned to understand "difference" in these mountaineering texts. It is cast in terms of race, which is explicitly referenced; class status, which is obvious; and nationality, which is implied, to be read as danger, violence, and immorality. It is also what naturalizes in these texts the superiority of the masculine European self, in terms of knowledge, ingenuity, and daring.

It is this natural supposition that would have us take for granted that Paul Güssfeldt, who in 1883 stopped about 400 meters short of the summit due to severe windstorms, "very nearly conquered Aconcagua . . . virtually alone" (Irwin 1950, 301; FitzGerald 1899, 7). Although the Chilean arriero Gilberto Salazar made the first summit attempts with Güssfeldt, he is rarely, if ever, mentioned as a cofounding father of Aconcagua mountaineering. To celebrate the centennial anniversary of the first successful summit (made in 1897, fourteen years after Güssfeldt), the Spanish sportswriter Juan José Zorrilla (1997), writing for *Desnivel*, the most important Spanish-language mountaineering magazine, proclaimed Güssfeldt to be the "discoverer" of the mountain (30), ignoring any pre-Columbian, colonial, or national knowledge of the mountain. Even if we were to believe that Stuart Vines had to identify Aconcagua (and its importance) to his local porter, the fact that the mountain already had an indigenous name would obviously discount a Güssfeldt claim on the peak. Still, a century later Zorrilla continues to invoke that original understanding of mountaineering in which explorer-adventurers are sent out from the metropolitan core to the unknown and "nonmodern" spaces of the periphery to stake a claim for self, nation, and modernity.

Trust in Modernity

The account sent by Dr. Paul Güssfeldt to the Berlin Academy of Sciences, of his recent journey in the Central Chilian Argentine Andes, contains so much that is new and strange that the American reader is led to wish that this continent could be made the scene of more thorough geographical exploration than has yet been accorded to it.

—"GEOGRAPHY AND TRAVELS" (1885, 158)[8]

There was the expectation by the North that scientifically grounded travel narratives that focused on geology, natural histories, and racial differences would provide important new discoveries for comprehending Spanish America (Salvatore 1999, 213). The desires for knowledge and the expansionist visions instigated by these new discoveries fed into the construction of an imperial masculine ethos (borrowing from Bayers 2003) that underwrote the first Aconcagua mountaineering narratives, as part and parcel of Western modernity, and fixed national and racial hierarchies where white European upper-class males were, literally and figuratively, on top. Within this scheme, late nineteenth-century Mendoza remained distant from the world of mountaineering in which it was either absent or represented as backward, lazy, dangerous, and personified by the underclass racially ambiguous arrieros.

The worldview provided by the first Aconcagua mountaineering narratives is in conflict with Mendoza's own vision of its modernization at the time. However, European mountaineering initiatives on Aconcagua and Mendoza's drives toward a future based on a faith in progress were not exactly at odds, as they are two currents of the same surge. They both illustrate basic modernist precepts: the establishment of core-periphery relationships, the validation of the nation-state, the definition of "modern" itself, and the advent of tourism.

Just as mountaineering on Aconcagua grew out of European modernity's affirmation of national superiority contingent on the privilege of travel and the erasure of native and local peoples, the 1880s in Mendoza saw these same ideological processes played out internally. In the introduction of the Mendocino newspaper *Los Andes*' special series on the collective history of Mendoza over the last 120 years, *Memoria de los Mendocinos* (Memory of the Mendocinos) (Campana, Compana, and Boggia 2004) (Mendocinos sent in stories, pictures, diaries, ads, and anecdotes that the editors used to compile the series), the editors describe Mendoza's situation at the moment of the newspaper's founding in 1883 and repeat the traditional creed from which contemporary Mendoza derives its origin.

> El fin de la conquista del desierto y el arribo de los inmigrantes facilitado por el ferrocarril, aceleraron el proceso de transformación de la

> provincia, sumado a la consolidación de la vitivinicultura. . . . Un cambio que obligó a un esfuerzo de adaptación, y a un precio que pagar: la desvalorización de los trabajadores nativos, desplazados por otros, más calificados, provenientes de Europa. (Campana et al. 2004, 1:4)
>
> (The end of the conquest of the desert and the arrival of the immigrants, which was facilitated by the train, accelerated the process of transformation of the province, as well as the consolidation of wine production. . . . A change which required an effort of adaptation, a price to pay: There was a devaluing of local workers who were displaced by more qualified ones coming from Europe.)

In the description above, it is the "disappearance" of the indigenous peoples with the end of the Indian Wars known as the "conquest of the desert" that not only foments a sense of Argentine nationhood, but also opens the door to a new progressive future symbolized by the train and, in terms of supporting a white liberal *criollo*, or creole, understanding of the modern nation, an outpouring of immigration from the European core to the Latin American periphery.[9] Mendocino collective memory, expressed by the *Los Andes* writers, reinforces the belief that in the 1880s Argentina's vision of its future as a Westernized modern state was validated once its native peoples were no longer seen as a threat, culturally or politically, to a unified nation. Although the great numbers of immigrants during the late nineteenth and early twentieth centuries would bring about dramatic conflicts and changes to Argentine society, the underlying assumption of a shared race, Western "culture," and belief in European-based modernity allowed for this kind of sociocultural mixing and heterogeneity while it excluded native difference.

Travel and Urban Modernity

> *The train in Mendoza populated and founded towns and cities in the period in which Argentina found itself among the 10 richest countries in the world and everyone looked towards the future.*
>
> —CAMPANA ET AL. (2004, 1:8)

The appearance of the modern symbol of travel, the train, not only allowed the first successful Aconcagua summit expedition, led by Edward A. FitzGerald, to reach the mountain area in 1896 in "relative" comfort, it also meant a new ease in communication, in every sense of the word, for

Mendoza. When the first train arrived in Mendoza in April 1885, bringing with it the president of the nation, Julio Argentino Roca, Mendoza's connection to the nation and national progress was symbolically re-affirmed (Campana et al. 2004, 1:9). Information, letters, business documents, and passengers could now make the trip to the capital, Buenos Aires, in a matter of twenty hours instead of two days (1:9). Agricultural products and wine could now be transported faster and more securely to the east, which helped Mendoza consolidate its wine industry. Another important factor for wine production was the new facility with which European immigrants could travel westward from the port of entrance in Buenos Aires to Mendoza, as many of them came with knowledge and experience in vineyards and wineries.

Mendoza's love affair with all things European, except mountaineering, reverberated in its urban planning and renovation during the 1880s. Mountaineering made its appearance in Mendoza in that same decade, a moment of "accentuated trust in progress" according to the Mendocino historian Jorge Ricardo Ponte (1987, 235), that could be defined by Mendoza's embracing of the Western project of modernity. This was most visibly evidenced by Mendoza's urban and architectural planning and renovation. Colonial Mendoza had been totally destroyed by a devastating earthquake in 1861. During the years to follow, city planners sought out scientific and geological analyses and based their decision to transfer the city center to the southwest area, a zone hypothesized by the science of the time to be less vulnerable to seismic disturbances (Ponte 1987, 236–237). Eventually, in the 1880s, city officials decided to reconstruct the destroyed center of Mendoza known as "Ciudad Vieja" but rejected any return to its former colonial appearance, choosing instead, a more "modern" look that would accompany its new entrance into the world-market and spotlight the class divisions associated with the rise of the middle classes.

> Mendoza se transformó . . . se instalaron sucursales y agencias de bancos extranjeros, aparecieron los clubes sociales para la gente "distinguida," los cafés, etc. Las nuevas burguesías que se avergonzaban de la humildad de las ciudades coloniales, dictaban normas que prohibían por ejemplo, pintar de blanco edificios para no rememorar aquella Mendoza blanca y chata que describieron las crónicas. (Ponte 1987, 236)
>
> (Mendoza transformed itself . . . branches and agencies of foreign banks were installed, social clubs, cafés for the "distinguished" appeared etc. The new bourgeoisie who was ashamed of the humbleness of the

colonial cities, dictated norms that prohibited, for example, painting buildings white in remembrance of that white and squat Mendoza that the chronicles described.)

Mendoza's middle class marked its "distinguished" status through the modernness and exclusivity of the places in which they were seen and where they spent their leisure time. The development, location, and practice of its leisure activities such as croquet, rowing, and soccer—modern British sports that began to interest the middle classes and that could be practiced within the city—were also cultivated as signs of social status and modernity (Ponte 1987). Mountaineering, which also was a European import, however, was one in which local participation was only represented by the arrieros, which disrupted Mendoza's self-conceptualization of its urban modernity and its consolidation of the bourgeoisie.

Modernity for both mountaineering and Mendocino urbanization purposes drew from the cultural valuing of positivist science. Positivism, understood as faith in the certainty of systematic observation and methodologies, together with the view of knowledge as unfinished, progressively accrued, logically verifiable, positive, and technically utilizable (Bernstein 1983), drove Mendoza's push to acquire the latest scientific information in order to urbanize, sanitize, and modernize. Positivism also validated Northern mountaineering as a quest for geographic, geological, and physiological data for the knowledge banks of the metropolis that would inform and finance progress.

Nineteenth-century tales of Aconcagua connected with the North's thirst for the lucrative, the novel, and the new and as such found a wide-ranging audience in the Northern metropolis. Accounts of Aconcagua exploration were well disseminated in the United States and Europe beyond specialized venues like the Berlin Academy of Sciences, the Geological Society, or the Royal Geographic Society. These first Aconcagua mountaineering narratives were also popularized in reviews, reprints, and citations in journals and magazines, such as *Quarterly Review*, *American Naturalist*, *Appleton's Annual Cyclopædia*, *Harper's Monthly*, and in books and anthologies ranging well into the twentieth century. In this respect the European monopoly on mountaineering science and the monodirectional flow of scientific information away from the mountain zone clearly marked the peripheral status of Mendoza in this exchange. Mendoza was the purveyor of primary scientific resources but was not imagined as recipient or implied as reader of the published reports.

Nor did Mendoza or Argentina enter into the national competitiveness geared toward a compilation of "firsts" that characterized the representation of mountaineering science in the Northern journals. Here the imperial masculine ethos of mountaineering, in the name of positivist science, rendered evermore "natural" the disregard of the previous or contemporaneous presence and knowledge of indigenous or local peoples and sanctioned the explorers' presence, observations, and accomplishments as "firsts." Within this context, "firsts" consisted of pioneering descriptions of flora, fauna, geology, geography, the effects of altitude, and economic possibilities, the issue of nascent hypotheses concerning these topics, correction or corroboration of ideas and opinions of previous explorer-travelers, first summits, and the trial and use of instruments and technology.[10] It was especially the testing and employment of technology that became a trope in the Aconcagua narratives to represent mountaineering as both modern and scientific.

By 1877 all the first ascents of the European Alps had been claimed, mostly by British mountaineers (Johnston and Edwards 1994, 462), and the competitive nature of mountaineering to collect firsts had become a culturally prestigious activity, perhaps even more so than the actual "science" it purportedly set out to accomplish. In fact, science often served only as a veneer to render the expedition more socially relevant and modern. Among the first explorations of Aconcagua, the geologist Paul Güssfeldt was the only trained scientist to lead an expedition. FitzGerald, although accompanied by a naturalist and a surveyor, was, like Conway, an upper-class Englishman with a penchant for travel who made a name for himself through expeditions to exotic locales.[11] Regardless of the actual qualifications of mountaineer narrators like FitzGerald or the reliability of the "valuable information [his expedition] collected concerning climate, topography, geology, and botany" (Irwin 1950, 301), it was the prestige of the positivist purport and the modernist bent of their activities, more than the actual data, hypotheses, or conclusions, that defined mountaineering science in these texts about Aconcagua.

Modernity in the Mountain

Sir Martin says that while he is interested from only the scientific standpoint, he believes the country to be so rich in minerals that American and English capitalists must soon look to that region as the most promising field for investments.

—"GEOGRAPHICAL PROGRESS" (1902, 260)

The mountain hotels were a true social success. From the entire country and even abroad, members of the elite arrived to strengthen their social identity and status.

—LACOSTE (2002)

The underlying ideologies of positivism that drove the first Northern explorers to the mountains also reinforced the expansion of capitalism and supported the core-periphery paradigm of world commerce. This trust in positivism, according to the Mendocino historian Pablo Lacoste (2000), served to justify Mendoza's lack of interest in the mountain zone (and for that matter, mountaineering) by encouraging the internalization of the region's position within the dynamics of world capitalism. Lacoste (2000) posits that the delay in constructing a trans-Andean railway at this time through the Aconcagua pass to connect Chile and Argentina reflected the fact that both nations were more interested in modernizing transatlantic transportation routes and securing their roles as suppliers of natural resources for European industrialization (2000, 78–81). For this reason, according to Lacoste, Chile and Argentina preferred to focus on improving trade with Great Britain rather than on strengthening binational communication and transportation or developing the high mountain area (2000, 81). This focus played into a long-standing conflicted relationship between Argentina and Chile, especially with regard to Mendoza. Ultimately, Northern subjects rather than Mendocinos sought out the high mountain area for economic and scientific gains. British commercial interests financed and began constructing the trans-Andean railway in 1887, which would drastically change the mountain topography, its functions, and the representation of the mountains in the Mendocino collective imaginary.

The trans-Andean rail line not only improved communication and transportation with Chile, it also was an important instigating factor in the development of mountain tourism in the Aconcagua region (Lacoste 2002). In his study of the social changes in the mountain zone associated with the construction and completion (1909) of the trans-Andean railroad, Lacoste (2002) explains that with shortened travel time upper middle-class Mendocinos began to frequent the high mountain as tourists. The Compañía de Hoteles Sudamericanos, a subsidiary of the British-owned FCBAP that had already constructed and been administering the Hotel Puente del Inca since 1903, built the Hotel Termas de Cacheuta in 1913 (later a third hotel was opened in Uspallata in 1936). Many Mendocinos took their summer holidays at these spa hotels funded by British interests, which came complete with piano halls and croquet lawns (Lacoste 2002).

This kind of mountain tourism generated through the connection of Mendoza to a world economic market and European capital, practiced by the upper middle classes, and built upon the most modern conveniences, projected the mountain space as a reflection of Mendoza's own material advances. Lacoste provides a broad overview of how the spa tourism in the mountain area functioned, which I paraphrase below:

> The elites of Buenos Aires and Mendoza came to Puente del Inca or Cacheuta for the thermal baths and to socialize. The hotels provided mail service and a telegraph, a chapel, a pharmacy, medical services, a barber shop, hair salons, and electric generators which ran the elevators and washing machines. The zone's snob appeal to the upper classes was even more accentuated by the passing through of European royalty, such as Edward, Prince of Wales, in 1924. Both sites became especially known for fomenting summer romance and making marriage connections. (2002)

This use of the mountain serves as a mirror of Mendoza's sense of progress based on British entrepreneurship and the practice of leisure activities bound by clear class divisions. Mountain tourism in the area was patently reserved for a minority, the upper middle classes with both the time and money to spend, while service to tourists provided employment and income for local workers and entrepreneurs.

It was only much later, in the latter part of the twentieth century, that the interest of the Mendocino middle classes turned toward their own exploration and exploitation of the mountain zone. While this newfound protagonism in the adventure tourism market marked a modification in how Mendocinos used the mountain area touristically, it did not signal a radical change in the direction that Mendoza's relationship with its mountains had begun to take since the beginning of the twentieth century. For Mendocinos, first as turn-of-the-century tourists (and tourist industry service providers) and later as mountaineers and mountaineering entrepreneurs and service workers, the provincial mountain region had come to function as a sign of Mendocino progress and especially come to be understood as a space of economic possibilities. The substitution of mountaineering for spa tourism in this equation depended on Mendoza's appropriation of the North's understanding of the mountain area and mountaineering, with the concomitant glossing over of the traditional positioning and functioning of Mendoza within the legacy of the modernist mountaineering framework.

Adventure, Nation, and Class

Both mountaineering and Mendoza's incipient mountain tourism were products of the modern age; both were sponsored by international capital, and they both maintained clear class divisions between practitioners and service providers. However, the discourse of mountaineering highlighted the idea of adventure in the name of a higher moral goal that further separated itself from the comfort and ease of middle-class tourism bought and sold for diversion.

Nevertheless, the practicing of "adventure" is understood to share a common factor with tourism in general. According to Swarbrooke et al. (2003), "Adventure is entered into freely, without coercion, and in this respect shares some of the characteristics of leisure. Also, like leisure, adventurers are to a large degree inner-directed and self-motivated" (11). Then again, the notion of adventure generally conjures up contradictory images to those of families enjoying the thermal baths, spa services, socializing salon games, afternoon tea, and all the modern amenities that were part of early Mendoza mountain tourism. Bayers (2003) has described the idea of adventure in early mountaineering as an activity through which masculine identity could be measured according to the tenets that supported Western national imperialism. He cites varying examples such as rationality, leadership, ruggedness, and self-sacrifice as defining traits in this kind of masculine adventure (2003, 3–5). Thus, the women, children, and croquet-playing men of Mendoza's mountain tourism, who contrasted with the stalwart mountaineers in terms of opposition to masculine traits like self-sacrifice, level of activity, risk, and often nationality (as most mountaineers at this time were not Argentines, but many of the mountain tourists were), were excluded from adventure in the way that mountaineering understood it. The idea of adventure still retains some of these exclusionary qualities, and contemporary tourism campaigns today play off this, even as they paradoxically market adventure as inclusive activities, open to all, that are associated with the outdoors and new experiences radically different from the daily routine.[12]

The conjoining of adventure and mountaineering with personal and national identity construction, then, has had an uneasy fit with Mendoza's historical experience and symbolic valuing of the mountain. When the first European expeditionaries traveled across oceans and continents to Aconcagua for adventure, early Mendocino mountain tourism was generally setting its sights a good deal lower, geographically speaking, as the upper middle classes preferred to spend their leisure time in traveling thirty-eight kilometers from the city to the foothills of Cacheuta to picnic, soak in thermal baths, or perhaps find romance. While those enjoying the hotels' delights formed a more homogeneous social group across nationalities (although it could be argued that European finance and nobility would always trump national elites), mountaineering maintained class differences more strictly along national lines.

Differences between Argentines and Europeans in the first decades of the practice of mountaineering in Mendoza, in terms of class status and patterns of interactions with the mountain (in that Argentines did not initiate or finance exploration, their high-altitude work as muleteers or porters formed part of their daily life rather than an element extraneous to it, and they were motivated to take risks by economics rather than intellectual or spiritual challenges), obscured and silenced stories about the arrieros' contributions to the history of mountaineering, or *andinismo* as it is called locally, on Aconcagua.[13] This erasure reflects the colonialist dynamic inherent in early mountaineering's history and exemplifies the fact that service workers have traditionally "been excluded from the role of proper travelers because of their race and class, and because theirs seemed to be a dependent status in relation to the supposed independence of the individualist, bourgeois voyager" (Clifford 1997, 33). In addition to the erasure of Güssfeldt's Chilean arriero, Gilberto Salazar, is the ignoring of the arriero Mario Pastén in discussion about the first Argentine summit of Aconcagua, although the Chilean-born Argentine resident accompanied that 1934 expedition and summited with Nicolás Plantamura and the other members of the group (García 2003b; Randis 1991).

It was not until 1919 that Argentines moved beyond a subordinate role in the traditional hierarchy of mountaineering when Alfred Koelliker joined with European explorers to brave the heights of the mountain as an explorer-adventurer, rather than in the service of explorers (Zorrilla 1997, 32). Later, Argentine participation in mountaineering on Aconcagua, in a heroic masculinized sense, was predominantly military until the second half of the twentieth century.

Today, Mendocino mountaineering has replaced the train and the spa as the symbol and legacy of regional modernity in the mountain zone. Mendoza's spa-like elite mountain tourism ended decades ago when the Hotel de Puente del Inca was destroyed by an avalanche in August 1965. The trans-Andean train stopped carrying passengers in 1979 and halted international cargo runs in 1984 (Lacoste 2000, 421, 425). These symbols of modernity, as icons of travel and flows of international capital and tourism, lie in ruins, some would say much like the dreams of influence

Figure 1.2. The ruins of Puente del Inca Hotel above the Mendoza River. Built in 1903, the hotel was destroyed by an avalanche in 1965.

and prosperity that Argentina harbored in the early part of the twentieth century. Mountaineering and adventure tourism, including activities such as trekking, mountain biking, rafting, rappelling, and kayaking, have supplanted the gentrified social scene and the luxury hotels that first brought tourism to the region.

Indiana Jones and Butch Cassidy

The pairing of adventure and modernity may be what buttresses the attractiveness of the scientist-explorer origin stories for the Aconcagua mountaineering industry, because it enhances the legacy of those first mountaineers with a greater sense of modern and masculine elitism that still resonates today. "They all want to be Indiana Jones" is what a Mendocino mountain guide recently told me when asked about the motivations of the international clients he leads up Aconcagua. While such fantasies may bolster numbers for the Aconcagua market, these kinds of mountain "tourist" expectations become problematic when clients come face to face with Mendocino-enforced restrictions, regulations, and routes that limit their freedom and their imagination for high adventure in the "Indy" style. In promoting mountaineering today, Mendoza is faced with juggling the tenacity of Western narratives of modernity and adventure that fix the region in an imagined past where it is subordinate, exotic, distant, unknown, and dangerous, together with its contemporary self-promotion as modern based on provincial authority, use of technology, and professionalization of the industry.

The echoes of that nineteenth-century modern outlook presented by the first mountaineering narratives, where science and adventure were recombinant elements in an exclusionary worldview, continue to reverberate in contemporary Aconcagua mountaineering. They are heard when international travelers arrive at Mendoza airport expecting to see Butch Cassidy and the Sundance Kid appear (Taplin 1992), or when climbers who would like to donate their medical skills as a sort of repayment to the host community are surprised to find that Mendoza's own medical specialists make their services unnecessary, or when mountaineers are disappointed at the social and safety-driven infrastructure of the Aconcagua base camp that makes it too "civilized," or when they choose to employ more expensive international guides with no Aconcagua experience over fully accredited Mendocino guides, or when they question why the province would even have a guide school.[14] It is also this paradigm that validates pressuring the province (by Mendocinos and clients alike) to open ecologically fragile areas of the park that were previously off-limits, so as to accommodate international demands for a more uncivilized, "wilderness" experience. This modernist legacy factors into regional tensions between national agencies about international accreditation of guides and park rangers, and federal control of the park. The paradigm supports the continued Mendocino belief that "la montaña es netamente de hombres" (the mountains are clearly men's domain) with the subsequent restriction of most Mendocino women to base-camp cooktents.[15] And it also facilitates the continued erasure of the indigenous heritage of the mountain region, except for those vestiges of the Incan civilization that, like the mummy found on Aconcagua, tie into Mendocino mountaineering's construction of itself as modern.

Contemporary Mendocino protagonisms in local mountaineering, which now supervise and run the show, seemingly turn on its head that modern opposition that absented Mendocinos from early endeavors and that validate the kind of climber expectations that I cite above. However, simply substituting Mendoza for European merely reinscribes the hierarchical nature of this paradigm and reinforces the neocolonial status of the local industry by aligning it with the very tradition that previously excluded it and would still position it as subordinate. In this way it re-invokes the modernist origins of mountaineering, which maintained racial, national, classist, and gendered hierarchies, thus justifying the local effacing of the history of the arrieros and the primacy of the scientist-explorers in the origin stories of Mendoza mountaineering.

The arrieros, as the first local participants of mountaineering, are still stigmatized by the history of their subordinate position in the understanding of mountaineering as a modern, middle-class, professional project that incorporates the latest technical and scientific advances, which the managing of mules and the transport of equipment do not satisfy. There are also questionably racist undertones in the marginalization of the arrieros in the mountaineering origin stories that efface them. Diego Escolar (2007) has found that in the high mountain area the region's indigenous peoples often were designated through nonethnic identity categories, like rural worker and arriero (113–117). The preference by Mendocino mountaineers to link themselves back to the European explorers in contrast to the "ethnically suspicious" arrieros and their long-standing local tradition of transport in the mountains may be that the European scientist-explorers better served to connect Mendocinos to mountaineering by conferring a modernist and nationalist meaning to their participation in this imported sport that represented European progress but that also embodied racial homogeneity and imperial expansion.

Debriefs

If we read the tales of Aconcagua's European mountaineering pioneers against the history of the sport's development and practices in contemporary Mendoza, the narratives that converge fracture the fairy tale of an unproblematic and coherent linking of mountaineering's origins to the present. This re-reading of mountaineering narratives from Darwin to Conway reveals how the traces of the expansionist subtexts of imperial modernity, inscribed through the discourses of adventure and science, have conditioned the growth and understanding of mountaineering in Mendoza. It also illustrates how the implicit embracing of the hierarchical social codes and cultural valuings of European-based mountaineering easily tied into ideas about race, class, and manhood that constructed modern Argentine nationhood and complemented Mendoza's drive to constitute itself as modern.

Mendocinos who have set themselves up as the heirs to the early scientist-adventurers have, until recently, had little problem ignoring the racial and classist undertones and the subalternization of Mendoza in the early mountaineering texts. The exclusive essence of those narrations is perhaps made more tenable by the fact that their hierarchical worldview also plays into traditional suppositions about Argentine nationhood and the region's integration of the national. In this regard, the referencing of the nineteenth-century European scientific explorations as founding events of Aconcagua mountaineering is often complemented in local venues by two other originary mountain stories: the history of the Incan presence on Aconcagua, dating back to the mid-fifteenth century (approximately the 1460s) and specifically tied to the Incan mummy found on the mountain in 1985, and the momentous crossing of the Andes here by General José de San Martín's troops in 1817 to liberate Chile and spread the flame of revolution. All these threads of mountaineering's origin story spool out comfortably from the hegemonic discourse of late nineteenth-century Argentine nation building, in which the indigenous is inscribed as absent or exotic and past, the mastering of nature and geography gives definition to the national, and science and travel hold privileged places as master tropes of modernity.

CHAPTER TWO

No Longer the Lettered City

San Martín and the Touristic Imagination

Mendoza went from being a province with tourists to being a touristic province.

—TAPIA (2006)

For many Argentines, one of the consequences of the economic crisis at the beginning of the new millennium was the collapse of a collective sense of national identity. How indeed was one to be Argentine in this southernmost nation, envisioned at the turn of the twentieth century as one of the ten most modern countries in the world, but by the close of 2001 confronted with bankruptcy and flanked by the demands of the International Monetary Fund on one side and the complaints of a demoralized and betrayed populace on the other? According to Beatriz Sarlo (Mariño 2001), there were few alternatives left to answer such a question in the twenty-first century. She argues that a collective sense of "Argentineity" vanished into an unending present separated from both a nostalgic and idealized past and an imagined future now made impossible. Argentina has become, in Sarlo's terms "a country without a project" (Mariño 2001). More than twenty years after the dictatorship, and after the debacle of the Menem transformation, there is only left, according to Sarlo, a broken imaginary of a pulverized Argentina where perhaps the only nationalism remaining is the athletic (Mariño 2001).[1]

But it may be that in addition to sports there is another forum in which Argentine identity is being sanctioned or is reconfiguring itself, in spite of, or maybe due to "the twenty-first century Argentine failure." Although Sarlo sees the athletic arena as one of the last vestiges of a project that creates a sense of national belonging, she leaves on the sideline another vital and vigorous mission that even in these desperate times continues to promote a sense of nationality and national pride. And it is this venture that may perhaps serve better than sports to demonstrate how the notion of the national is being constructed out of the Argentine financial crisis and in collusion with neoliberal market practices and the culture of mass media. It is tourism, or the discourse of tourism marketing, that synthesizes "the Argentine" based on cultural patrimony and tourist expectations, that I suggest provides an exemplary way to study how a sense of nationalism is being created, and deconstructed, by the economic, political, and cultural cross-currents of globalization.

Positing tourism as a discourse that projects and configures the nation is taking Benedict Anderson's (1983) conceptualization of the imagined community one step further into the twenty-first century. Anderson has theorized that the sense of nationhood began to flourish with the rise of print capitalism that set the stage for a wide and diverse populace of readers to imagine themselves as part of a limited and sovereign community that united them. This community, which could never be fully known by any one of its individual members in a material sense, could be "imagined" fully by each one. It is this imagined community that generates the concepts of nation, nationalism, and national identity. Anderson sees the model for this process originating in nineteenth-century Latin America. After independence, creole leaders, no longer colonial subjects, sought to differentiate and define a coherent and homogeneous image of an individual nation and citizenry adherent to the values, codes, and desires of a Europeanized, white, liberal intelligentsia. In Anderson's paradigm this image of the nation, constructed on the basis of liberal economics, modernity, and republican ideals that most often did not translate to democratic equalities, was represented in the vernacular language of the region, especially through newspapers and print narrative. Today, in the twenty-first century, sources in print no longer dominate communication, national or otherwise. Methods of communication and media have changed, diversified, and globalized, and any imagined community intuited from within contemporary systems of communication would necessarily be reflective of the heterogeneity of the media's nature.

Tourism, as it is practiced and marketed today, cannot be articulated only through the kind of print narrative that dominated the nineteenth century; it is also represented through visual texts, iconic systems, and by the flows and movements of peoples, images, services, and goods. It is read through posters, postcards, pamphlets, websites, TV ads, videos, architecture, urban planning, street signs, museums, gross national products, and tourist bodies. These discourses of tourism project a different kind of imagined community, one that adheres to the exigencies and principles of commodity culture and transnational markets rather than to the ideals of writers, journalists, and statesmen who sought to create a national identity that reflected their beliefs about the world and self. Obviously, world economic schemes did also underlie the national visions that the creole intellectuals held. However, their imagined communities encompassed the open market debates of liberal economics stemming from the core-periphery model of Western modernity. Nineteenth-century Latin American elites endeavoured to define the nation based on their understandings of this model and how they saw the needs of the nation being satisfied. Their discussions, projections, models, and arguments came together within the newspapers, journals, and fictional narrative from which national readers could ingest these principles and visions of the nation's future and identify with one another as sharing common traits and beliefs.

The imagined community projected by tourism is much more volatile, and more relative to and dependent on the desires, imaginings, and needs coming from outside national territory. This makes identifying with one another as sharing national commonalities in this community more problematic as such imagined identities may be ones that are archaic, anachronistic, fictional, or that create divisions between tourism providers and participants, or because they emanate from such a variety of media, they may be antagonistic to or contradict each other. Tourism's imagined community highlights the neocolonial aspects of contemporary Latin America, especially in the cultural narratives and questions of sovereignty created by globalization. In contrast to solidifying a coherent and limited concept of the nation, tourism tends to fracture and open up the idea of the nation by imagining the national, not only as subordinate to international issues, but also as defined by its reinterpretations at the regional level, as this kind of imagined difference is the key to creating touristic interest and growth for specific locations. With a nod to Anderson, in this chapter I consider how the discourses and representations of tourism have come to inform, shape, and codify concepts of the nation and the region in Mendoza and how this has reflected and changed Mendoza's relationship and valuing of the Cordillera.

Image and Tradition

Over the last two decades Mendoza's tourist industry, media, and the provincial government have increasingly highlighted the significance of Aconcagua's economic potential and international draw as a mountaineering adventure destination. The economic returns for Mendoza from Aconcagua mountaineering are far-reaching in terms of revenue for service providers, restaurants, hotels, and mountaineering and adventure tourism agencies. With respect to environmental gains for the province, notwithstanding the use and degradation of the park's territory, the additional monies that the Aconcagua Provincial Park generates through admission permit sales provide support for the running of the park itself and add to the Department of Renewable Natural Resources' funds to administer the twelve other natural reserves of Mendoza province. Thus, the continued success of mountaineering has become crucial to the province and, consequently, the managing and marketing of Aconcagua have evolved into significant and salient features of Mendoza's mountaineering industry.

The marketing of Aconcagua forms a relatively new part of Mendoza's tourist initiatives and indicates a rift in the coherency of Mendoza's long-standing and traditional touristic images and self-representations. Although Mendoza has historically been connected to the nation via Buenos Aires, it has also been a territorial "other" for the nation's capital. In this model, a provincial and agricultural Mendoza is in opposition to the industrialized port city of Buenos Aires. From this duality, Mendoza, "la tierra del sol y buen vino" ("land of sun and good wine"), represents everything that is not *porteño* (pertaining to Buenos Aires). It is an inland, exotic place, Chile-anized, and at times idealized; Mendoza is the premodern idyllic countryside compared to the cosmopolitan urban sprawl of Buenos Aires. This model generates the narrative that Mendoza has traditionally used to define itself, a story based on European immigration and settlement, agricultural industries, and wine production. These narratives are principal components of the Mendoza origin story that is reenacted every year in the province's biggest tourist draw, the week-long harvest celebration, la Vendimia, held every March. This celebration includes the crowning of departmental Vendimia princesses and a provincial queen and court. Subsequently, provincial tourist enterprises have primarily derived out of these traditions, as illustrated by the tourist circuit, El Camino del Vino, and the ever-popular organized tours and visits by tourist agencies to the province's local wineries, which are estimated to number approximately one thousand. It is this historical and touristic image of a princess-laden, wine-sipping, sedentary, and what we might call a "feminized" Mendoza that contrasts with the presence and promotion of "masculinized" Aconcagua momentous adventure.

After more than a hundred years of mountaineering activity in the region, the touristic vision of Mendoza as the land of sun and good wine and beautiful women is now destabilized by the integration of mountaineering into Mendocino socioeconomic culture and its tourism project. This new profile of Mendoza is dependent on the many varied, sometimes complementary and often conflictive, national, international, and regional imaginings, past and present, that Mendoza's tourism industry has cannibalized to represent the Aconcagua zone. Mendoza tourism, as it digests images, discourses, and icons of Aconcagua and mountaineering, creates a polyvalent, hybrid, and fluid portrait of Mendoza in which we find transnational imaginings linking with regional routes of history and memory. As these competing imaginations and social practices have evolved and recombined over time they have reworked the way that Mendocinos see themselves in the context of the nation and the world, and they have reformulated the way that the mountains, and specifically Aconcagua, are seen in Mendoza. The junction of multiple understandings of Aconcagua and Mendoza, in response to the pressures of an international adventure tourism market, both invoke and disrupt mountaineering's imperialist modern legacy of exclusivity concerning nation, race, and gender, thus both sustaining and challenging the sport's traditional marginality for local society.

The Face and Facets of Tourism

While Aconcagua may lie hundreds of kilometers away from the capital city of Mendoza, it is easily located in the downtown urban landscape. Mountaineering equipment shops and adventure tourism agencies that promote Aconcagua with posters, pictures, signs, and displays of mountaineering gear in storefront windows have snagged prime positions in the city center's busiest shopping blocks. In addition, news kiosks flaunt postcards, photographs, and posters, many by Mendocino mountaineer-photographers, that show the gold-drenched West Face of Aconcagua at sunset, the snow-covered wall of the South Face, or Nido de Cóndores where a lone *andinista*, or mountaineer, stands at dusk looking out over the horizon toward the Pacific (see fig. 2.1). During the climbing season (approximately November 15 to March 30), the sunburned faces sporting white-circled eyes and blistered lips that congregate at the outdoor cafés on the tree-lined Peatonal, or Calle Sarmiento, clearly signal those who have returned from Aconcagua. Their air of relaxation contrasts with the hurried anxiousness of other, paler body types of international visitors, unmistakably on their way up the mountain, who crisscross the city center to rent equipment and clothing and buy the entrance permit. It was not a

Figure 2.1. This postcard of Aconcagua shows a mountaineer looking towards the Pacific Ocean from Nido de Cóndores (5,250 meters), the North Route. The postcard is from a series of photographs by the Mendocino mountain guide and conservation activist Mariano Nadalich.

coincidence that the city moved the permit-granting site to the city center from its previous location in the Parque de Independencia in 2004; this move was to keep the mountain visitors in town and spending money as long as possible. Mountaineering, once a marginalized activity, exclusive to Northern adventurers, and restricted to the Aconcagua zone 240 kilometers to the north, is now front and center in downtown Mendoza.

Mountaineering bodies, shops, gear, and images of Aconcagua have changed the commercial and demographic face of urban Mendoza by catering to the most international base of Mendoza's tourism industry. Mendoza's mountaineering industry attracts climbers from more than sixty countries every year, while other tourist attractions in Mendoza draw primarily from Argentina and other South American countries, especially Chile. This focus on international tourism and the emphasis on the Aconcagua industry reflect both national and regional touristic movements. In 2007 the official Argentine governmental website for tourism cited tourism as playing a central and fundamental role in the national economy for its capacity to generate a rapid intake of monies and create employment ("El turismo" 2008). While Mendoza's looking toward tourist revenues for a rapid economic fix mirrors national tendencies as a whole to promote tourism, it also underscores collective Mendocino support for increasing provincial initiatives to deal with chronic Argentine economic instabilities via regional projects and local-global connections rather than relying on national institutions or national solutions.[2] In keeping with national trends of development, Mendoza saw a 50 percent increase in tourism from 1999 to 2006 (Tapia 2006). As for Aconcagua mountaineering, there was a 20 percent increase in the 2002–3 season after the devaluation of the peso and until 2009 growth registered between a 5 percent and 10 percent increase every season.[3]

Tourism and the oil and agriculture industries have ensured Mendoza's economic survival when national coffers have failed to cover the federal share of regional expenses. By 2003 tourism revenues were already seen as being as important as wine exports (Sala 2003). While the oil industry and agriculture are more closely tied to national control of tariffs and restrictions, tourism generally allows for more autonomy in regionally based initiatives with global outlooks. An exception to this is the fact that during the national economic crisis of 2002–3 it was Mendoza's oil production that helped stabilize the regional economy. The issuance of the *petrom*, Mendoza's regional currency, was based on projected oil industry revenues and was used to meet provincial government expenditures when the federal government defaulted on its payments to the province. The governor of the province at the time, Roberto Iglesias, ordered the emission of a provincial bond, the petrom, to replace the *lécop*, the national bond, citing the inability of the federal government to send the funding that corresponded to the provinces. The loss of faith in the national government also implied a challenge to the International Monetary Fund (IMF) that demanded that the national government prohibit the provinces from emitting their own currencies.[4]

In the twenty-first century, Mendoza has tended to turn its back on the capital city in its battles with the IMF, similar to how it denies its resemblance to Buenos Aires in order to promote itself touristically. In the same vein it has also distanced itself from the capital when looking to make economic, extraterritorial connections. Mendoza has also put its eyes on Chile, in the past a tourist destination for Mendocinos, but now, since the devaluation of the peso, converted to a provider of tourists for Mendoza. The old colonial connection with Chile, which until recently was always vehemently rejected, has now been resuscitated as the road to the future. Thus, tourism trends in twenty-first-century Mendoza reflect how economic endeavors that provide a way for the province to assert some local control in a neoliberal globalized economy may also serve to fracture the national-regional nexus by forging regional-international bonds that are not brokered explicitly through national channels.

There is little doubt that the tourism industry, not only in Mendoza but within Argentina in general, has intensified as a result of the country's twenty-first-century economic crises and the devaluation of the Argentine peso that, until January 2002, had maintained parity with the dollar for a decade. Since that time tourism's potential to benefit from an unfavorable exchange rate has been routinely touted as a hopeful and immediate opportunity for an otherwise bleak economic forecast in Argentina. This was especially true in Mendoza, with its population of approximately 1.5 million and its borders with Chile, where optimism in tourism's capacity to fill the economic void held sway with regard to both international and national travel to the province. Speculation was that with the devalued peso Argentines would find it more difficult to travel abroad and national destinations would become a practical alternative. With regard to international travelers, it seemed likely that Argentina's depressed economy would make the country's tourist destinations more attractive and accessible to foreign pocketbooks. However, in Mendoza, the tourism industry's wager on Aconcagua as an international destination was placed even before the devaluation occurred as part of a comprehensive strategy by the tourism industry to speculate on those kinds of high-end international tourist markets that would be least tied to Argentine economic cycles (Lledo 2001).

In its five-year planning document, *TurPlan 2000–2005*, the Mendoza Tourism Subsecretariat, now the Ministry of Tourism, heralded Aconcagua as a magnet for international mountaineering whose presence should provide one of the most important touristic advantages for the province (2000, 217). Amidst *TurPlan* speculation about prospects for provincial tourism growth in general, the Aconcagua market has lived up to, and at times surpassed, the most optimistic of the plan's predictions. *TurPlan* projected for the province an 8 percent yearly growth in tourism, with even a minimum 3 percent increase during the worst economic situations (2000, 264). Although 2001 brought unexpected obstacles to the Argentine tourist industry on both national and international fronts, the tragedy of 9/11, the war in Afghanistan, and Argentina's subsequent political and economic crisis that occurred in the middle of the climbing season did not provoke a drastic decrease in Aconcagua activity. In fact, park admissions for 2001–2 registered a 2 percent increase. The following season's growth, a 20 percent increase in admissions to the Aconcagua Provincial Park during the 2002–3 climbing period, more than doubled *TurPlan*'s highest expectations when not even the threat of a US war with Iraq in 2003 curtailed travel to Aconcagua. (Emotional or material obstacles to

US travel are fundamentally important to the Aconcagua industry because US nationals consistently register the highest numbers of international climbers every year.) In the period 2002–2008 the park saw yearly growth vacillate between 5 and 10 percent, which has meant at least an annual addition of over a million dollars to the Department of Renewable Resources budget (after expenditures) for the administration of the twelve provincial areas under its jurisdiction.[5]

The new mountaineering dimension of Mendoza may be seen in this increased success of Aconcagua and in the celebratory register of the stories and articles by local twenty-first-century Mendocino media, especially in the two major daily newspapers, *Los Andes* and *Uno*, that have openly speculated about the future of mountain tourism by professing that the international recognition of Aconcagua and the regional growth of tourism in the mountain region are of lucrative significance for the development of regionally beneficial international connections.

Tourism Blueprints

In Mendoza the official provincial policy of the twenty-first century was laid out in *TurPlan 2000–2005: Plan Estratégico de Desarrollo Turístico de Mendoza* (Strategic Plan for Touristic Development of Mendoza), a document designed in 1999 through collaborative consultation between the private and public institutions involved in the tourism industry. *TurPlan* referred to tourism as "the great alternative to generate investments and jobs" (2000, 18). However, the former governor Roberto Iglesias warned in 2000 that this touristic growth would depend on the capacity of Mendoza to sell its attractions to a global audience. "For this," said Iglesias, "we should reconvert ourselves, because the demands today are different" (Fiore 2000). The touristic conversion that Iglesias advocated in the abstract suggests for the material world an increased attention to the practical necessities of touristic infrastructure, and it also hints at the altering of the scope of regional self-identification. While Mendoza regional identity has previously been forged on confirming local Argentineity according to the parameters of the nation, promotion of its touristic potential must now be looked at in accordance to those different demands of today, as Iglesias put it, which most necessarily translate to those of globalization and the exigencies of the international tourism market.

In Mendoza this touristic reconversion has been implemented through the directives of the official document, *TurPlan*, which was meant to guide the steps of both government and business tourism initiatives. *TurPlan* defined itself as a plan of "organization, professionalization, and coherency" and proclaimed that "the Province of Mendoza definitely needs to situate itself in the global market" (2000, 17). Mendoza´s *TurPlan*, a document of more than two hundred pages of graphics, diagrams, and economic projections, established itself as a regulating tool to program and narrate Mendoza, especially to itself, as a worldwide tourist destination. That *TurPlan 2000–2005* was successful in this endeavor was publicly acclaimed in 2007 with the announcement that tourism had increased by 50 percent since 1999 and that its successor, *TurPlan 2007–2011*, was in the wings. Mendocino officials spent the year in between the two plans, 2006, in open planning meetings and workshops, and in a lengthy evaluation of *TurPlan I*, which was found to have functioned satisfactorily by more than 67 percent of those involved in the evaluation process ("Fue presentado" 2007).[6] An advisor to *TurPlan 2000–2005*, Rafael Fuentes García, proclaimed that Mendoza had radically readjusted its profile with regard to its touristic identity during those years: "When I arrived, tourism lacked importance at the institutional level, in the media, and among entrepreneurs and in society. Today there is a Ministry, it is covered in the media, the activity is respected among entrepreneurs and society values it. It is a drastic change" (Tapia 2006).

TurPlan, in fashioning Mendoza for tourism with respect to its mountain heritage, postulated three foci that were most advantageous for the market: Aconcagua, adventure tourism, and General José de San Martín. While the promotion of Aconcagua mountaineering and adventure tourism skews toward future possibilities of a more globally connected Mendoza, the highlighting of the historical significance of General José de San Martín for Mendoza's claim to the mountain region harkens back to a more traditional interpretation of local Argentineity based on its function within the construction of Argentine nationhood.

Tourism's Patriotic Heights

In the early twenty-first century the vindication of Mendoza´s link to José de San Martín, as much a nineteenth-century national Argentine hero as a transnational champion of South American independence, was encouraged as a way to resuscitate the province's most epic and patriotic past as touristic capital. Mendoza considers San Martín to be a native son. Although he was not born in the region, he served as governor of the province from 1814 to 1817, during which he was readying his army to cross the Andes and continue the continent's struggle for independence from Spain. Mendoza takes much pride in its contributions to and support of San Martín's Army of the Andes. The provincial and city governments have commemorated the great sacrifice and triumph of this army in crossing the Cordillera to liberate Chile, as well as Mendoza's own role in the campaign. This is evidenced in the various San Martín historical museums and in the reenactments, such as "History in Its Place" and "The Preparations for the Crossing of the Andes," at the museum of site at San Martín's Plumerillo camp. This veneration is especially confirmed in the huge monument gracing the top of the hillside of the Cerro de la Gloria that depicts Mendoza's supportive role in the army's crossing of the Cordillera.[7]

These historical memories and commemorations of San Martín, a figure most familiar to tourists from the Southern Cone, are evoked by museums, monuments, and dramatizations, and these collective memories are what *TurPlan* sought to make more visible in Mendoza. This was accomplished with the creation of a program of signage, Las Rutas Sanmartinianas, inaugurated in 2001 at a cost of more than 70,000 dollars.[8] This new touristic mapping proposed to "value places of educational, touristic, and cultural appeal and show the visitor, in an orderly fashion, a program of routes and activities that would have him live the past in a different way" (Hidalgo 2001). The signage program divides the region into five routes whose points of interest along the way are explained through seventy-five signs that summarize the history of each site in three languages: Spanish, English, and Portuguese. The signs, through drawings and narrations, illustrate and interpret the vision of San Martín, and especially his association with the Andes, held in the Mendocino imaginary and as interpreted by Mendocino tourism officials. These San Martín signs bring history, collective memory, and the mountains into the city by changing the urban cartography and inserting other imagined timelines. In this way, Mendoza reorganized and reinvented itself according to *TurPlan* as an out-of-the-ordinary location of Sanmartinian touristic import. As such, it fashioned itself for the touristic gaze (Urry 1997), which was to be directed and instructed by the signage roadmaps that interpreted its importance for the visitors. According to Mendoza's Subsecretary of Tourism at the time of the inauguration of the signage program, Gabriel Fidel, "in this way the magic of the landscape unites with history through the image of the Liberator. . . . Mendoza doesn't sell by itself unless it is accompanied by a product that makes it attractive" (Hidalgo 2001).

It is what is not seen, or what is seen only through the help of new maps, routes, signs, and explanations, that makes Mendoza appealing to tourists.

Typically, in order to promote interest in a place, it is what does not exist that is often explicitly highlighted. On Las Rutas Sanmartinianas this is the case, both implicitly and explicitly. A *Los Andes* journalist, Mariana Gil, reports that "in those cases in which the historical sites have been destroyed by the earthquake, they have been reconstructed with images and portraits so that the tourist can know the Mendoza of that era" (2001, 19). Barbara Kirschenblatt-Gimblett (1998) explains that "both heritage and tourism deal in the intangible, absent, inaccessible, fragmentary, and dislocated. . . . Guides routinely refer to what cannot be seen—the people and events and places of years ago" (187). *TurPlan*, its media campaign, and the signage program construct not only a historical Mendoza for the touristic view, but also an imagined future Mendoza as the hub of a multitudinous and diverse international (thus the trilingual explanatory texts) cultural tourism associated with San Martín, as well as hiding the current-day Mendoza, in which only an average of 1,700 tourists visit the Sanmartinian sites annually.[9]

This use of the past patrimony as present-day capital or economic investment for the future contrasts with the disconnectedness from history that Sarlo sees in Argentine society today (Mariño 2001). For Sarlo, whatever national cultural project may exist, present or future, it can no longer benefit from the traditional relationship between the reading public and an intellectual elite capable of reimagining the country and legitimizing it. Certainly, Sarlo is right when she insists that the traditional reading public has diminished drastically before the acute conformist pressures of global economies and mass media. Nor does the state, as Sarlo puts it, have the "necessary force to intervene from the perspective of general interest when today the fight is every faction against the rest" (Mariño 2001). Reformulating the postulations of Angel Rama (1982) and in reply to Sarlo, I suggest that there might be a new matrix from which to forge the symbology of a national spirit and in which the touristic public would replace the reading public as the recipient of the nation-building discourse, fractured though it might be, pronounced by the new men of letters, the new *letrados*, the directors, ministers, subsecretaries, and businessmen of the tourist industry.

In Mendoza, the tourism elites are those who invent, reveal, and validate cultural patrimony as a touristic destination, offering visitors the experience of living the past in the present. The use of the history of San Martín as tourism does just this. Following the Sanmartinian routes, a *Los Andes* journalist, Celeste Polidori (2001), asserts that "anyone can, through his/her imagination, become part of the feat and even fire rifles

Figure 2.2. A Rutas Sanmartinianas (Sanmartinian Route) sign in downtown Mendoza. The image of Argentina's Liberator, José de San Martín, who crossed the Andes to defeat the Spanish, signals sites of historical importance. The signs are in Spanish, English, and Portuguese.

and cannons of the period." Kirschenblatt-Gimblett finds that an experiential factor is most urgent in assigning touristic value to heritage (1998, 167). Experience is made possible by the signage that promotes "becoming acquainted with revolutionary-period Mendoza," "getting to know San Martín as a man, an officer, and a father," and of "living history" (Polidori 2001). In addition to the new look that the signs give to Mendoza, it is this experience of passing time in an earlier period, albeit constructed through dreams, wishes, texts, and graphics, which tourist officials package to surreptitiously convert Mendoza into a kind of Sanmartinian theme park.

Epic Visions

TurPlan, in its promotion of Mendoza's ties to San Martín, has set its sights on those heroic images of this history that might best promote Mendoza within a globalizing tourist economy. Besides the neoliberal practices employed by the multinational industrial complex and international financial institutions, García Canclini (2000) suggests a broader characterization of globalization that goes beyond the purely economic. He sees it as a space where a vision of the present, as well as the future, can be reformulated. With respect to tourism, this type of reformulation may be especially fruitful, since it can benefit, according to Canclini, the growth of cultural industries that are able to homogenize while preserving regional diversities, which, in essence, would offer peripheral cultures a way to maintain their local traditions (2000, 24).

The local memories and projections of San Martín as he prepared to take revolutionary war to Chile and Peru that are mapped by Las Rutas Sanmartinianas are uniquely Mendocino in origin. Yet, at the same time, they project a more expansive image of the Liberator that directs itself toward South American independence as a whole. In this way, Mendoza's claim to San Martín invokes both Argentine national unity and transnational cooperation. In other words, as a cultural commodity, San Martín has the capacity to homogenize a sense of both nation and pan-Americanism through the evocation of a distant epoch that is ideologically neutral with respect to the present. His memory harkens to a period that remains beyond the reach of present-day nationalist antagonisms and fractures and recriminations against history. Nevertheless, at the same time that the San Martín image projects an idealized, united, homogeneous national, and continental citizenship linked to independence and victory, it also attends in detail to secular and regional diversities by highlighting Mendoza and its unique participation in the army's crossing of the Andes. Thus, Mendoza is positioned in a place of privilege within a patriotic national scheme and in an overarching idea of South American freedom that is constructed by the signage. In this way, Mendoza is differentiated from the rest of Argentina at the same time that it reaffirms its connections to both the nation and the transnational region. This capacity to spotlight its uniqueness, as well as its common appeal, is a vital touristic strategy. The routes especially create interest for the two main groups of tourists who visit Mendoza: Argentine nationals, who since the devaluation of the peso in 2002 make up approximately 75 percent of Mendoza's visitors, and Chileans, who since the same moment in time have come to see Mendoza as a viable and affordable destination.[10]

TurPlan's (2000) characterization of the potential of tourism in the mountain zone juxtaposes its reverence to San Martín with its spotlight on Aconcagua. As a lure for international mountaineering, Aconcagua, according to *TurPlan*, provides one of the most important touristic advantages for Mendoza (2000, 217). Thus, patriotic heritage and contemporary adventure come to define present-day Mendoza's official engagement with the mountain as strategies to participate in a globalized tourism market. This mix of history and adventure are not as contradictory as they might seem at first glance. In terms of history, *TurPlan* chose to emphasize an epic discourse about a particularly epic period: the crossing of the Andes by San Martín. Although local newspapers speak of the guiding thread of the signage plan that weaves "a complete picture of the Father of the Nation" (Gil 2001), the image stamped on each sign is that of the exalted victor, the Liberator on his rearing stallion, with his arm extended like a saber, a super-patriotic and hypermasculinized image of the conqueror of the Andes.

The tourist elites of Mendoza use this heroic San Martín as their trump card to market, sell, and validate their products. It is the manner in which the story is narrated, according to García Canclini (2000), that leads us to understand how the process of globalization integrates itself into the local. He points out that the various disciplines used to study society and culture, which he codifies as epic (economics, sociology, communications) or melodramas (those that mark the fissures, violences, pains: anthropology, psychoanalysis) are of no value alone, but only in conjunction in order to evaluate the recompositions that are being produced between the local and the global (2000, 34–35). Nonetheless, in its evocation of Mendoza, the *TurPlan* tends to ignore the melodramas and emphasizes history as its referent, an epic discourse about a daring moment, the crossing of the

Andes by San Martín. In terms of Mendocino tourism, this not only serves as an impetus to change the face of Mendoza through the Sanmartinian signage but also to promote adventure tourism, which takes advantage of the association with San Martín.

This virile stamp of San Martín's patriotic and victorious image easily links to the imperial masculine appeal of mountaineering adventure. The heroic discourse of the association of San Martín with the mountain effectively complements *TurPlan*'s strategic marketing of Aconcagua and adventure tourism in general to a more internationally diverse, yet homogeneous, public that feeds on adrenaline, challenge, exploration, and conquest.[11] This is especially exemplified by the growing popularity of the touristic facsimile of San Martín's feats, or the horseback excursions across the Andes organized by Mendocino adventure tourism agencies that follow the trails of the Army of the Andes.

TurPlan's focus on Aconcagua and adventure tourism, together with the implementation of the signage cartography that physically inserts San Martinian-style mountain adventure into Mendoza and its suburbs, serves to instruct Mendoza's contemporary understandings and uses of the mountain zone as an area of expanded touristic potential. *TurPlan* models superimpose times that highlight both the heritage of the past and the activities of the present, situating multiple fantasies in the same scenario. With these strategies, coupled with the signage of San Martín that projects an ideal, united, homogeneous citizenship linked to independence and victory, but also attentive to secular and regional diversities, Mendoza seems to be "re-converting" itself following the necessary guidelines, according to García Canclini (2000), to be favored by globalization.

Other Discourses of Tourism

Without a doubt, *TurPlan* officially remains within epic discourses, specifically in respect to historical references to San Martín and the mountains, and to the economic, sociological, and media studies that form its base. Although *TurPlan* as a document does not intimate any doubt about the meta-discourses that construct it as possibly reflecting ideologically bound and genre-associated truths, there are other present-day touristic initiatives that insinuate a partiality and arbitrariness in any "official" discourse. These touristic efforts in recuperating ethnic identities and reconfiguring economic borders imply a broader and more multicultural perspective than the epic stories that San Martín and mountaineering promote. In the last fifteen years, there has been a vindication of indigenous Mendoza, which has repercussed in the cultural tourism sector. The most visible proof that Mendoza is reaffirming its existence as an ancient Huarpe settlement is El Museo del Área Fundacional, which opened its doors in 1995. Nearly half of the museum is dedicated to the telling of the indigenous past of the region through dioramas, sketches, and narration, and the other half contrasts pre- and post-earthquake Mendoza. In addition, during the last decade the provincial government named the Guaytamari Huarpe commune as the guardian of three historical sites in Uspallata and began conceding land to the Huarpe communities of Lavalle and supporting them in developing a cultural and adventure tourism industry as an economic outlet (see chapter 3).

Mendoza has not just seen a return to its indigenous past in recent years, but also a reaffirmation of its links to Chile. In order to create a global Mendoza, it became necessary to redefine movement across cultural, historical, and national borders in order to facilitate transit (of ideas, people, goods, etc.). Although the Mendocino mountain region with its claim on San Martín is enshrined in national patriotic history and is seen as having predominantly served as a geographical and climactic barrier separating Argentina from Chile, various attempts at binational collaboration have emerged. For example, the IVA (Impuesto al Valor Agregado, or value-added tax) for the winter season of 2001 was rescinded to increase and facilitate tourist travel; in mid-2003 there was an initiative to create a macro-region with Chile in the vicinity of the Valle de Uco; there is an ongoing multinational project to have the Camino del Inka declared a World Heritage site; and there continue to be rumors of other binational touristic collaborations in the high mountains closer to Aconcagua. Mendoza, with its eye on the world market, is rediscovering its erased pasts, its ethnicities, its links to Chile, and its local particularities. What was denied or hidden before in order to seem more "Argentine" (the erasure of the country's indigenous populations, Mendoza's historical association with Chile) is now being revealed to offer other images that are more pluricultural and cooperative. Whether or not these new images result from their attractiveness as a lucrative viability in a global market, they still take on oppositional positionings in the traditional paradigm of Argentine national identity that evolved out of a white creole modern imaginary, the belief in the nineteenth-century desert campaigns' "extermination" of Argentina's native peoples, and the legacy of European settlement.

It appears that the tourism industry, in terms of diversifying its cultural agenda and representing the history and people of Mendoza, has realized that in order to invest in globalization it might be beneficial to diversify from those grand epics and the traditional identity categories, be they cultural, discursive, or geopolitical, that they support. At the same time, however, tourism's most visible policies clearly seek to benefit from repeating the same narratives, relationships, and categories that are already established and functioning in the national collective imagination, which facilitates marketing Mendoza as a tourist destination where you can experience history and pleasure. Of course, these traditional imaginings seem to be formulated with the assurance that the "tourist" who is looking or observing or desiring is masculine and will feel attracted to the beautiful women, the good wine, an ennobling patriotism, and the challenge of adventure and conquest that discounts women in the equation.

Military Visions

History of Aconcagua, *written with realism, vivacity and color by the men who have dominated the highest peak in America, is a book that honors its authors and honors the Nation.*

—JUAN PERÓN (1953, 9)

The high esteem in which General José de San Martín and his Army of the Andes are held for having braved the cruelty of the mountains in the name of liberty has a decidedly masculine tone. San Martín's especially proud place in Mendocino memory projects the grandiosity of patriotic fervor to the mountains and easily links to the long-standing history of the militarization of the Aconcagua zone and Argentine mountaineering as a military endeavor. General San Martín is routinely referenced by local andinistas, or mountaineers, when discussing the origins of mountaineering in Mendoza, and he is referred to, as in the title of Orlando Mario Punzi's book (1978), as the region's first andinista (*San Martín: El primer montañés de América* [San Martín: America's First Mountaineer]).

This invocation of San Martín and the history of Argentina's first state-backed initiatives on Aconcagua and beyond Latin America connect the sport to masculinist and military traditions. The first Argentine to actually summit Aconcagua was another military man, Lieutenant Nicolás Plantamura, who reached the mountain's pinnacle in 1934. (He participated in a European expedition and was accompanied by a Chilean-born local arriero, Marío Pastén.) Subsequent military participation in local mountaineering reached international levels when President Juan Perón sent several Argentine military mountaineering expeditions to the Himalayas in the 1950s. The military's endeavors on and administration of the Aconcagua region remained paramount until civilian control and the Aconcagua Provincial Park were established in 1983.

The approximation of the Argentine military to the kind of interaction with Aconcagua initiated by international expeditioners earlier in the century was not a radical disruption in tradition. Whether a celebration of Anglo-European adventurer-explorers or Argentine military heroes, the hierarchical nature of international mountaineering remained intact in that it still privileged the experience of mountain adventure for an elite group that is patriarchal in structure. In fact, according to Ortner (1999), "the dominant mode of the mountaineering expedition was derived from military practice. Expeditions were modeled on army campaigns . . . and the language of mountaineering is full of militarisms such as assault, attack, conquest" (159). The romantic legacy of the mountaineer adventurer and the shadow of the military man overlap in a sharing of characteristics and assumptions about the nature of adventure and mountaineering that transcend First World and Third World and civilian and military differences. Fearlessness, the ability to deal with unexpected or chance occurrences, the notions of honor and personal sacrifice, the patriotic rhetoric of their stories, as well as the maintenance of strict hierarchies of leadership and compliance, are common traits of both these climbing archetypes. Intrinsically, both of these models retain the notion of mountaineering as serving a higher spiritual and national purpose or goal that disregards material gain.

The traditionally positive association of the military with mountaineering and Aconcagua clashes with the more troublesome perception of the Argentine military in the twentieth century. In Argentina, the role and function of the military, past and present, has always tended to be conflictive, but the most recent painful Argentine memory is that of a repressive dictatorship (1976–1983), known as the Proceso de Reorganización Nacional (Process of National Reorganization), that lost the Falkland Islands War and kidnapped, tortured, and disappeared thirty thousand of its own people.

The generalized military demeanor of a mountaineering expedition, as well as images that play to the underlying values of sacrifice, courage, and honor that drive both mountaineering and military rhetoric, may not be so innocently discounted in a country with recent memories of a military's oppression of its own people. Postcards, pamphlets, and adventure agency websites abound that depict Aconcagua in the discourse of valor, honor, and noble gesture: a lone (masculine) body profiled against the setting sun at Nido de Cóndores; other solitary male bodies shot vertically on the steep grade of the Polish Glacier; and the lone man on the ice wall, which graces the official poster of the Aconcagua Provincial Park. The most visible image on pamphlets and posters is of the mountain hero as a solitary individual struggling against the dangers of overwhelming nature. That lone man on the postcard juxtaposed with the majestic mountain leads one down the historical memory path to that of another Argentine solitary character, the military man. Diana Taylor explains that

> it is not coincidental that the Junta's dismantling of a constitutional system of collective decision-making (such as the dissolution of Parliament and the Supreme Court in the days following the coup) should have been represented in terms of the lone male, situated in a dark vacuum beyond the boundaries of communal life, with only the stars to guide him. Nor should it surprise us that the emphasis on the solitary hero coincided with Argentina's economic drive toward privatization, consumerism, and international capitalism. As civil society "disappeared," members of society were pushed into the "individual" and "private" sphere. (1997, 285–286)

In tourist campaigns for Aconcagua, more than just marketing an idealized mountain body is going on. Taylor's reading reminds us of the capitalist and military undertones of the imagined solitary body on the mountain that is created for tourist consumption. However, this association of the military and the mountain for Mendocinos is not as one-dimensional as allusions to Taylor's reading of the lone military man might suggest. It is also associated with the adventures of heroic rescues, with international dealings, and a perspective turned outward to protect, unlike the forces of the Proceso that turned inward to police the national body.

The painful collective memory of the Dirty War is especially countered by the mountaineering museum of the 8th Mountain Brigade's First Lieutenant Ibáñez Company of the Cazadores de los Andes, which is located in Puente del Inca, the main staging area for Aconcagua expeditions. This informal museum, open to the public, displays mostly photographs, newspaper clippings, and documents of the Brigade's climbing celebrities, its rescue missions, its international collaborations, and especially of its favorite son, Francisco Ibáñez. The museum clearly represents the history of the military mountain man as a protector of the people and as a national and international icon of Argentine achievements. The Brigade's museum and the opening to the public every year of its two short ski-training slopes, at an incredibly low price, project a positive image of the Brigade's role on the mountain as one of support and accomplishments.[12] Additionally, that other particularly Mendocino and undeniably patriotic military icon that counters the Junta's image of control, order, and violence is the presence of General José de San Martín, the Liberator. Route markers along Highway 7 note the passage of San Martín's troops on their way to cross the Andes and liberate Chile. At Puente del Inca there is a sign marking a stop on one of the five tourist itineraries mapped by Las Rutas Sanmartinianas. And in 2010, a bust of San Martín was officially placed at Horcones, the entrance to Aconcagua Provincial Park. These official Mendoza government initiatives reinforce the projection of regional and national patriotism on Aconcagua by framing it within the discourse of homage to Mendoza's favorite adopted son, General San Martín. His presence is invoked in an image that projects freedom, independence, and a turning toward international connections as the Argentine forefather of andinismo.

Debriefs

The memory of San Martín, the continued presence of the military, and the traditional work of the arrieros are the most consistent and longest-lasting Argentine images of the Aconcagua region for Mendoza today. But only the first two feed into an epic discourse of patriotism, valor, and masculine authority that has been ceremoniously upheld in collective memory and in tourism campaigns as representing Mendoza's mountaineering patrimony. Mendoza's tourism policies create an image of Argentineity that highlights the individuality of Mendoza and demonstrates the history of its modernity as an internationally linked center, in the past as a base that San Martín connected to Chile, Peru, and independence, and in contemporary times as the base where international travelers mingle with Mendocinos in the name of adventure.

However, touristic promotion of traditional Mendoza, "the land of sun and good wine," downplay its image as a modern global center and tend to emphasize a rhetoric of escapism that complements Aconcagua as adventure, a remote, dangerous, unknown destination of personal quest.[13] While a modern mountaineering industry that takes pride in its global connections may highlight these for marketing purposes, paradoxically, tourist propaganda, the touristic imagination, and especially postcards of Aconcagua, also cultivate the mountain as the premodern, antimaterialistic, unexplored solitary territory of the Victorian-age expeditionary hero.

The Argentine identity forged by Mendoza's new men of letters, the tourism administrators, is a mixed bag of seemingly contradictory images that especially draw from modernist and nation-building paradigms but, ultimately, do not serve to consolidate a coherent, inclusive national spirit. In other words, touristic discourses and promotions do not interpret the past to mold a heterogeneous citizenry toward an imagined homogeneous future. Instead, they interpret the tourism market and reformulate a sense of the Argentine past and present according to those economic guidelines, not only national but also global, that favor the specificity of the region. In Mendoza the grand deeds of history that have lost their polemical charge and that imply transnational associations, like those of the epic of the Liberator, San Martín, take the lead in constructing the Cordillera-Mendoza association as a symbol of the Argentine. This construction suggests a national unity dependent on an epic homogeneity of regional history in which the sociohistorical melodramas, in García Canclini's (2000) terms, are not acknowledged. But the fissures and cracks of this unity, while not necessarily front and center, are becoming more present as cultural tourism projects and provincially backed and privately administered museums and archaeological ruins have begun to spotlight Mendoza's indigenous origins.

Sarlo names Argentina as a country without a project with respect to its own identity (Mariño 2001), but I propose that there is something more to consider here. Tourism is indeed projecting a marked sense of what is Argentine. It is an Argentina that has become multiple and fractured, defined by regional and atemporal mixes of past and present, and whose sovereignty is explicitly conditioned by outside sources. This Argentina is now looking in the mirror at the new face of twenty-first-century neocoloniality. During the period of European imperial expansion in the late nineteenth and early twentieth centuries, Argentina envisioned itself as one of the ten most modern countries in the world with a bright, prosperous, and independently driven future ahead. Now, in its bid to develop tourism, Argentina has become one of the countries for which the United Nations World Tourism Organization's 2007 Strategic Message finds resonance in its affirmation to "consolidate tourism as a key agent in the fight against poverty and a primary tool for sustainable development."[14] Although Argentina's inclusion in this global community of "developing" and impoverished nations, imagined as potential "service providers" for international visitors, is a real blow to the traditional sense of what Argentine meant, tourism, in another more positive sense, provides Argentina with an outlet for reconstructing and vindicating its patrimony and its self-image in spite of the severe economic and political crises that have spurred citizens and cultural critics alike to bemoan the demise of the nation and national identity. It is a different kind of identity for sure, but it is not totally disconnected from Argentina's past nor is it alien to its future.

In the example of Mendoza's mountain tourism industry we can see that traces and memories of Mendoza and its mountains during the periods of colonization, independence, modernity, militarization, and globalization have been incorporated and represented in tourist campaigns as self-portraits of the region that benefit both the present and the future economies of Mendoza. However, these self-images are no longer materialized through a nationally bound literary-cultural project like that of Angel Rama's (1982) nineteenth-century men of letters, but rather through a transnational capitalist-entrepreneurial one whose imagined community of tourism is where "lo argentino" is sold, according to local geopolitical specificities and not national ones, in the global market of tourist destinations.

CHAPTER THREE

Indigenous Identities

The Mummy, the Mountaineer, and Re-ethnification

Aconcagua (6,962)
With its almost 7,000 meters, is the highest summit in the western hemisphere. It is situated 240 km. west from Mendoza city, 600 km. east from Santiago de Chile and 1,300 km. from Buenos Aires. This peak was considered a sacred sanctuary by the Incas; it was there that they offered sacrifices to their deities. (In 1985 a momified [sic] *body of an Incan child was found by an expedition at more than 5,000 mts. high, it contained golden ritual objects 500 yrs. old.)*

—CONSTELACIONES AGENCY

The Mendoza poster cited above pointedly situates Aconcagua for mountaineers journeying from afar by pinpointing both its distance from Argentine and Chilean cities and from Anglo-European tradition.[1] Highlighting the Incan ties to Aconcagua rather than some other mountaineering fact to sell adventure rearticulates a long-standing discursive economy in which a premodern image of "the Andes" is exported to satisfy North American and European expectations and desires of pre-Columbian empires and exotic difference. Accordingly, both kilometers and the Incan mummy serve as coordinates of distance to chart Aconcagua on the map of international mountaineering. This selling of Aconcagua in terms of ethnic and temporal distance relies on a virtual re-indigenization of the high mountain region, which for nearly four hundred years has not been home to its original native peoples and communities.

However, there has also been another kind of re-indigenization taking place in the region. The boom in Mendoza's mountaineering industry since the mid-1980s coincides with a national "ethnic reemergence" (Gordillo and Hirsch 2003, 5–6) that has both informed and contested the representations of indigeneity in the Aconcagua zone. A legal and cultural movement of re-ethnification emerged in the Uspallata Valley, near the Aconcagua Provincial Park, in the mid-1990s, when the commune of Guaytamari gained official recognition as a Huarpe community and began developing a heritage industry to chronicle and display both pre- and post-Incan occupation of the area. The resurgence of local indigenous identities in the *alta montaña*, along with their own touristic projects, complicates the ways in which the area's indigenous past and present are read. The very presence of a modern-day Huarpe commune challenges the privileging, by governmental tourist projects and, especially, by mountaineering, of the Incan heritage of the region to characterize the indigenous nature of the area.

The uneasy coexistence of mountaineering rhetoric and practices and Guaytamari's undertakings in the high mountain zone speak to tensions in contemporary Argentina's self-identification, that is, its coming to terms with a past founded on the myth of a white European homogeneity and a present being forged by an ethnically diverse society (Gordillo and Hirsch 2003; Quijada 2004, 425–430). Moreover, the dynamics of mountain tourism that contextualize the process of re-indigenization in the Aconcagua zone serve to exemplify the ways in which the business of tourism intervenes and mediates in the political, social, and cultural negotiations of national and ethnic identity construction.

Indigenous Aconcagua

The equating of the mountain with a premodern indigenous past in order to imbue it with an exotic, "other worldly" spirituality encourages the understanding of mountaineering as an activity that allows its practitioners to transcend the mundane and the ordinary of the world below. The indigenous on Aconcagua, a mountaineering site, is not visibly or physically manifested through the presence of bodies, ceremonies, practices, or language use. Rather it is imagined and elicited through textual, linguistic, and topographical cues primed for tourist consumption. It is drawn from the texts and images in pamphlets and posters and on websites that are produced by Mendocino mountaineering service agencies and by international groups and individuals. These varied media narrate accounts of the Incan presence on the mountain, as well as the etymologies of its name, in order to create a dislocated and fragmented indigenous history that reconstructs Aconcagua's indigeneity as virtual and intangible.

Most salient in mountaineering's emphasis on the indigenous characteristics of Aconcagua is indeed the discussion of its name, clearly an indigenous term, whose origin and meaning are contested. Some sources claim it is a Mapuche term meaning "from the other side," corresponding to the Aconcagua River in Chile. However, many Mendocino mountaineering agencies, both online and in print, explain that the roots of "Aconcagua" presumably trace to the Incan occupation of the area and are attributed to both the Aymará phrase "Kon-Kawa," translated as *centinela blanca* or *monte nevado* (white sentinel, or snow-capped peak, respectively), and the Quechua "Akon-Kahuak," as *centinela de piedra* (stone sentinel). The most commonly accepted and recognized translation in mountaineering lore is the latter, which gives the name, both in Spanish and in English, to a variety of websites and several books about Aconcagua mountaineering such as *Aconcagua: The Stone Sentinel* (Taplin 1992) and *Aconcagua: El Centinela de Piedra* (Randis 1991).

The construction of Aconcagua as indigenous is also visually and linguistically cued by the mountaineering landscape of Aconcagua itself, which is overlaid with reminders of the area's Incan past. Mountaineering service agencies have ensconced themselves in indigenous-named locations, using Los Puquios and Puente del Inca as two of the three primary staging areas for all Aconcagua routes.[2] In addition, some Mendocino mountaineering agencies have chosen to invoke the indigenous past by adorning themselves with names such as Aymará, Mallku, and Inka Expediciones, all major agencies in the Aconcagua industry. The indigenous toponomies, together with the prominently located base-camp settlements of Aymará, Inka, and Mallku, contour the mountain with constant allusions to its pre-Columbian connections. In this way signs of the indigenous are plotted onto the mountainside in a symbolic reclaiming of its heritage that does not, however, articulate a revisionist or indigenous narrative to counter the official history of colonization and European settlement. Instead, it sets up Aconcagua within the semiotics of mountaineering as an oppositional sign to the trappings of modernity and the materiality of everyday life.

According to Sherry B. Ortner (1999), the foundation for mountaineering and its development throughout the twentieth century has been a countermodern discourse where "the point of climbing is to find something that one cannot find in modern life, that indeed has been lost in modern life" (36). The vindication of Aconcagua's pre-European indigenous past by the adventure tourism industry plays into this critique of modernity when it evokes and revalues the mountain's "lost" Incan character.

Lost Origins

Although theories of Incan presence on Aconcagua had been suggested by military climbers to Mendocino archaeologists as early as 1972, the general scientific conclusion at that time was that the mountain had been an area ignored by the Incas (Schobinger 2001c, 358–359). It was mountaineering itself that confirmed and reclaimed Aconcagua's Incan heritage as "lost" with the discovery in 1985 by local climbers on the peak's West Face of an Incan mummy, "something one cannot find in modern life," as Ortner (1999) characterizes mountaineering. The discursive power of the discovery story of the Incan mummy, along with the indigenously named topographical areas and mountaineering agencies, renarrativize Aconcagua's Incan past into its commercial present. These "newly found" indigenous roots remove Aconcagua from the ordinary and routine and can be read, in mountaineering terms, as extraordinary difference, remarkable discovery, and ennobling adventure. It is this kind of "sublime and transcendental experience," that finding an Incan mummy represents, that allows mountaineering, as in Ortner's equation, to oppose the vulgar materialism of modernity (1999, 38). In addition, it is the discovery of the mummy that most closely ties Aconcagua to a reading of the indigenous that fortuitously underwrites the traditional myth of a white Argentina.

An Incan sacrifice over five hundred years ago on Aconcagua serves to re-voice that commonly held Argentine adage that in Argentina "no hay indios" (there are no Indians). There has been the collective understanding, held for over a century, that Argentina's native peoples were all killed in the nineteenth-century "desert campaigns" to provide freedom for "progress, territorial integration, and modernization" (Quijada 2004, 426).[3] The belief in this foundational fiction of the modern Argentine nation served to facilitate the late nineteenth and early twentieth-century integration of new European immigrants into a criollo-based social order forged on race and European models (Quijada 2004; Gordillo and Hirsch 2003; Carrasco 2000). As a consequence, the space left by the supposed absence of indigenous populations from the modern period until the present day allows for the evocation of the Incas as representation of South American authenticity and difference, which plays especially well to international adventure tourism markets.

The memory of a long-absent pre-Conquest Incan Empire also supports a traditional vision of Argentine nationhood and modernity. This is a modernity based on the "civilization," understood as extermination or acculturation, of Argentina's "barbaric" indigenous elements and its self-representation as European (Pigna 2004; Gordillo and Hirsch 2003).[4] However, the privileging of this memory of the Incas is dependent upon an erasure of Argentina's native peoples who, despite the myth of their extermination, account for nearly 1.5 percent of the population, numbering over 900,000 (Carrasco 2000, 9; Gorostiaga 2003, 18).[5]

The mountaineering stories of the mummy on Aconcagua inscribe indigeneity there based on this same kind of erasure. The stories' focus on the Incan roots of the region ignores the native peoples of the zone, the Milcayac Huarpes, who were subjugated by the Incas and enslaved by the Spanish.[6] The descendants of those Huarpes who avoided being sent in *encomiendas* to Chile during the early colonial period settled in Lavalle, in the eastern deserts of the province, and they eventually acculturated to Western ways of language, dress, religion, and lifestyle. In other words, both the Huarpes and the Incas have seemingly been absent from the mountain zone for centuries. However, it is the forgetting of the Huarpes, in favor of the memory of an idealized and imperial indigenous tradition, that sets up the Incan to be the principal historical sign of indigeneity in the Aconcagua zone and thus confirms Aconcagua's uniqueness from an Anglo-European world.

Sacrifice, Ritual, Pilgrimage

The Way I See It #116

Mountains preserve the heritage of the past, enhance the beauty of the present and inspire actions for the future. Near a sacred peak everything reveals its most essential meaning.

—CONSTANZA CERUTI, HIGH-ALTITUDE ARCHEOLOGIST AND *NATIONAL GEOGRAPHIC* EMERGING EXPLORER (PRINTED ON A STARBUCKS COFFEE CUP)

Mendoza-based mountaineering agencies and websites especially stress the Incan ties to Aconcagua by drawing attention to the mummy.[7] Despite the fact that the Camino Incaico is nearby, and that ruins of an Incan tambo, or way station, lie just meters from the trail leading in and out of the Confluencia camp on the heavily traveled Normal Route, it was the discovery of an Incan mummy on Aconcagua, according to mountaineering websites, brochures, and common mountain knowledge, that confirmed the Incanness of the peak and the area. Few climbers have any knowledge of the remnants of the Incan Empire in Mendoza province, yet

Figure 3.1. Aconcagua's West Face, seen here from the Hotel Refugio Plaza de Mulas. In 1985 a Mendocino expedition, following Aconcagua's southwest ridge, found an Incan mummy at the base of Cerro Pirámide.

most Aconcagua mountaineers know the story of the Incan mummy and its sacrificial burial on the mountain. If they have not read about it beforehand in mountaineering publicity and marketing texts, they do hear about it once they are on the expedition. It is a common practice for guides and other Plaza de Mulas (base camp) officials and workers to point toward the West Face of Aconcagua and tell climbers the story of the discovery of the Incan mummy.

Undoubtedly, the mystery of the mummy reinforces the mystique of mountaineering. This is nowhere more evident than in the "official" recounting of the discovery of the burial site, in the multidisciplinary study of the Aconcagua mummy, *El santuario incaico del cerro Aconcagua* (The Incan Sanctuary of Mount Aconcagua)(Schobinger 2001f). Gabriel Cabrera (2001), a Mendocino mountain guide, in his retelling of the events implicitly, but indelibly, connects mountain climbing to the Incan ritual by highlighting both the reverential and the sacrificial nature of mountaineering. In his narrative the singular and extraordinary act of veneration that the Incan sacrifice supposes is uncannily paralleled by the special expedition that Cabrera led in 1985 to pay homage to the modern ancestors of mountaineering on Aconcagua. Cabrera writes that in order to commemorate the fiftieth anniversary of the Club Andinista Mendoza (CAM), four different expeditions were organized by Mendocino climbers to complete previously established routes. Cabrera led a group composed of two sets of brothers—Fernando and Juan Carlos Pierobon, and Franco and Alberto Pizzolón—to extend the southwest ridge route inaugurated by Francisco Ibáñez, Fernando Grajales, and Frédéric and Dorly Marmillod in 1953 (Cabrera 2001, 20). In essence, the expedition set out to honor the past of Aconcagua mountaineering while establishing a Mendocino claim to the present and future of the mountain. During the expedition, the mummified remains of a male child, approximately six years old (Cruz 2001, 93) were found at an altitude of approximately 5,300 meters on January 11, 1985, by Alberto Pizzolón, who spotted what he thought was a patch of grass. The grass turned out to be feathers emerging from the earth and the top of a human skull partially covered by snow. The mountaineers realized the archaeological importance of what they had found, took pictures, and decided to contact specialists in Mendoza before returning to remove the mummy (Schobinger 1995, 3–4; Cabrera 2001, 20).

The significance and functions of these celebratory mountaineering activities of the CAM mirror the purposes attributed to the rites of the Incas on Aconcagua. María Constanza Ceruti explains that in the Andean region of the Incan Empire there existed a generalized belief that the spirits of the ancestors dwelt in the mountains and that high-altitude sacrifices were often made to venerate them, as well as to petition for rain, climate moderation, and fertility (2001a, 379–383).[8] Additionally, Ceruti posits that the pilgrimage to the mountains of a ceremonial group to offer sacrifice also served to sacralize the space and the new borders of empire, consolidating and legitimizing Incan appropriation of territory (2001a, 386).[9] In a parallel manner, the ceremonial activities of the CAM, which ended up tracing the paths of the Incan ritual in its attempt to honor the efforts of early Aconcagua mountaineers, mimic a pilgrimage along "sacred ancestral" routes that functioned to mark new frontiers of Mendocino authority and territory on Aconcagua and symbolically undermine the hegemony that Anglo-European activity on the mountain had maintained since its inception in 1883. In essence, the expedition set out to honor the past of Aconcagua mountaineering while establishing a Mendocino claim to the present and future of the mountain.

The importance to the mountaineering industry of the discovery of the mummy and the recognition of Aconcagua as a site of sacred ritual and sacrifice may be better understood in light of how contemporary perceptions of ritual and pilgrimage, especially as theorized by Victor Turner (1969, 1979), have been used to characterize the mountaineer's journey as a liminal and transformative act (Houston 2006; Beedie 2003; van Vuuren 2000). Houston (2006) views the mountaineer as a pilgrim, in a Turneresque interpretation, as one who exits an ordered, complex system of social relations to initiate a mountaineering endeavor, then enters into the liminal state (without the accustomed social structures of everyday life) that defines the expedition, accepts a definite end to the activity, and subsequently undergoes transformation (2006, 151). This reading of the mountaineering process is not far removed from Nelson Graburn's (1995) reading of touristic travel in general as symbolic pilgrimage. Graburn, taking from Durkheim, examines tourism against its complement—everyday life—and sees tourism as a symbolic ritual in its alternation of the sacred and the profane (1995, 28).

All the rewards that Graburn theorizes for modern tourism as ritual, "mental and physical health, social status, and diverse, exotic experience" (1995, 28) are interpreted at a higher value, figuratively and literally, by mountaineering as the superlative manifestation of adventure tourism. These recompenses come at an elevated cost due to the liminal nature of the sport that takes place in a dangerous, risky, and "structureless" domain that promises a transcendent experience. It is especially this expectation of transcendence that connects Aconcagua mountaineering to the sacrifice of the Incan mummy. It is also what projects mountaineering, similar to how Graburn saw touristic travel, as a sacred journey that "emphasized the process of leaving the ordinary, i.e., sacralization that elevates participants in the nonordinary state wherein marvelous things happen" (Graburn 1995, 24–25).[10]

Within a paradigm of ritual travel and transcendence, Cabrera's original discovery of the mummy and the mountaineers' subsequent returns to the burial site are the sacred pilgrimages within a mountaineering epistemology that echo Incan interactions with Aconcagua. Cabrera details the heroic spirit of the expeditioners and the physical sacrifices and ingenuity demanded of them to confront the inscrutable powers of nature as they delved into the extraordinary world of the Incan ritual.

Cabrera's tale narrates the following event in El santuario (2001, 21–24). After finding the mummy at the base of the southwest wall, known as Pirámide, and deciding to contact archaeologists in Mendoza to coordinate its retrieval, Cabrera's team was hit by a snowstorm so severe that the two pairs of brothers became disheartened and returned to Mendoza without completing the route that they had proposed. Cabrera remained to continue alone, but inclement weather also eventually forced him to desist. On his descent, upon reaching the low camp of Confluencia,

Cabrera suffered an attack of blindness that lasted for more than twenty-four hours. During the expedition's return to the Incan sanctuary a few weeks later with Juan Schobinger, an archaeologist from the Universidad Nacional de Cuyo (UNC), nature and the mountain seemed to continue the assault on the expeditioners who had determined to take the mummy from the mountain.[11] While the expedition rested at base camp, Mendoza suffered its largest earthquake in recent history on January 26, 1985. When there was a follow-up expedition attempted by Cabrera and Roberto Bárcena, another UNC archaeologist, in 1997, as part of the centenary celebration of mountaineering on Aconcagua, one of the peak's glaciers had moved to such a degree that it was impossible for them to access the area where the mummy had been found. On the group's descent a raging rainstorm and heavy winds hampered their trek across the Playa Ancha back to Horcones. (A subsequent effort to reach the site in 2000 by Maria Constanza Ceruti, as part of a Japanese documentary project, was also unsuccessful in its attempt [2001b, 438].) On the whole, the tale of the discovery and retrieval of the mummy is a story of mountaineers suffering and persevering in a liminal space against all odds and every kind of obstacle that nature can throw at them. In Cabrera's chronicle of its discovery and recovery, the Incan mummy becomes forever entwined with Aconcagua mountaineering in the evocation of sacrifice, ritual, and the struggles between nature and the human will to survive.

The sense of transcendental awe that the Incan ritual projects on Aconcagua is also tied to the wonder of a new Mendocino mountaineering present and future. This is especially characterized in Cabrera's report of his return to the sanctuary site a year after the mummy's first discovery in order to complete, alone, the route that his team had planned for the 1985 celebration. At the base of the Pirámide wall, Cabrera found a semiburied red cord that seemed to lead to the summit, which he theorizes was the goal of the original sacrificial mission or of subsequent Incan visits (2001, 24). Cabrera explains that his successful bid on this occasion to become the first to link the West ridge to the South and North summits on one route was not just realizing the original goal proposed by the Ibáñez, Grajales, and Marmillod team of thirty years before, but that of continuing the Incan ritual in an act of mountaineering that was "following a destiny outlined by a red cord" (2001, 24). With Cabrera's completion of this route of "destiny," the Incan past is reinscribed in Aconcagua's mountaineering present as its mystical origin and potential for future transcendence. Cabrera concludes the tale by leaving the future of both the Incan ritual and mountaineering possibilities open, suggesting that the mystery of the red cord, or the lost Incan nature of Aconcagua, is still to be unraveled by scientists and mountaineers alike (2001, 24).

It is the possibility of stepping out of time and into the mythic realm of a sacred peak, the burial site of an Incan mummy, where, according to Ceruti's coffee cup, "everything reveals its essential meaning," that especially informs the interpretation of indigeneity on Aconcagua. The mummy marks Aconcagua as a mysterious and inspirational place of discovery and sacrifice, not just for the Incas, but for the mountaineers themselves. As such, the mummy inspires and justifies the extraordinary physical and mental sacrifices that climbers pay on Aconcagua where mystical things might be revealed, like an Incan mummy, a conduit through which mountaineers may achieve personal transcendence.

The Mummy Debates

The archaeological find of the mummy as cultural commodity and as evidence of Mendocino accomplishments on Aconcagua has held other significance for Mendocinos as well. Mendoza's construction of the mummy as a sacrificial artifact imbued with transformative powers reflects a common use of the indigenous as a fetishized commodity that bestows special knowledge, privilege, or status to an owner.

Mendocino sociocultural valuations of the mummy were perhaps best illustrated during the centenary celebration of mountaineering on Aconcagua. The celebrations took place in January 1997 at the Plaza de Mulas base camp, at 4,300 meters, where the then-governor of Mendoza, Arturo Lafalla, an ardent andinista, promised to "pagar una deuda," or pay a debt, to the mountain in recognition of its great value to the province and to return the mummy to its burial place on Aconcagua (Ayassa 1997, 9). Local news reported that the announcement was met by great enthusiasm on the part of Mendocino and international andinistas who were present, and journalists also suggested that the restitution of the mummy could take place within the following months (Ayassa 1997, 9).

This pledge to restore the mummy to its resting place was never fulfilled, as its pronouncement brought about a huge polemic that exploded in the Mendoza press during the last three months (January through March) of the 1997 climbing season. Discussion about jurisdiction over the mummy and the meaning of it as a "debt owed to the mountain" became a hotbed of contention. The media speculation about the return of the mummy to Aconcagua revealed that there was a growing belief among some sectors of

Mendoza that this act might help to bring about the end of a long-reigning drought in the zone. People argued that restoring the mummy to Aconcagua would restore balance to nature, appease the spirit of the mountain, and in this way promote precipitation. There was also conjecture that the governor's "promise to the mountain" was motivated purely by a plan to increase tourism to Aconcagua (Oviedo 1997).

The polemic played out on two fronts: who had the right to interpret the significance of the mummy, and who could lay claim to its guardianship? Journalistic articles, editorials, and letters to the editor exposed the strident competition between institutions, discourses, and economies for control of the young child the Incas had offered in sacrifice approximately 550 years before. Folklore, religion, law, science, politics, capitalism, indigenist spirituality, history, and morality were all invoked in the questioning of the authority of the governor to make decisions concerning the location of the mummy in Mendoza's geophysical territory, as well as in its social imagination.[12]

As the controversy raged on, science aligned itself with moral patriotism, civic duty, and modernity. This complex of arguments was buttressed by a recitation of laws and regulations that, on the one hand, could establish the mummy as a national monument or that, on the other, could declare it to be the property of the province of Mendoza. State and provincial rights to the mummy were then juxtaposed with the authority that world heritage institutions such as UNESCO and ICOMOS might have to determine the mummy's fate (Pincolini 1997). On moral grounds Catholicism was invoked to examine whether or not there had been profanation of a grave site, and ecumenical spirituality was posited as sufficient reason for reburial.

At the forefront of the debates, representing the voice of scientific reason, was Juan Schobinger. Schobinger, who had supervised the mummy's retrieval from Aconcagua in 1985, spearheaded the subsequent scientific analyses of the mummy and funerary objects and had self-published a forty-six-page study of the mummy only two years before, *Aconcagua: Un enterratorio incaico a 5.300 metros de altura* (Aconcagua: An Incan Burial at 5,300 Meters) (1995). Schobinger's response to the governor's ideas primarily served to assert the authority of science over politics, adventure, and economics, in interpreting cultural and archaeological information to theorize the mummy's significance. In a letter to the editor of *Los Andes*, Schobinger (1997a) discounted any legitimacy that indigenous traditions or mountaineering practices might have for interpreting the mummy.[13] As an artifact of the past and object of scientific study, the mummy, according to Schobinger, should remain under the care of the UNC archaeologists, whose actions were guided by scientific methodology in the name of knowledge and preserving national cultural heritage (Schobinger 1997b). He instructed readers that even in Peru the idea of returning mummies to their high-altitude sanctuaries was unheard of, and that although the governor was an avid andinista, his enthusiasm for the mountain had gotten the better of him.[14] His citing of Peru, implied as an area with a long-standing and continuing indigenous presence, supports two basic assumptions on his part: that there is no authentic indigenous objection to the removal and analysis of the mummy, and that Mendoza has no authentic indigenous peoples. Instead, Schobinger positions Mendocinos, as the discoverers and researchers of the Aconcagua mummy, as supreme moderns, participating fully as initiators of and contributors to unique advances in both mountaineering and science, and as guardians of the origins of an imagined ethnically homogeneous national community.

During the debates the province's self-identification with the hegemonic understanding of national ethnic identity indeed came to the fore. This was most clearly articulated through an appeal to universal humanitarian rights by a few concerned citizens who sought to counter the many and diverse fetishized and utilitarian interpretations of the mummy that formed the basis of the polemic. Their letters criticized the arguments about the needs of science and the desires of newly formed convictions that gave little dignity to the human remains of a six-year-old child and failed to respect his culture. While this counterargument suggests a cultural sensibility to ethnic difference and indigenous beliefs (which itself became a fulcrum in the debates), it also validated the construction of Mendocino identity as fixed by the duality of Mendoza Self and Native Other. One of the letters suggested that readers consider how they would feel if one of "our ancestors, a Spanish conquistador, was put on display in a museum" (Raía 1997). While the letter sets out to critique the objectification and commodification of the Incan mummy, it does so by affirming the racial homogeneity of "our" Mendoza, descended solely from its European ancestors. The absence of indigenous peoples in the conceptualization of regional identity reiterates the belief that indigeneity in Mendoza, as well as in Argentina, has only been visible in the past (Escolar 2007; Briones 2006).

Consequently, the absence of the indigenous, or its relegation to the Mendocino past, also facilitates the construction of Mendoza as modern. In this way it served handily to refute the "curse of the mummy," as the notion of the mummy's role in the drought had come to be called. If there were no descendants of the Incan Empire in the area, the fervor for restoring the mummy to the mountain to end the drought could not form part of a living indigenous belief system. Therefore, the "curse" could instead be disavowed as a spontaneously constructed urban myth based on superstition and ignorance rather than on lack of respect for indigenous traditions.

Despite the governor's promise and subsequent arguments for its relocation, the mummy has remained under the jurisdiction of science, in its freezer in the Regional Center for Scientific and Technological Research (CRICYT), in the Reproduction and Lactation Laboratory (maintained at −10 degrees Celsius and 60 percent humidity).[15] However, echoes of these mummy debates reverberated in the academic sphere nearly four years later when the scientists had the last public, official say on the matter. Two years after the 1997 exchanges, a decade-long drought of academic funding for the UNC archaeologists' project on the mummy ended and research was reinitiated. The culmination of these efforts was the 450-page anthology *El santuario incaico del cerro Aconcagua* (Schobinger 2001f). Here, Schobinger, in tracing publication records of the project, again returned to the mummy polemics of 1997 when he explains that "another series of newspaper articles had to be published during the first months of 1997, within the frame of a polemic unraveled by a hairbrained proposal to restore the mummy to the mountain" (Schobinger 2001b, 48).

Within the context of the debates of 1997, the anthology reads as a deconstruction of indigenous and folkloric mythologies associated with the mummy. Arturo E. Corte explains through dendrochronology (climate analysis based on the examination of tree rings) that the period in which the mummy was sacrificed (approximately 1471–1493) did not correspond to a cycle of drought that had occurred earlier (1400–1460) (2001, 63). Ceruti argues that the sacrificial ritual, rather than merely seeking to appease "Mallku, caretaker and dispenser of the waters of the mountain" (2001a, 382), or to ask for climate moderation and fertility, was more than likely carried out to confirm Incan territorial claims (384), and Schobinger theorizes that the sacrifice was a symbolic act to celebrate the presence of the Incan imperial god on the mountain within the terms of the Incan religious-belief system (Schobinger 2001e, 431–432).

While *El santuario incaico* debunks the mythology of folklore, it also grounds itself in the mythos of mountaineering. Within Schobinger's anthology, the legitimacy of science to define the mummy in terms of data and quantifiable deliverables is always framed by the discourses of adventure and self-transcendence constructed by mountaineering and its evocation of ritual and sacrifice. Schobinger dedicates the anthology to the "andinistas of Mendoza y San Juan" and uses the mountaineer Gabriel Cabrera's account of the mummy's discovery to initiate the series of studies. Schobinger's report of the 1985 excavation is followed by a general history of mountaineering on Aconcagua (Videla and Suárez 2001, 51–53). Further reference to the practice of mountaineering proper on Aconcagua that is not directly linked to the mummy is also evidenced by a reproduction of Edward A. FitzGerald's 1899 map, made on the first successful European ascension of Aconcagua, that is included in the narrative of later visits by archaeologists to other Incan sites within the Aconcagua park (Bárcena 2001, 365). The collection closes with more mountaineering exploits chronicled in Schobinger's 1985 expedition diary (2001a, 436–437) and in Ceruti's fieldwork notes on the unsuccessful attempt to reach the burial site in 2000 (2001b, 438). While *El santuario incaico* may be a "high five" to science in its rebuttal of folklore's appropriation of the mummy, it also privileges mountaineering's relationship to science and the mummy. The scientific discourse of the anthology is exalted by a variant of what I like to call the "Indiana Jones effect" when it incorporates the glamour of mountaineering and adventure into the practice of science. In this realm the attractions of danger, risk, and the wondrous discovery of self, and even a mummy, are, like the Starbucks cup, signs of cultural status.

The Huarpes

The Huarpes in San Juan and Mendoza are a particularly noteworthy case in this spectrum of re-emergent ethnic identities, for it involves a group that had been considered extinct for centuries.

—GORDILLO AND HIRSCH (2003, 20)

While the mummy debates reflected the strength of hegemonic discourses on race and national and regional identities, they also revealed the multiplicity of perspectives and the contestatory social disposition evolving throughout the 1990s in Argentina in its reassessment of its ethnically diverse heritage. At the core of the deliberations about the mummy was a questioning of authority in the interpretation of Argentine social reality that has become ever more acute since the economic crisis of the early twenty-first century.

This critical engagement of Argentine society with its own heterogeneity is particularly symbolized by the constitutional reform in 1994 that recognized cultural and territorial rights of Argentina's indigenous communities.[16] It was this reform, specifically Article 75, Incise 17, that allowed for what Argentine anthropologists are calling a "re-ethnification" of the central Andes of Mendoza, which both differs from and parallels the indigenization process in the mountaineering circuit on Aconcagua.[17]

In 1996 a group claiming its rights as descendants of Argentina's native peoples became the first Huarpe community to gain both national and regional governmental recognition as an ethnic community. Subsequently, the group was granted land in the Uspallata Valley, contiguous to the Aconcagua zone, to establish the commune named Guaytamari.[18] In asserting their claim to the area, the members of Guaytamari also requested and were granted guardianship of nearby archaeological sites, one being the colonial foundry, known as Las Bóvedas, which they have since converted into a museum of the area. The other guardianships included two nearby sites of Incan ruins (tambos) and an area of petroglyphs called Tunduqueral. These three areas had been previously studied, cleared, and organized with interpretive signage by archaeologists from the Universidad Nacional de Cuyo, who received material for instructional, security, and preservational use of the petroglyph site from their collaboration with the Hollywood production of the movie *Seven Years in Tibet*, which was filmed in the zone. Within the last decade Guaytamari has, for a small entrance fee, opened its own doors to the public as a site where traditional art and artisanry can be viewed as they are practiced by the members of the commune. The fees for entrance to Guaytamari's sites of guardianship and tours that they offer of the area, together with the sale of their ceramics and weavings, based on the traditional practices and materials of the Huarpes and other Andean peoples, form the basis of Guaytamari's economic livelihood.

The sociopolitical factors and the historical processes that conditioned the "emergence" of Huarpe communities during the 1990s in Cuyo (the region consisting of the provinces of San Juan, San Luis, and Mendoza) are what Diego Escolar (2007) treats in his seminal work *Los dones étnicos de la Nación: Identidades huarpe y modos de producción de soberanía en Argentina* (National Ethnic Legacies: Huarpe Identities and Means of Production of Sovereignty in Argentina). In discussing alternating historical moments of Huarpe visibilization and invisibilization, contemporary movements for indigenous rights, and changes between the Argentine state and its citizenship as factors in the reemergence of the Huarpes, Escolar names Guaytamari as one of the militant Huarpe organizations that since the 1990s has been developing an ethnic-based discourse as well as political strategies (2007, 185).[19]

The visibility of Guaytamari in the mountain landscape counters the erasure of the Huarpes by traditional heroic narratives in which the Incas,

Figure 3.2. Petroglyphs at Tunduqueral in the Uspallata Valley. Guardianship of the area has been contested by the Huarpe commune, Guaytamari.

General José de San Martín, and mountaineering have taken the forefront. However, the commune members' self-definition is problematic, contested, and sometimes accused of being as "virtual" as the Incanization of Aconcagua. The legitimacy of the six families predominantly of European and mestizo ancestry to characterize themselves as Huarpe and their authority to represent the indigenous history of the area has been a point of contention for academics (historians and archaeologists) and a generalized public who point to a supposed silence of nearly four hundred years that has been accepted as the disappearance of the Huarpes.

Mendocino academic and intellectual discourses have traditionally held that there were no more Huarpes in the province (Escolar 2006). My own findings from interviews with Mendocino academics strongly coincide with Escolar's (2007) research in San Juan that shows a marked reluctance on the part of local academics to accept the historical continuity of Huarpe identities thought to have disappeared in encomiendas to Chile in the sixteenth century or to have been acculturated into criollo society. Despite the consensus on the extinction of the Huarpes, Escolar (2006, 2007) argues that their invisibility in the Mendocino social imagination was due to the machinations of the hegemonic discourses of history and nation of the period and not to the actual disappearance of the Huarpes. He documents several moments throughout the last 150 years in which local peoples emerged in the public eye on the basis of their identification as Huarpe.

Nevertheless, the generalized belief in the extermination of the Huarpes is the most popular explanation given to justify the hesitancy of many to accept the people living in the Guaytamari commune as an indigenous group. In fact, in 1998 Guaytamari was publicly denounced as a cult in a court case by a grandmother who was seeking her granddaughter's return after the girl's mother decided to join Guaytamari. According to the grandmother, Guaytamari was "a group that tries to profit by assuming a false Huarpe identity, when through its veins only run Spanish and Italian blood" (Fioquetta 1998). This same argument has also been leveled against Guaytamari from a representative of a Mapuche community who accuses the group of "making a business out of being indigenous" in order to receive land and national and international privileges and subsidies (Centro de Documentación Mapuche 2001). Such accusations, especially those coming from other ethnic communities, challenge the process of ethnic reemergence that has engendered communities like Guaytamari by positioning them in opposition to other groups that do have a visible historical tradition of indigenous lands, customs, practices, languages, and beliefs.

At the crux of the argument about the Guaytamarians' indigeneity is the fact that, in accordance with the 1994 Constitution, rights to land control are specifically linked to indigenous identity. A traditional connection to land and the reestablishing of indigenous rights to communal territories have been especially significant in the reemergence of ethnic communities in Argentina since 1994 (Occhipinti 2003). This issue is problematic for the Huarpes of Guaytamari, because their relationship to the land and their right to guardianship of indigenous areas are principal points of contention in discussions of their legal status as indigenous.

The Huarpes of Uspallata, in terms of their historical and economic connections to the land, differ from other indigenous communities in the Argentine Northwest who can claim land based on traditional agricultural or hunting practices (Occhipinti 2003). And unlike the eleven Huarpe communities of eastern Mendoza whose ancestors settled in the lowlands of Guanacache centuries ago (Michielli 1983, 135), the Guaytamarians cannot profess a continuity of location. In fact, Guaytamari's claims to the mountain area and to Huarpe heritage have been disputed by the archaeological community that argues that there is little physical evidence to suggest that traditional Huarpe settlements were ever located at these altitudes of the zone.

However, while the Huarpes of Guaytamari cannot assert continuity of settlement or of land use, Catalina Teresa Michielli's (1983) scrutiny of the earliest colonial chronicles and the foundational documents of Mendoza offers evidence that when the Spanish arrived there were indeed Huarpes present in the valley of Uspallata. She also found that some were "encomendados" ("given" as laborers to Spanish conquistadors and colonizers) across the mountains as early as 1562 (1983, 68–70).[20] In addition, Escolar (2007) has found that in oral histories the Cordillera, in general, has traditionally been seen by the region's native peoples as an indigenous zone and the last historical refuge of escape, but its inhabitants have often been subsumed into nonethnic marked categories of rural worker, muleteer, or mountain "guide" (113–117). Nevertheless, the lack of a continued historical Huarpe presence in the mountain, whether as a result of colonial policies or not, is still a thorny issue for other projects who use and inhabit the mountain zone. The Guaytamari cooperative has not been warmly embraced by members of the mountaineering community who have tended to align themselves with the archaeologists and have been reticent about recommending Guaytamari to their clients as a site for mountaineers' pre- or postexpedition visits.

In 2000 when I attended a Guaytamari-sponsored presentation to university-level students about indigenous Mendoza and I asked about the decision to form Guaytamari, Claudia Herrera, the vice president of the cooperative, responded with the same explanation that Francisco Candito, the president, has consistently reported to the press. Although Herrera pointed to her own mestizo heritage she did not offer that as the principal factor in the formation of Guaytamari. Rather, she explained that the group wanted to recuperate, preserve, disseminate, and follow ancestral traditions and that their decision to create Guaytamari as a commune, or cooperative, was based on what they saw as the best approximation to the organizational traditions of the area's native peoples.[21]

In defense of Guaytamari's rights to legal status and land, Herrera invokes the INAI's (Instituto Nacional de Asuntos Indígenas; National Institute of Indigenous Affairs) definition of ethnicity: "'ser indígena' no es una cualidad intrínseca sino una identidad que sólo se define por oposición a los 'no indígenas'" ('being indigenous' is not an intrinsic quality but is an identity that can only be defined in opposition to the 'non-indigenous') (Bossi 2003). Herrera emphasizes Guaytamari's self-perception of difference from the nonindigenous, and she openly and self-consciously addresses their own protagonism in the process of re-ethnification. This is a process by which groups assume an indigenous identity without having lived as such previously, but who reconnect with their roots and take on traditional ways of life (Gorostiaga 2003, 24). In Guaytamari's educational programs, presentations, and videos, spokespersons explain how they reconstruct Huarpe history and traditions and discuss the sources that they have used, such as colonial chronicles and oral narratives. In this way the Guaytamari members construct their own autoethnographic narrative when they connect the Huarpe past with present representations of themselves and their present activities.

As a principal spokesperson of Guaytamari, Herrera, who in educational presentations about the Milcayac Huarpes describes them as a peaceful group who incorporated and integrated the language, religion, culture, and practices of other, dominant, cultures with which they have had historical contact, engages the rhetoric of transculturation by highlighting indigenous agency and the hybrid nature of identity. Taking place in the contact zones, where marginalized groups do not just assimilate hegemonic meanings and practices but also exercise agency in selecting and inventing from a dominant culture (Pratt 2008, 7), the transcultural process accentuates mutability, flexibility, and racial-cultural mestizaje. Herrera's emphasizing of contemporary Huarpe identity in this way allows re-ethnification to be sketched as the vindication of a historical fluidity and cultural hybridity that speaks to the continuity of contemporary Huarpe subjectivity and negates its representation as a disconnected and anachronistic invention.

However, transculturation as legitimization of indigenous identity is problematic on several levels. The kind of hybrid identity that transculturation produces, mestizaje, "a critical source of the ambiguities surrounding indigenous identity" (Postero and Zamosc 2004, 12), has historically been constructed as an identity category in opposition to the indigenous (García and Lucero 2004), and in Cuyo it has not traditionally been used for self-designation (Escolar 2007). According to Escolar, mestizaje has served in Mendoza as an "ethnic passport" that allows either white or Indian identity to be articulated and thus avoid the claims of inauthenticity that being seen as "mixed" attracts in local understandings (2007, 105). The Guaytamarians' openness about the fluidity of their "mixed" heritage, paralleling similar processes in Latin America where mestizaje has generated self-characterizations of indigenous identity (De la Cadena 2000; Warren 2001), demonstrates the indeterminancy of this construct, as the group's self-identification both invokes, as well as unsettles, the regional conceptualization of mestizo, which has been to see it as a stand-in for either indigenous or white, but not both.[22]

Beyond the Guaytamarians' reframing of regional understandings of mestizaje, the cooperative is creating seemingly "new" ethno-based connections to social activism, similar to those defining other indigenous movements in Argentina and across Latin America that have primarily been forged on demands for territory, autonomy, political participation, reforms to state organization, and cultural recognition and survival (Briones 2006; Postero and Zamosc 2004; Langer 2003). However, in basing their authority to engage such issues from an indigenous subjectivity, Guaytamari's members cannot assert long-standing visibility or identification as indigenous, which historical continuity in language, land use, social customs, governance, or religion could more easily legitimate in the public's eye.

Nevertheless, since the mid-1990s the Guaytamarians have constructed their self-representation as indigenous in both traditional and nontraditional ways. In the commune itself Guaytamari members perform their cultural identity through their practice and explanations of traditional artisanry and their maintenance of an Andean fauna reserve. When tourists visit the cooperative commune, members explain that they use traditional techniques and materials in making their ceramics, although they clarify that they draw not only from Huarpe traditions but also from those of other Andean peoples. This is also true of the weaving that they do.

In addition, as an ecological reserve and guardian of indigenous patrimonial sites, Guaytamari is reinventing and reimaging its cultural and spiritual relationship to the land in ways that attempt to reconstruct or create anew the kinds of indigenous ecological knowledge and spiritual beliefs about the natural world that serve to differentiate indigenous communities from other rural Argentines (Occhipinti 2003, 169). Escolar has found that highlighting an indigenous cosmovision and recuperating or reinventing rituals and practices have especially served as strategies of authentification among Huarpe groups (primarily urban-based organizations) (2007, 197), and such a case could be made for the Guaytamarians. While the Guaytamari Huarpes' claims to the commune area and the guardianship of nearby indigenous ruins, which the province has officially recognized, legally serve to justify their indigenous difference, it is also their endeavors to recreate indigenous ecological and spiritual connections to the natural world in ways that differ from other mountain communities that would ground their claim to an indigenous cultural identity. It is this difference that members of Guaytamari focus on in their video *El sueño del Millcayac* (The Dream of the Milcayac) (Candito ND) (presented to visitors of Las Bóvedas and in educational presentations), that highlights and personifies the Uspallata Valley. The video's traditionally clad protagonists, in symbolic and ritual-like performances that connect the present to the pre-Hispanic period, voice ecological concerns, in the reconstructed Milcayac language, about the health and survival of the natural area.

However, it is particularly through community members' self-identification as indigenous in social, academic, and political spheres that again leads back to INAI's interpretation of indigeneity as being self-defined in opposition to the nonindigenous, which serves to validate their cultural and ethnic difference. The Guaytamari cooperative, which cites itself as a cofounder of the Organización de las Naciones y Pueblos Indígenas (ONPIA; Organization of Indigenous Nations and People of Argentina), participates actively in pan-regional projects that are identified as indigenous initiatives.[23] In this respect Herrera has explicitly declared that she consciously seeks opportunities to increase the visibility of the Huarpes as the importance of representative indigenous organizations that recognize the Huarpes' continued existence (Davison and Cuyul 2007, 79–80) serve to contextualize and politicize her public activities and those of Guaytamari, in general, within the broader scope of national identity politics. In addition to national participation, at the regional level Guaytamarians' endeavors as an ethnic community have included instructional programs about the region's indigenous history presented to the Mendocino community and provincial schools, the production of a video about Huarpe customs and beliefs, a weekly radio show, and outreach to the traditional Huarpe communities located in the eastern desert of Mendoza.

Guaytamari's recognition as an indigenous community via its presence, commitment, and involvement at the national and regional levels of indigenous organizations is a justification in practice of the INAI's determination of indigenous as "recognized difference from the non-indigenous." Guaytamari members cannot rely on the more commonly accepted ways of distinguishing this difference based on historical visibilities. Instead, they depend especially on a recognition of their legal status, which then endorses current involvement and membership in indigenous projects that, in turn, serve to justify and validate the ethnic identity of Guaytamari's members. These strategies connect to what Escolar has found to be a common thread in the political efforts of the Huarpe communities: using the possession of juridical recognition as a principal factor of legitimization for public opinion, as well as for national, provincial, and transnational organizations (2007, 187).

Mountain Tourisms

The Guaytamari commune itself, as an open museum, suggests the plurality and dynamism of the Andean region and the historical blending of Incan and Huarpe cultures, in contrast to the fossilization of indigenous identity read on Aconcagua. It is just such a fossilized past that is being mapped onto plans of the recently created Ministry of Tourism and Culture, whose primary initiatives in the mountain zone have been to expand focus on the vestiges of Incan presence. One of its first ventures in the Aconcagua area is a transnational collaboration motivated by Mercosur to promote as a UNESCO World Heritage Site the Capac-Ñam, or Camino Incaico, described by the ministry's director as "an indigenous cultural topic that is much valued by Europeans and Asians" (Manoni 2004). The Ministry is also supporting plans to ready and interpret for tourism the ruins of the Incan way station near the trailhead in Aconcagua Park. The direction of these initiatives has been further strengthened by the founding of the Provincial Department of Historical and Cultural Heritage in 2003, which cited as its primary functions the care of Mendocino identity and the integration of cultural heritage into the tourist circuits (Manitta 2004). However, the only public mention of indigenous heritage at that time by the department's director, the archaeologist Valeria Cortegoso, was the presence of human occupation of the area 12,000 years ago, which should be included in the concept of Mendocino heritage (Manitta 2004).

For the purposes of a coherent provincial tourism project, there seems to be a homogenizing of claims to legitimacy for representing the region's ethnic heritage. Emphasis on the prehistoric and the Incan pasts supports a consistent, unified, unproblematic regional image of its indigenous history that absents native peoples from the present and modernity. Instead of promoting a new awareness of the plurality of Argentine culture, official discourse, as well as mountaineering narratives, seem to support an alta montaña cultural tourism project where indigenous origins exoticize the zone and promote it as a destination for national and international tourism. In other words, they create difference that will sell, and Incan difference already has a well-established market.

Guaytamari has not yet been mentioned in plans for a provincial cultural tourism route to accompany other official tourism circuits such as the wine route and San Martín's routes. On the provincial government's touristic website, www.turismo.mendoza.gov.ar/quevisitar, the petroglyph and Incan sites of Guaytamari's guardianship are included under cultural points of interest in Uspallata; however, the commune itself is never

Figure 3.3. Souvenirs for sale at the Las Bóvedas Museum, whose guardianship is held by the Guaytamari commune.

mentioned or offered as a cultural tourist stop for the zone. Guaytamari does, however, show up on the government's website in a different location under the rubric of "rural tourism." Nonetheless, Guaytamari does form part of the "un-official" alta montaña touristscape and is now included and designated as a Huarpe community on many tourist agency circuits of the zone.

Tourism remains especially important for Guaytamari because tourism revenue helps to provide the resources to continue its educational work in Mendoza's schools, to strengthen its solidarity with other Huarpe communities in eastern Mendoza, and to participate in national and international indigenous projects. It is tourism, however, that is also presenting the biggest obstacle to Guaytamari's survival. Guaytamari has received its most vociferous attacks on its ethnic authenticity due to battles over touristic control of its areas of guardianship. Local inhabitants of the Uspallata Valley have railed against paying a small entrance fee to sites that were previously free. They have protested Guaytamari's right to the areas based on ethnic difference. Their critiques are ones that have continuously plagued Guaytamari. Local opposition cites the commune's European and mestizo heritage as negating Guaytamari's claim as an indigenous community and accuse its members of political pandering to receive government subsidies.[24] Stemming from these disputes, the Las Heras municipal council rescinded in 2006 its grant to Guaytamari of guardianship of Tunduqueral, the area of petroglyphs.

Guaytamari's other Incan sites could also be threatened by the bid for official UNESCO recognition of the sites as part of the Capac Ñam if the provincial government were to choose to remove those areas from Guaytamari's control. The revoking of Guaytamari's guardianships would not only be significant in terms of tourism for the community, but it would also undermine its legitimacy as indigenous based on its relationship to traditional land.

In official plans for a cultural tourism circuit in the alta montaña, the Guaytamari commune continues to be ignored. It may be that, despite governmental recognition of its legal status, Guaytamari's openness about its self-construction renders it less than "authentic" for official agencies. A series of December 2003 *Los Andes* articles about the direction of the new Ministry of Tourism and Culture highlighted the importance of "singularity" and "authenticity" for tourism in Mendoza, which would not support the pan-Andean and hybrid outlook of Guaytamari.[25] In what seems to be a direct critique of Guaytamari's hybridity, one *Los Andes* reporter writes that travelers to Mendoza want to "look for artisan products with the certainty that they are legitimately derived from the originary peoples of the region and not a pastiche of styles and origins" (Ramos 2003). In this vein Mendoza has established the "Mercado Artesanal de Mendoza," created by the Subsecretariat of Social Development, to certify the authenticity of local indigenous artisanry, improve the quality of local products, motivate creativity, and create a larger and urban market (Pastor et al. 2006).[26] Authentification, then, is also contingent on skewing production to better serve the consumer and touristic market.

In contrast to official projects, public tourism agencies have little problem with Guaytamari's invention of itself, as they continue to re-create it through touristic marketing by identifying Guaytamari in a wide variety of ways, from Indian reservation to a "curiosity" (Taranto 2002). When agencies translate the Guaytamari Cooperative, its self-designation, to Guaytamari "Indian reservation," Argentina's history of genocidal warfare against its indigenous peoples, at least for English speakers, is reinscribed. There is the temptation to suppose that the North American historical connotations of "reservation" could reconstruct and reterritorialize the memory of the nineteenth-century desert campaigns, which did not actually occur in this area but that very much have conditioned the social reality and collective Argentine memory of its indigenous peoples. However, this reading of Guaytamari, and by extension, of Argentina's indigenous communities, is directed toward an outside group of international tourists as a marketing ploy (or as the result of doubtful translation skills) that exoticizes Guaytamari and subsumes it to a North American context. It also erases the very real social, economic, political, and historical marginalizations suffered by the majority of Argentina's indigenous peoples living in the Northwest. Nevertheless, although Guaytamari spokespersons are very clear about their re-ethnification process and the founding of the cooperative, the imagined historical exploitation and repression associated with Indian "reservation" may serve to entice a larger international tourist public to consider visiting Guaytamari's enclave on a tour of the high mountain region.

Debriefs

The Guaytamarians' openness about their reconstruction of Huarpe culture, the hybrid nature of their re-ethnification, and their decidedly modern approach to indigenous activism make the commune unattractive to official touristic projects that seek a coherent premodern "authenticity" and also complicate mountaineering's privileging of the mythos of the

Incan mummy. Guaytamari destabilizes an exotic, premodern, unchanging indigeneity located in the past that would benefit the touristic projects of the Mendocino Department of Cultural Heritage and mountaineering's discourse of adventure and transcendence.

In the complex alta montaña zone, tourism has become a key mediator of the way that indigeneity is understood. The province's invention of an indigenous past, mountaineering's cult of Aconcagua's Incan heritage, and the strategies and practices of Guaytamari are all based on reconstructive methodologies that integrate interests and concerns of the tourist market. The tensions among these touristic projects also speak to the uneasy renegotiation of provincial identity and ethnicity. They suggest that it might be easier for the province to "authenticate" an invisible Incan past through science, signage, myth, and market demands than to work through issues of historical social marginalizations, the sociopolitical meanings of re-ethnification, and the disjuncture between the national government's definition of ethnicity and local collective beliefs and practices.

CHAPTER FOUR

Fashioning Adventure

CREATING MOUNTAINEERING IN THE 1980S

Tailoring the Image

Dear Listeners, I am telling you about this "Fashion Mountain" Aconcagua.

—RADIO BEROMUENSTER INTERVIEW WITH DORLY MARMILLOD, C. 1953[1]

In the 1986 mountaineering narrative, *Seven Summits*, the chapter about Aconcagua concludes at the top: "For at that moment, Frank Wells and Dick Bass were the two highest men standing on any point of land in the western hemisphere of the world. . . . 'One down and six to go,' Dick rejoined, and then he let out his Tarzan call. 'Aah-eah-eaahhh'" (Bass et al. 1986, 104). This metaphorical voicing of white male supremacy over both nature and modernity, a call made popular through Hollywood's ventriloquism of romanticized Western imperialism, ends the recounting of Frank Wells's and Dick Bass's successful ascent of Aconcagua in 1983, the first in their attempt to scale the highest peak on each of the seven continents. This shout of jubilation and triumph, however, did not just mark the taking of the topmost point in the Americas; it also signaled the setting in motion of drives toward other heights. It inaugurated the Seven Summits Route that Wells and Bass had set as their climbing goal, imprinted an image of Aconcagua on an international public, and targeted a bright new era in the mountaineering industry for Mendoza, Argentina.

It was during this decade, the 1980s, in which Bass and Wells sought to make mountaineering history, that key global, regional, and national circumstances came together to lay the groundwork for Mendoza's development of a thriving mountaineering business. Growth and change in the international climbing market, advances in communications technology that brought the globe closer in terms of access to information, and newfound international awareness of Aconcagua, the highest peak of the Americas, coincided with an ambitious generation of Mendocino climbers emerging out of the 1980s to energize the local climbing scene and take advantage of the mountaineering capital held by the area.

The 1980s marks a new beginning, or even a kind of contemporary origin for Mendocino mountaineering. It was not that prior to the 1980s locally based mountaineering was absent in Mendoza or, for that matter, that it did not participate at the international level. Previously, local mountaineering activity had first been represented by service providers and porters for foreign expeditions and later spearheaded by the military in both national and international arenas. However, both the service and military activities of Mendocino mountaineering differed radically from the nature of the civilian group of Mendocino climbers, or the Generation of the 80s, as I have come to call them, that came into ascendancy during that decade. This generation of young climbers was instrumental in popularizing climbing within the local area both for pleasure and as a profession. They also played essential roles in creating the economic and educational infrastructures to support the sport in Mendoza. Coincidental, or perhaps causal, to the Generation of the 80s coming of age was the end of the Argentine military dictatorship in 1983 and the subsequent "opening up" of the nation to new political, cultural, and economic forces. These national and regional moments of the 1980s intersected with a surge in international interest in mountaineering, innovations in gear, and changes in attitudes about the sport that would redefine Aconcagua's position and reputation on the contemporary map of international mountaineering. This new mountaineering map would especially chart how the prominence of capital, the commodification of adventure, the effects of globalization, and the doggedness of modernist legacies would locate Aconcagua and Mendoza.

Capital Endeavors

"It's our victory together," Dick said between gasps. "You got me up—and I know you'll get me down."

—DICK BASS TO DAVID BREASHEARS ON EVEREST SUMMIT (BASS ET AL. 1986, 319)

Considering the forces at play in the dramatic outgrowth of the mountaineering industry on Aconcagua is to take a look at the kinds of negotiations and articulations that occur at a global-local-national nexus. Globalization, in its most generalized sense, can be understood as a worldwide network in which flows of commodities, information, people, and images are driven across national borders by the markets and finance capital of neoliberal economics. Within this grid, the sovereignty of the nation-state to provide services, protect rights, and anchor identity is undermined by machinations of transnational financial institutions, such as the International Monetary Fund and the World Bank, and the dynamics of a world market. Of course, within this globalized market not all participants are equal nor are all categories of nation and nationhood broached in the same way. Indeed, the most unyielding border still resisting in a globalized world is not the frontier between nations, but one that continues to set apart First World consumers from Third World producers (Rodowick 2002, 16). This hierarchical duality reproduces the consequences of modernity's imperial project where political and/or economic colonization of great parts of the world were carried out and justified by belief in Western progress. Within the scheme of globalization, however, it is not the guise of an assumed national superiority, but rather the impetus of transnational finances that tend to maintain the asymmetry of this relationship. Although globalization supposedly decenters modernity's center-periphery binary, First World capital still defends its hegemony within the globalized system.

The preeminence of capital in establishing market and social value is what especially marked the 1980s as a moment of transformation in mountaineering. The 1980s not only registered changes in the parameters of the mountaineering market with the consolidation of equipment and clothing industries and the growth of its clientele base, but this decade also especially recorded differences in how climbers related to the mountains and the sport.

Capital's fundamental role in mountaineering was nothing new. From the start, mountaineering tradition stemming out of the late nineteenth century could not be divorced from the economics of Anglo-European imperial expansion. Mountaineering generally took place in those areas considered the periphery of Western modernity, where Western occupation and influence could be rationalized for the benefit of science, knowledge, progress, and the future. In terms of Western subjectivity these faraway, outlying areas provided the necessary distance and perspective for confirming and authenticating the modern Western self. Thus, as a reflection of modernity's project abroad, notions of climbing for patriotic duty for the benefit of country, knowledge, and especially in search of a heightened sense of self-awareness allowed the politics of finance, as well as those of race and culture, to remain obscured.

Within this tradition, Anglo-European climbers' connections to mountaineering have largely been defined through a competitive playing out of national masculine identity and superiority (Bayers 2003; Ortner 1999). This masculine competition was driven by a "natural" assumption that only the bravest, strongest, and most intrepid would dare to participate in it. In assessing the stories of early British and American expeditionaries, Bayers finds that "because of their supposed racial and cultural superiority or both, imperial adventurers could, it seemed, tackle any challenge that came their way—whether the rigors of the 'wilderness' or the 'savagery' of 'natives'" (2003, 2). This special and hierarchical relationship to the mountain and other "natural" dangers, such as "natives," was supposedly divorced from the base interests of capital and carried out in the name of privileged and elevated purposes. Although the social and cultural understandings of the sport necessarily evolved during the twentieth century, climbers' relationships to mountaineering have held on to the basic ideological premises of its earliest beginnings. Indeed, Ortner has found, when speaking of the tradition in the Himalayas, that the constants in Western mountaineering, through periods of romanticization, hypermachismo, and the counterculture of the 1970s, have been masculine competitiveness and the critique of middle-class values and modernity (1999, 281–282). Paradoxically, mountaineers' "rejection" of modernity does not undo mountaineering's originary configuration as a modern construct. A rejection of the industrialized urban metropolis as a path to self-knowledge is an inherent trait of modernity itself. The modern Western mountaineering self would seek to define its subjectivity in contrast to an other deemed less modern and to validate its "inherent" superiority over the unmodern and the accompanying dangers of the unknown, unseen, unexplored, or uncivilized.

The advent of jet travel in the 1960s, which shortened distances and reduced the possibility of anywhere being left as "unknown," is generally heralded as spurring the boom in the international tourism industry (Gordon 2006, 10). At this time the space-time compression afforded by fast, easy, and relatively inexpensive travel is also cited as marking a moment of change in the conceptualization of adventure and mountaineering to now be more explicitly linked to consumerism and status accrual (Gordon 2006, 19; Houston 2006, 147–152). By the 1980s the modern mode of traditional mountaineering with its inherited assumption of a unique and elitist nature was definitively breached when the ability to buy adventure became more determinant than ever and overshadowed any sense of dedication to a national moral high ground, the achievement of superior physical prowess, or individual transcendence. That the clique had been violated was no more clearly emphasized than when Dick Bass paid David Breashears to lead him up Everest and become the first person to complete the Seven Summits Route. This event is repeatedly discussed and critiqued in climbing books, magazines, and websites as representing the moment when the "real" spirit of mountaineering was tarnished. When Dick Bass was guided to the top of the world to gain renown as the first to complete the Seven Summits, the vestiges and traces of what Bayers (2003) calls "heroic imperial masculinity" clashed head-on with the middle-class values of experiencing mountaineering as adventure tourism. Gordon (2006) calls adventure tourism a hybrid, "a contradiction since adventure is about dealing with uncertainty, yet planned tours minimize this. Adventure tourism is marketed for those who have neither the time nor the desire to take the risk fully upon themselves" (7). Ultimately, adventure tourism cannot be considered apart from the enterprise of business (Beedie 2003; Cloutier 2003). Thus, the very essence of the Aconcagua mountaineering industry is hybrid in a variety of complex and complicated ways, but it especially hinges on the kind of hybridization that Gordon discusses as being at the heart of adventure tourism. The syncretic nature of Aconcagua mountaineering is prominently noted in its partnering of the guided expedition and its built-in safety nets with the mystique of mountaineering as an exercise in freely negotiated risk. It was in the 1980s, this period of surge in the commercing of adventure and its elision with mountaineering, that the mountaineering industry on Aconcagua began to take the form and shape that it has today.

Hybrid Identities

During the eighties, climbing changed from a fringe activity to a sport that attracted thousands of new enthusiasts.

—"BLACK DIAMOND 'ORIGINS'" (www.blackdiamondequipment.com)

Although Aconcagua can trace its international mountaineering history back to the 1880s it was not until a century later that it became a major destination for mountaineering (Secor 1999, 21; Zorrilla 1997, 35). Since the 1980s adventure seekers from the United States have consistently ranked first every year, in terms of numbers, among international climbers attempting to summit Aconcagua. Their numerous and continued presence implies that North American interest in mountaineering and the state of the mountaineering industry in the United States have held real consequences, in terms of generating revenues and cultural meaning, for the development of Aconcagua as a mountaineering destination.

While a more complete picture of Aconcagua mountaineering might also include a detailed look at other national mountaineering projects such as those of Britain, France, Germany, Spain, Italy, and Japan, countries especially present today on the Argentine mountain, this chapter primarily focuses on a broad overview of the representations of the mountaineering industry in the United States. I believe that the example of the United States offers a representative way in which to look at the appropriation, modification, and/or rejection of hegemonic traditions and discourses in Aconcagua mountaineering. In many respects the forceful presence of the United States in Mendocino mountaineering parallels the political, economic, and sociocultural importance that the United States has had for the extended region over the last century. Historically, since 1898, the United States has held a prominent (if not dominant) place, with regard to Latin America "in the structure of the modern/colonial world system" (Mignolo 2002, 89). The historical usurpation of European influence by the United States in its southern neighbors reflects the evolution of US protagonism in the history of mountaineering on Aconcagua. Although early expeditions on Aconcagua were predominantly European, currently, and over several decades now, the United States has led the way in foreign activity there.

I do not mean to give primacy to "First World" endeavors or to use them as the standard against which local Mendocino enterprises would be judged as derivatory, subordinate, or inferior. Instead, I look at the mountaineering industry on Aconcagua as a high-altitude borderland (Ortner 1996) in which international and local traditions compete, diverge, merge, and evolve. In this borderland, differing mountaineering products, strategies, and styles create and share meaning about the sport, the mountain, the nation, the self, and the body. Within this globalized community, configured by the practices of international mountaineering, national, gendered, ethnic, and racial identities replay and reshape relationships as they negotiate difference.

In this kind of globalized contact zone, such processes of transcultural fusion and hybridization are based on unequal power relationships (Pratt 1991, 34) and correspond to First World tendencies to dominate economics and values of sociocultural relationships. Therefore, examining how

Mendocino mountaineering has evolved means acknowledging its neocolonial relationship with Anglo-European mountaineering and its development from a geopolitical position that has traditionally been the periphery (Southern, Latin American, Argentine) for Northern (Western, Anglo-European) modernity. In this way I have come to think of Anglo-European mountaineering and the Mendocino project within the relational frame that Mignolo set for Latin American and European philosophy during the colonial period, "separated and linked simultaneously by the epistemic colonial difference [that] can account for the fact that, for instance, European Thought does not need Latin American Thought, but Latin American Thought cannot be such without European thought" (2002, 78).

I do not extrapolate from this that Mendocino mountaineering is merely a dependent imitation of Northern tradition. Rather, Mendocino mountaineering has also identified itself with the origins and practices of the Northern mountaineering tradition while recognizing the neocolonial relationships of power and status it has maintained within this tradition. Taking these practices for their own does not render their interpretations of them as second-rate duplicates. Bhabha's (1994) conceptualization of mimicry informs us that the colonial imitation inevitably, to lesser or greater degrees, reworks and disrupts the hegemonic discourse of the colonizer. In its own manifestations of mountaineering, Mendoza has interpolated local practices and values to create a new syncretic version of mountaineering that in its hybridity is uniquely Mendocino, but also recognizable according to international standards and expectations.

Mendocino mountaineering has never maintained a static relationship with Anglo-European traditions, nor has it emerged from purely mimetic impulses. It is, however, the meaning of its difference from the North that is often contentious. The unquestioned integration of Anglo-European traditions reverberates in the neocolonial consciousness of some Mendocinos who tend to mark any difference as inferior, substandard, and immature. Conversely, there are other mountaineering currents in Mendoza that, in the name of national and regional pride and revisionist history, laud the distinctiveness of the local mountaineering culture and challenge its assumed subordinate location in the world of mountaineering.

Whatever its resistance to Northern hegemony might be, the concept of difference in Mendocino mountaineering is also problematic on another level. Mendocino mountaineering masks its exclusionary foundation in the same way that, according to Mignolo, the terms "Latin America" and "Latinidad" hide the silencing of indigenous and minority voices for both the North and South (2002, 79). With respect to the Mendocino climbing industry, these kinds of erasures and mutings are derived from international mountaineering traditions, national historical practices, and local identity politics that see Mendoza as a blend of criollo and immigrant cultures and imaginations. Other chapters look more fully at these silences and at how Mendocino mountaineering engages indigenous participation, women's roles, and class hierarchies within mountain culture and adventure tourism practices in the region.

The Seven Summits Effect

It was serendipitous that Aconcagua was put on the map of a new kind of mountaineering growing out of the 1980s, one based on the daydreams and fantasies of middle-aged American businessmen with the time and the means to look for "something big" to give a sense of accomplishment and a rapid payoff (Bass et al. 1986, 10). The linking of the highest peaks of the continents of the world as a mountaineering route was cemented by the endeavors of Frank Wells, the ex-president of Warner Brothers, and Dick Bass, a Texas oil and energy mogul.[2] *Seven Summits*, written by Bass and Wells with Rick Ridgeway, chronicled the team's efforts from 1981 to 1985 to reach the highest points of each of the seven continents: Everest in Asia (8,848 meters), Aconcagua in South America (6,962 meters), Denali (Mt. McKinley) in North America (6,195 meters), Kilimanjaro in Africa (5,963 meters), Elbrus in Europe (5,633 meters), Vinson in Antarctica (4,897 meters), and Kosciuszko in Australia (2,238 meters) (some mountaineers now prefer to include Carstenz as the highest peak in Oceania [4,884 meters] rather than Australia's Kosciuszko). The setting up of this route and the conferring of prestige to its completion were both arbitrary and artificial. Many climbers have pointed out to me that a better proving ground for validating mountaineering's elite would instead be a route of the seven highest peaks in the world, regardless of their location, or one made up of the seven most technically difficult ascents. Either one of these itineraries would exclude Aconcagua.

Although the escalation of Aconcagua's draw for international adventure tourism in the last twenty years cannot be directly attributed to Bass's and Wells's notoriety, the mountain's inclusion in the highly publicized account of their expeditions fixed Aconcagua on the itineraries and in the imaginations of international mountaineering devotees. Through their book, the Mendocino peak became known as a unique and appropriate challenge for international mountaineering and one especially attainable

Figure 4.1. A t-shirt display, marking completion of the Seven Summits Route, in the Hotel Refugio Plaza de Mulas.

for novice climbers. In *Aconcagua: The Stone Sentinel* (Taplin 1992), Mark Cornwall explained his decision to attempt Aconcagua: "*Seven Summits* has influenced a lot of people. It certainly influenced my decision about both Mt. McKinley and Aconcagua. . . . I . . . knew Aconcagua would not be as dangerous as McKinley; there aren't the crevasses, and there is not constant ice and snow. I expected Aconcagua to be better because on McKinley you are always roped in, you have no freedom of motion, you cannot leave camp, you have no privacy at all" (23). While Aconcagua mountaineering was never dependent on its inclusion in the Seven Summit Route that *Seven Summits* promoted, its appeal as one of the continental highests has certainly profited from it. (In 1982, a year before Bass's and Wells's summit, there were only two expeditions on Aconcagua's Normal Route; in 1991–1992 the park granted 2,600 permits [Balf 1992; Johnston and Edwards 1994, 463].)

The establishment of Bass's and Wells's chosen "fantasy" circuit of continental summits as a naturalized and prestigious goal of high-altitude mountaineering was promoted worldwide when Bass was the first to complete the circuit. For many in the climbing community, this moment marked a before and after in mountaineering, the point at which mountaineering became a possibility for the mainstream. When the story of Bass's completion of the route (on Everest in 1985) became public knowledge, it signaled the moment when "people who never thought about mountaineering were suddenly inspired to try it" (Norman 2000, 101).

The undertaking of this enterprise by Bass and Wells was made possible by the lucrative and transnational scope of the North American energy and entertainment industries that supported them. Since the book's publication in 1986, many mountaineering enthusiasts have censured the high profile it garnered for a route mapped by a pair of amateur sportsmen whose skill and knowledge were far inferior to those of most professional mountaineers of the day. These critics point out that it was the fiscal power of the two businessmen more than fortitude, experience, and technique that allowed them to pioneer and champion this route (Norman 2000, 101).[3] Financial resources, leisure time, and access to media coverage allowed Bass and Wells to imprint their "dream" tour onto collective popular memory and open up mountaineering to a much wider and nonprofessional audience.

Despite its detractors, the Seven Summits Route today remains a symbol and goal of mountaineering prestige and a viable marketing tool for mountaineering agencies. The competitive nature of mountaineering and the importance of this route are demonstrated by websites such as www.everestnews.com and http://7summits.com which maintain a list of those who have completed the Seven Summits. This list includes the name and country of the summiteer and the date of completion. Everestnews.com also reports on records such as the oldest and youngest to summit, and the shortest time to complete the route. Although the list may not be complete, accurate, or consistently updated, as inscription is voluntary, it assumes a global audience, and everestnews.com states that its website is "the largest mountaineering publication in the world." Stature for both the individual and nation are conferred by being named on the Seven Summits list. Beyond the jockeying for position for personal and national recognition that the list conveys, the route itself is contested. The artificiality of the route is highlighted by the argument over whether Carstenz in Indonesia or Kosciuszko in Australia should be included as the highest, which depends on whether Australia or Oceania is used as a continental marker. Thus, there are actually two lists held on the websites and by collective mountaineering memory for the Seven Summits. (By 2011 7summits.com reported that there were approximately 179 people on the Carstenz list and 200 on the Kosciuszko list, with numerous climbers listed on both.)

The hegemony that the Seven Summits Route (whether with Carstenz or Kosciuszko) has gained within contemporary mountaineering circles to confer status exemplifies the globalizing reach of capital to establish a market and determine value, demand, and prestige across national boundaries. In other words, access to financial and media capital created a global mountaineering itinerary that was not initiated or promoted by expert, local, regional, or national needs or interests. Interestingly, this globalized route still allows for national competition and identity politics traditional to mountaineering to be played out within its confines as climbers continue to strive to put themselves and their nation on the list. Yet, within the route itself, nation and territory are virtually disconnected and displaced on its globalized map of mountaineering. Here, Aconcagua is reterritorialized within the imagined terrain of the Seven Summits Route where only continental location and height are salient, and where Argentina, Mendoza, and Mendocino climbers do not figure. Or if they do, it is to reenact a subordinate role of Southern other for Northern self, in repetition of the well-worn playing out of imperial adventure.

Seven Summits, more than narrating the first success on the route of the continents, especially commemorated a change, conflictive for many, in attitude toward the sport. The "Seven Summits effect," which reterritorialized Aconcagua into the global imagination, promoted the belief that the risk and danger of mountaineering could be mitigated by access to monetary resources. With expendable capital and leisure time, anyone with a modicum of athletic ability could climb a mountain and buy status as an adventurer. While the Seven Summits effect did not erase the nationalistic and patriotic overtones of mountaineering as exploration or do away with North-South oppositions and First World–Third World divisions, it did expand the mountain climbing pool, or increase its market potential, across a new and broader-based community, one whose only commonality, as Beedie (2003) has explained, is "the financial capacity to pay for their expensive holidays" (210). This has meant a challenge to the previously elitist attitude held by and about mountaineering and its participants (Johnston and Edwards 1994; Beedie 2003; Gordon 2006; Houston 2006). The Seven Summits effect of the 1980s and the boost in interest in mountaineering at that time, in the United States and abroad, promised a greater role for Aconcagua within international mountaineering and signaled a push for development in Mendoza's adventure tourism industry.

Fashion and Gear

The Seven Summits effect, the coupling of capital and adventure, exacerbated earlier tendencies in mountaineering that equated the commodification of adventure with the dilution of mountaineering status. In the

1980s this coupling process intensified as new and expanded connections and networks meant for a heightened and changing awareness of the sport. In other words, the mountaineering imagination no longer was emanating from and restricted to the preexisting climbing community; it now was mutating and being constructed by media, celebrity, business, and fashion trends to encroach into other kinds of social spheres. This also meant that mountaineering narratives, which have traditionally held the principal role in constructing the ideological underpinnings of mountaineering (whether it be "imperial heroic national masculinity"; racial, cultural hierarchies; or late modernity's antimodern stance), now shared representational potential with other cultural, visual, and financial discourses.

Profitable business endeavors in the United States in the areas of technical gear and apparel, especially during the 1970s and 1980s, helped to refashion the way mountaineering was envisioned and practiced by many new aficionados, some of whom would eventually make their way to Aconcagua.[4] In North America this growth in mountaineering paralleled two movements: radical improvements in gear and the founding or expansion of what are now the major US mountaineering equipment and clothing companies, among which figure Patagonia, The North Face, Marmot, Black Diamond, Mountain Hardware, and Columbia.[5]

The tone for the 1980s that brought new respect for mixing big business acumen and the allure of mountain adventure was especially exemplified by Yvon Chouinard. Chouinard, who formed part of the Bass and Wells Aconcagua team of 1983, was founder of both Chouinard Equipment and the outdoor clothing company Patagonia. In *Seven Summits,* Rick Ridgeway described Chouinard at the time of the Aconcagua expedition as "the most internationally recognized climber in America" whose two businesses gained him "annual sales of $30 million" (Bass et al. 1986, 85). Chouinard was a longtime, experienced climber whose business ventures developed out of his personal quest to improve basic climbing and mountaineering tools. Although some might argue that his commercialization of the sport was unlike that of the relative novices Bass's and Wells's "buying" of mountain experience, the linking, in one way or another, of big finance and mountain climbing came to characterize the popularization and expanded practice of mountaineering in the 1980s.

Chouinard began to redesign climbing materials for his own use in the late 1950s. By the 1970s, with improvements in pitons (and the subsequent move to aluminum chocks), carabiners, crampons, and ice axes, Chouinard Equipment became the largest supplier of climbing hardware in the United States.[6] This was a significant moment for the US climbing scene as previously most mountaineering hardware had to be imported from Europe. According to A. David Napier (2006), when Chouinard started out tinkering in his garage,[7] "[t]here were no climbing stores or books on technique that you could find at your local mountaineering shop because there were no mountaineering shops. There was no money in the sport because there was no market. There was no market because no one had yet invented . . . all the . . . gadgets that have turned climbing into a safe, highly popular, and profitable enterprise" (85). Without a doubt, new equipment and easier accessibility to the necessary specialized tools of the sport created an encouraging environment for the business of mountaineering to prosper.

Chouinard's outdoor clothing line, marketed with the Patagonia label, was equally as successful as his hardware line. According to Chouinard, he chose the name Patagonia because "it was a name like Timbuktu and Shangri-La, far-off, interesting, not quite on the map. Patagonia brings to mind, as we once wrote in a catalog introduction, 'romantic visions of glaciers tumbling into fjords, jagged windswept peaks, gauchos and condors.' It's been a good name for us, and it can be pronounced in every language."[8] The exotic allure of the distant, unchartered territory of "Patagonia" hinted at the idea of exploration, risk, and escape from modern urban civilization. This imagined and imaginary place invoked the vestiges of imperial adventure where modern subjectivities could prove their mettle against the dangers of the unknown, "uncivilized" (and relatively uninhabited, except for gauchos and condors) world. Wearing Patagonia meant you could imagine yourself taking on those characteristics attributed to this kind of adventurer—the daring, free-spirited, heroic (and imperialistic) risk taker. Tellingly, Patagonia was no longer just a place to go; it had become an ideology to wear.

The 1980s marked a significant moment in design and development for Patagonia. In 1985 Patagonia introduced its trademark Synchilla fleece (a synthetic boiled-wool blend) outerwear and its Capilene (polyester-based) underwear. These two items signaled a huge improvement in mountaineering and outdoor cold weather apparel: they could be easily layered, were lighter in weight, better at wicking away perspiration, and more efficient at holding in warmth. Patagonia's web page explains that in the late 1980s these innovative technical fabrics, coupled with the company's new use of bright vivid colors for men's adventure wear, caused a "fashion craze" with "the Patagonia label becoming as much of a fad as the rugby shirt and extending beyond the outdoor community to fashion consumers."[9] Patagonia's high-tech, ultra-modern connotations of stylish superiority that combined with the idea of escape from the modern that its name implied broadened its attractiveness. In this way the cachet of mountaineering was popularized and romanticized through Patagonia's brand appeal to a diverse and broad clientele who formed an expanded potential market of buyers for mountain adventure.

I am not suggesting here that simply wearing Patagonia garments motivated people to become mountain climbers. (Although in ethnographic work at base camp I have found some rather humorous anecdotal evidence to the contrary.) The fact that Patagonia garb was popular and trendy and projected an image of the "bold and free spirits" that mountaineers were purported to be (and were suggestively illustrated as such in the company catalogs) was probably only significant to company marketers and not to the adventure tourism industry. However, the widespread popularity of Patagonia did make knowing *where* to go to buy technical clothes much easier, for those who might be so inclined. And Patagonia's appeal to those who *were* mountain enthusiasts was not just limited to its greater accessibility. Patagonia's reputation for having some of the most up-to-date and technologically crafted materials for climbing also conferred on the body that was wearing its label an easily recognizable status, regardless of the wearer's skill level.

Equal to or even greater than the snob appeal of the Patagonia brand is The North Face label, a company that also offers both technical and fashion wear. About the same time that Chouinard Equipment was established in Southern California (1965), The North Face began its operations in San Francisco (1966). By the end of the 1980s The North Face had become the only US supplier of both a technical outerwear line and a backpacking line (packs, sleeping bags, tents), and today it has branches in more than thirty countries.[10] International recognition for The North Face came as early as 1969 when the company began organizing environmental, climbing, and mountaineering expeditions. Nowadays, The North Face also sponsors a stable of "North Face athletes" (including Argentine brothers Damián Benegas and Willy Benegas), whose international feats while wearing and using The North Face gear are highlighted in its catalogs, on its website, in climbing and adventure magazines, or even in articles in *National Geographic*. In mountaineering tradition, this kind of expeditionary and individual economic support and public forums of recognition and honor were previously given through the auspices of local clubs or national governments or institutions like Britain's National Geographic Society. High finance, marketing instruments like catalogs and websites, and fashion trends have usurped their roles.[11] This disassociation from official state institutions parallels how the state's responsibility is usurped by transnational capital in globalization and characterizes what some refer to as the postmodern moment of mountaineering.[12] Mountaineering is no longer underwritten by, nor explicitly tied to, national projects or concepts of national sovereignty. Instead its practice and success are contingent on the influence of transnational capital and the modes of popular culture. While the shell of imperial masculine adventure still encases mountaineering, it no longer performs for the sake of empire, but rather for individual esteem or to increase profit margins.

High Profiles

The increased visibility and status for mountaineering in the 1980s were disseminated within the arena of popular culture through global media's cult of celebrity. The media's promotion of climbing stars and Hollywood's embracing of mountaineering allowed a disparate and diverse public to more easily imagine themselves as insiders in a group formed by mountaineering. According to Rodowick (2002), "[t]he globality of the media state—the transnational sale and circulation of images and information—transcends and unifies otherwise heterogeneous cultures and communities" (16). There exists a kind of transnational mountaineering community whose common factors are determined by the entertainment and communications media. When asked, most climbers today can cite any number of books, magazines, movies, and celebrity icons that have served as inspiration. And in my experience on Aconcagua, these kinds of high-profile images and facts are most often called up by members of climbing groups of mixed nationalities who search for common threads to engage conversation and create a sense of *communitas*.

With the publication of *Seven Summits*, print media combined in new ways with the power of Hollywood to project an iconic and glamorous image of mountaineering. The coauthor of *Seven Summits*, Frank Wells, financed his trip through his previous presidency at Warner Brothers Studios, and he received a great deal of publicity for the sacrificial nature of his resignation from such a high-profile post to go scale mountains. The front cover of the book that recounts his efforts, *Seven Summits*, includes a quote by Clint Eastwood, himself a famous movie mountaineer: "A hell of an adventure. A book for everyone who's ever dreamed of accomplishing great feats." The book's back cover contains a quote by Robert Redford, another famous movie mountain man. Being sandwiched between Eastwood and Redford in the late 1980s, the story of Bass's and Wells's summit bids was tinged by a Hollywood, rugged leading-man aura that romanticized mountaineers (and anyone else "who's ever dreamed of accomplishing great feats") with a Hollywood-ese, super-achieving loner, or "one-against-nature-and-all-other evils," "but-ready-to-sacrifice-all-to-save-a-friend" masculine veneer. This Hollywood image holds true for the portrayals that Michael Biehn, Sylvester Stallone, and Chris O'Donnell make in the mountaineering films *K2* (1992), *Cliffhanger* (1993), and *Vertical Limit* (2000), respectively.

The combination of Hollywood, the outdoor gear industry, and increased visibility for mountaineering in US popular culture is exemplified in Marmot's "origin" story. The founders of Marmot were originally from Southern California and their first year in business was a huge success due to an order for 108 "puffy jackets" from the producers of Clint Eastwood's mountaineering-spy movie *The Eiger Sanction* (1975).[13] Marmot, although not as internationally well known as Patagonia or The North Face, now has over 650 dealers in the United States and sells its products in twenty-seven countries. A major contribution of Marmot to the improvement of mountaineering gear was that it was one of the first companies to produce outdoor apparel with Gore-Tex.[14] Its claim to fame is that Clint Eastwood was one of the first to use its line.

In addition to the Hollywood hype, new achievements of world-class mountain athletes marked this period of growth and change. The excitement surrounding the feats of world-renowned international climbers complemented and competed with media and entertainment icons. Many armchair adventurers, as well as practicing mountaineers themselves, talk about how the stories of mountaineering icons like Chouinard, Glenn Exum, and Alex Lowe have sparked their imagination about mountaineering. Perhaps the greatest and most widely reported and acclaimed achievements during this time of transition in mountaineering were those of the Italian climber Reinhold Messner. In the 1970s and early 1980s, mountaineering was energized by the darings of Messner who was the first climber to summit, and without oxygen, the fourteen 8,000-meter mountains of the world. The completion of this fourteen-summit route, which Messner chronicled in his book *All Fourteen 8000ers* (1999), sets a mountaineering standard that many feel outranks that of the Seven Summits, which, of course, Messner has also done. Messner's adventures were reported in international journals, in national mountaineering magazines (both *Climbing* and *Outside* began during the 1970s), in Werner Herzog's documentary *The Dark Glow of the Mountains* (1984), and in the numerous books that he has written about his experiences.[15]

For many climbers it is Messner who set the standard against which Bass and his crew and the consequences of the Seven Summits effect are measured.[16] As a "real" mountaineer, Messner climbed without the use of a guide (often without the help of supplemental oxygen), attempted the most difficult peaks, and opened up new routes, such as the Messner Direct on the extremely difficult and snow-covered wall of the South Face of Aconcagua in 1974. His incredible feats that awed the mountaineering public and made him an international icon also provided the hallmark from which the accomplishments of climbers like Bass would be held in contempt by "those in the know."

The promotion of mountaineering celebrity in all of its forms helped the sport to gain a foothold in the collective popular imagination. Today there are countless articles, books, and websites that talk about why people climb: to escape the dreariness of a routine and dull life, to mark a birthday milestone or a midlife crisis, to get over a divorce, to celebrate newfound health, to support a charitable foundation, to find self-understanding or transcendence in life, or to look for physical challenges that entail the idea of thrill and risk. As a cultural archive, mountaineering represents historical moments of social, cultural, and economic systems that provide the structure and potential for all these dreams, desires, and imaginings.

In the 1980s, the prestige of sufficient economic power to buy adventure, a superior sense of knowledge represented by technically advanced and accessible equipment and clothing, the lure of celebrity, together with the vestiges of affirming masculine and national prowess and individual transcendence, all formed part of the cultural capital that practitioners of mountaineering could accrue. As a cultural commodity, there was a certain positive status, or symbolic capital (Beedie 2003, 212), associated with mountaineering that made it attractive to a widespread audience that eclipsed (but that did not erase) its imperialist, racist, and sexist undertones.

Locating Aconcagua in the Text

It's obvious, that under these conditions where all that's really asked for to climb the highest mountain in America is money, time, and the weather forecast, there is a big crowd of mountain climbers every summer.

—RADIO BEROMUENSTER INTERVIEW WITH DORLY MARMILLOD, C. 1953[17]

The 1980s marked a period of increased visibility for mountaineering, improved and easier-to-access gear, an expanded popular base, brand appeal, and a new relationship between finance and adventure. Although

Mendoza had the advantage of Aconcagua being one of the seven summits, any attempt that Mendoza made at developing an appealing adventure culture for an international market would necessarily be bordered, constrained, and limited by both the evolution and the traditions of mountaineering, personified in the Tarzan yell with which Dick Bass christened Aconcagua's summit. The legacy of Western colonial imperialism, the commodification of adventure, the exoticization of the location, and the romanticization of the experience meant that in most mountaineering narratives Mendoza and its claim to Aconcagua would be absent.

Mountaineering is one of the most literary of sports (Ortner 1999, 14; Johnston and Edwards 1994, 461), and as a cultural construct it has largely been produced in language (Bayers 2003, 15). *Seven Summits*, as the best-known mountaineering narrative about Aconcagua, is particularly rich in generating meaning for the Argentine mountain. Aconcagua is first introduced in the book as a "practice climb" for Everest (Bass et al. 1986, 34) and the Normal Route as being "easy, maybe too easy" (34) to provide adequate training for Everest. This façade of relative ease has become one of the most distinctive stereotypes about Aconcagua, and one that does not give credit to the harshness of its climate and the difficulty of its altitude, which generally account for more deaths on Aconcagua than do falls, avalanches, or accidents.

In the retelling in *Seven Summits* of the two actual expeditions on Aconcagua, the fact that the mountain is situated in Argentina mostly goes unnoticed. During the second expedition the climbers never seem to cross the border into Argentina or find themselves in Puente del Inca, Los Puquios, or Penitentes, the staging areas for Aconcagua, before arriving at the trailhead. However, the Chilean geographical points of Santiago and Portillo are used to orient the readers. On the first expedition the team seems to locate the mountain in the northeast corner of the continent, as opposed to the southwest, and the only concession to being in Argentine territory at all is the mention of Patagonia, "that place not quite on the map," and gaucho attire: "One of the joys of expedition mountaineering is traveling to exotic places through offtrack regions, often accompanied by local porters or animal drivers. On Aconcagua the approach began at a trailhead off the trans-Andean highway connecting Merida [*sic*] and Santiago, where they hired mule drivers to pack their food and equipment to base camp. These mule drivers were dressed like the gauchos who ride the open ranges of Argentine Patagonia: . . . shoulders draped with ponchos woven of alpaca" (Bass et al. 1986, 37). This description is vague with no mention of local Argentine geographical markers and it even mistakes

Mendoza for Mérida, Venezuela. It does, however, chart the area firmly in a distant exotic elusiveness, not in the Andes of Cuyo that is traversed by arrieros or in a Patagonia roamed by misplaced gauchos but instead in a free, uncivilized, offtrack territory of the mountaineering imagination. It allows readers and climbers to imagine themselves both temporally and spatially distant from the urban, the everyday, and the modern. It does not seem to matter that gauchos traditionally were cattle-herding ranch hands of the pampas far-removed from the agricultural and mountaineering realms of Mendoza. What did matter was that the gaucho was far-removed from the daily and financial worlds of the North American climbers.

While *Seven Summits* was published in 1986, present-day mountaineering narratives, as well as expeditioners I have spoken to over the a span of six years, still continue to focus on the "gauchos." Invoking the figure of the gaucho in lieu of the lesser-known and less romantic arriero, the muleteers who transport gear to base camp on Aconcagua, is a commonplace occurrence. Geoffrey Norman starts his travel memoirs and sets the tone for adventure on Aconcagua with the image of a "gaucho" in *Two for the Summit: My Daughter, the Mountains, and Me* (2000): "A horse-mounted gaucho accompanied the defeated climber, and he seemed sublimely indifferent to the man's laments. But they made a deep impression on me" (2). The attitude of the enigmatic, different, and indifferent "gaucho" contrasts with Norman's more human response of compassion for the climber. This comparison between the "feeling" Norman and the inscrutable gaucho/arriero also forebodes the exotic, perilous, and mysterious adventure ahead for Norman. With this presage of danger goes the concomitant understanding that to undertake such a risk requires valor, courage, and strength of character in those, unlike the "gaucho," who are moved by human suffering.

According to Jean Franco (1999), the abstract gaucho has been taken as a global cultural symbol of Argentine folk culture to indicate Latin American difference and distance from the metropolis. In this way it serves to mark "'underdevelopment'—of tradition as opposed to progress—backwardness as opposed to modernity" (209). For writers and climbers alike, it has been more important to represent and highlight this sort of difference and distance than to locate accurately the people and places along the route up Aconcagua. Inevitably, these expeditioners, whose trip has been configured a priori according to traditional suppositions about where and how mountaineering takes place, follow a trail of the imagination where the expectations of backwardness and underdevelopment link back to nineteenth-century travel and mountaineering narratives and have led to many misconceptions for climbers. In *Aconcagua: The Stone Sentinel* (1992), one of the few mountaineering narratives entirely about an Aconcagua expedition, Tom Taplin, as his plane touches down, envisions Mendoza in the 1990s as the early twentieth-century South American hideout of some rather notorious North Americans immortalized by Hollywood: "Arriving at the Mendoza airport was like that scene in *Butch Cassidy and the Sundance Kid* when they flee to South America and disembark in the middle of the Bolivian boondocks: a hot, dry wind was blowing; dust was swirling around; shacks on the outskirts of town. . . . Once you cruise into town on one of the major boulevards, of course, the realization hits that Mendoza isn't a wild-west frontier outpost at all; it's one of Argentina's provincial capitals, and it has every modern convenience" (20).

Although Taplin's belief that time had stood still in western Argentina was quickly undone when he was confronted by Mendoza's urban landscape, this same imagined temporal dissonance between the climbers' point of origin in the northern hemisphere and the Mendoza region in the southern continues to resonate among those who come to ascend Aconcagua. While the actual time difference between Mendoza and the US East Coast is just one hour ahead, there is the perception by climbers that it is at least a century behind. Two experienced climbers whom I met at base camp, doctors who liked to volunteer their services in the local country of their climbing trips as a way to get to know the region and its people better, were surprised and somewhat disappointed to find the variety of medical specialists in Mendoza that made their services unnecessary. In this same vein, a journalist from North America I was chatting with at base camp about the Aconcagua mountaineering scene laughed out loud at the idea of a professional mountain guide school in Mendoza, asking, "Why would *they* need a guide school?" The emphasis on "they" was the journalist's and served to highlight the "apparent" difference between an "us" and "them." In this rearticulation of mountaineering as a construct of modernity, there is the assumption that adventure is carried out by a First World self in a distant "premodern" world of "others" whose backwardness renders their presence inconsequential or, at least, subservient to the "authentic" mountaineer.

For these reasons it is not seen as necessary to mention people or place names. Norman (2000) reports that a man whom he did not name (possibly from Rudy Parra's or Fernando Grajales's companies) was hired to transport them to the trailhead and to provide mules. On musing about the work of the unnamed Mendocino in their unnamed staging area, Norman was spurred to discuss the situation with a team member: "I talked,

Figure 4.2. On the North/Normal Route, *arrieros* herd mules laden with gear and provisions across the Playa Ancha twice daily on their way to and from base camp at Plaza de Mulas (4,370 meters).

on the way to the trail, with one of the men on our team, about how the American craze for adventure sports had provided an economic boost for remote places around the world. 'They probably think we're crazy,' the man said, 'and hope to God we don't get over it'" (208–209). Again the "we-they" dichotomy excludes Mendoza and Mendocinos from mountaineering proper and posits them all as merely service providers, in the First World consumers–Third World producers kind of way. In this opposition, Mendocinos are not seen to be actively involved in mountaineering themselves, but instead are reactionary to American initiative, adventure, drive, and money. The hierarchy remains clear.

Within this paradigm Aconcagua and Mendocino mountaineering are inevitably located at a great distance, measured not just in miles but also in time, from the North. Displaced from national Argentine territory by the Northern imagination, Aconcagua is reterritorialized in an exotic, dangerous site of the past. This reterritorialization allows for a geographical dislocation that is unconstrained by the specificity of the region or even the representational pull of the gaucho, that relocates Aconcagua anywhere on the globe that symbolizes the First World self's construction of the Third World other as strange, dangerous, and fixed in the past.

In *Seven Summits*, as the team enters what most probably is the Playa Ancha on the approach to base camp via the Normal Route, the "exotic" nature of the countryside is again emphasized. Rick Ridgeway narrates that "[t]his was a high desert. On the second day of our hike the air above the flat floor shimmered under noon heat and it was easy to imagine from this a mirage of camels carrying turbaned riders with curved swords through their cummerbunds" (Bass et al. 1986, 89). Aconcagua, under the orientalist gaze (Said 1978) of Western mountaineering, is located neither in the present day nor even the Americas. It can substitute for any remote, uncivilized location whose dangerous elements present a grave threat to the narrating mountaineering subject. The victory of the mountaineer over such hazards subsequently reveals the true nature of his adventurous spirit.

This same landscape is described similarly in *Aconcagua: The Stone Sentinel* (1992), where its most significant characteristic is the feeling of overwhelming danger: "It looked like a moonscape. The only thing missing were dust storms sweeping across that valley. Neil kept referring to the landscape as 'Let's go for a hike through Afghanistan.' We were expecting mortar fire to come overhead anytime, with Mujahideen horsemen riding out from behind the boulders, strafing us" (42). These two quotes come from expeditions made in 1983, and 1990, respectively, before either of the Gulf Wars or the US action in Afghanistan, and they underscore how the cultural stereotype for romanticized imperial adventure, premises that underlie mountaineering's origins, is often tied to an image of the Middle East.

Seven Summits and other mountaineering narratives relocate Aconcagua in order to amplify a fantasized sense of danger. In so doing they also construct an idealized masculinity by bringing to the fore the self who is willing to take on such perils. Theirs is a masculinity of elitism in terms of career, physical ability, mind, and spirit. In *Seven Summits*, masculine identity is connected to wealth generated by bold business acumen, perseverance, and intrepid, free-spirited risk taking. They do not test themselves for the benefit of nation, science, or progress, but rather to prove personal strength and valor that would transfer back to everyday life and business challenges. Bass (1986) explains, "Then when I persevere and prevail, when I overcome and make it, I come back down to the lowlands, back to the bankers and the regulatory officials, and by golly I'm recharged and ready to take them all on" (2).

In addition to equating business success with mountaineering, in what would seem at first glance a contradictory stance for participants of such a physical enterprise as mountain climbing, but one that continues a tradition held throughout the history of mountaineering, the team members consciously self-identify as well-read literary types whose psyches are uniquely constructed to appreciate the special bonds of male camaraderie that are only forged by risking life and limb at altitude. *Seven Summits* tells us that mountaineers are a special breed: they speak of Molière; they recite poems such as "Gunga Din," "The Rolling Stone," and "The Men Who Don't Fit In"—those who "break the hearts of kith and kin and they roam the world at will" (Bass et al. 1986, 89–90). Their love for a literature that projects an image of restless independence also serves to unite them. Although the Bass team sees mountaineering as boosting their personal esteem ("I'm telling you, this climb has given me a new found sense of self-respect and self confidence," 10), male camaraderie among the select few who are members of this club is extremely important, as Ridgeway muses: "There's a lot more to this mountain climbing than just that exhilarating moment you reach the summit. No, the parts that matter most are those intangible ones like tonight, those moments of camaraderie that are like sips of good brandy that give your body and spirit a nice, warm glow" (Bass et al. 1986, 94). For these elites, bonded through literature, friendship, business savvy, and self-esteem, novice climbers and "tourists," and, for the most part, women, have no place on the mountain and diminish the experience for these "real" climbers who "get stuck in rescues" (Bass et al. 1986, 90). This sense of manhood that is derived in part from Bayers's notion of heroic imperial adventure includes a new aspect, that of super achievement in business, or an excess of capital, that adds to mountaineering prestige. This factor is one that will be much debated among subsequent mountain writers and will come to reverberate in how mountaineering is practiced on Aconcagua in the twenty-first century.

Debriefs: The Design Template

We're going to knock 'em all off. . . . This is history.

—BASS ET AL. (1986, 104)

When the cultural capital and status of international mountaineering changed in the 1980s, it would translate to Aconcagua as an increase in income and a greater intimacy with the strategies and cultural values promoted by US mountaineering ideologies. The presence and influence of US mountaineering practices especially grew out of an increased accessibility to gear, visibility of fashion and celebrity, and the Seven Summits effect of commodifying adventure. This heralded a shift in the sociocultural construction of mountaineering that envisioned new ways to see mountain adventure and adventurers. Mountaineering became an option for a much broader, less professional, and less experienced public. Merchandising promotions by gear manufacturers replaced nationally or institutionally sponsored expeditions. Individual motivation to climb became linked to the selling of products, big business successes, or simply putting "your domestic baggage behind you for awhile" (Norman 2000, 105), instead of highlighting traditional mountaineering goals of spiritual transcendence, scientific exploration, or ennobling patriotism. Nevertheless, although the elite status of adventurer could now be bought, or worn, by anyone with the money, this "democratizing" trend in mountaineering still held within it the vestiges and traces of imperial adventure in its conceptualization and practice of mountaineering.

Both *Seven Summits* and the consolidation of the Seven Summits Route marked innovations at the same time that they reflected and supported traditional ideas about mountaineering. The hegemony of the Seven Summits Route as a test of merit within the mountaineering world became institutionalized via the globalizing reach of American capitalism. The vision of mountaineering and Aconcagua it proffered was also far-reaching in its globalized and deterritorialized vision of Aconcagua and its blindness to the mountain's regional or national specificity or endeavors. The Seven Summits effect made Aconcagua a "fashion mountain," a new viable and novice-friendly mountaineering destination in terms of financing and imagining the experience. Nevertheless, it also consolidated traditional North-South, metropolis-fringe binaries in which Mendoza would be portrayed as the inferior, negative, backward, uncivilized element, or not even found on the map.

When Bass let out his Tarzan yell as he stood on top of Aconcagua and Ridgeway projected its reach to those unseen peaks to be scaled in the future, it also signaled new heights for Mendoza. The pinnacles of mountaineering that lay beyond for Mendoza were not the same peaks of Bass's circuit, yet they would still be connected to the values that Bass's call of victory embodied. Mendoza had other routes to follow, to establish its own protagonism in local mountaineering, to develop its own adventure tourism industry, and to create a governing and educational infrastructure that would support these endeavors. To capitalize on the growth of international mountaineering, Mendoza would need to contour a space for itself that allowed it to conform to the parameters of an evermore homogenizing global adventure market and, at the same time, to showcase the region's specificity and difference. Mendoza would also have to reassess its relationship to national political, economic, and historical factors and its role in supporting or enhancing regional mountaineering or tourism of any kind. At the local level, regional institutions would be called upon to expand, or even new ones would be created, in response to the increase and internationalization of the adventure tourism industry. Moreover, the initiative and imagination of key individuals would be essential to navigate all these cross currents of needs and demands as they flowed together to power the mountaineering business. This multipronged project, which the following chapters discuss, would forge a distinctly Mendocino interpretation of mountain climbing. However, all these enterprises would reverberate with the echo of the ideological undertones of Bass's shout of conquest in that cultural borderland, as Ortner (1996) calls it, of high-altitude mountaineering.

CHAPTER FIVE

Local Heroics

Militarisms and Democratizations

El Aconcagua adquiere para Mendoza otra dimensión; se empieza a justificar que somos los dueños . . . las cuestiones de montaña se incorporan a nuestra cultura.

(Aconcagua brings another dimension to Mendoza; that we own the mountain is beginning to be justified . . . mountain issues are being incorporated into our culture.)

—FERNANDO GRAJALES (GARCÍA 2003A)

Myth and (New) Origins

In 1934 when the four-man Polish team returned to Mendoza from making the first summit of Aconcagua from the east, across what is now known as the Polish Glacier, they refused to talk to the local Mendocino newspaper, *Los Andes*, about their scientific expedition.[1] Instead, they issued a statement indicating that all data about the route and their ascent would be sent back to Europe. The attitude of the Polish team in withholding information from Mendoza illustrates the way that mountaineering on Aconcagua and Aconcagua itself were displaced from local materiality into a European imaginary that envisioned the mountain as a space for exploring, charting, and claiming in the name of national achievement. Knowledge about the Mendocino peak and mountaineering was classified "European." The actions of the Polish team were in accordance with the hegemonic discourse of mountaineering as a Western, modern project. The legacy of neocolonialism in the mountaineering world fixed Mendoza as subaltern within the paradigm of Western modernity and provided the parameters for Mendoza's relationship to mountaineering within its territory for many decades.

However, the advent of globalization and the increased and rapid exchange of information, capital, people, and values would undo the stability of the

Mendoza-Europe opposition in mountaineering. This is nowhere more apparent than in the emergence of the Mendocino Generation of the 80s who have provided the impetus for mountaineering and the adventure tourism industry in Mendoza to explode over the last thirty years. During an interview I had with one of the leading members of this Generation, Daniel Rodríguez, known simply in mountaineering circles as Danielón, explained how this ontological shift in Mendocino mountaineering came about:

> Antes no hubo protagonistas de acá-aunque había conocimiento en Suiza, Europa. Antes de los 70, la historia de la relación del hombre con la montaña era como un privilegio de personas de otra cultura. Había como un mito, los extranjeros tenían un secreto, un desarrollo físico y fisiológico y técnico que los habilitaban más a la alta montaña y las dificultades. Y los criollos no. El mundo se globaliza y hay protagonistas que quieren romper las fronteras. Empezamos a estudiar, estudiar, estudiar, y enseñar. Por ejemplo, casi todos los fundadores (EPGAMT) trabajamos más de 10 años gratis formando andinistas, trabajo de club, trabajo vocacional. Y después trabajé un par de años cobrando la miseria. En base de eso el intercambio de información, mejores comunicaciones, empezamos a hacer así logros. Record de ascensiones de dificultad. En vez de una cosa gringa pasa a ser una cosa de nosotros.
>
> (Before the '70s, the history of man's relationship with the mountains was like a privilege belonging to people from another culture. There was like a myth, the foreigners had a secret, a physical and physiological development and technique that prepared them better for high altitude and its difficulties. And the criollos didn't. The world globalizes, and there are protagonists who want to break down frontiers. We began to study, study, study, and teach. For example, almost all the founders [of the Guide School] worked for over ten years for free to prepare andinistas, work in clubs, vocational work. And later I worked a couple of years for a pittance. Based on that and with the exchange of information, better communications, we began to make achievements. Records on difficult ascents. Instead of being a gringo thing, it became something that was ours.)

Rodríguez recognizes the artificiality of the paradigm that excluded Mendocinos from mountaineering by calling it a myth. That alleged secret that foreigners held, that privilege of secrecy that the Poles invoked when they came down the mountain in 1934, was dependent on a restrictive exchange of information along a monodirectional course leading away from Mendoza. For Rodríguez, that secret is broken once new and freer flowing communication links afford Mendoza admittance to a globalized net of information. Rodríguez lists the easier access to previously unavailable knowledge, the power of education, and the drive to break down borders as the forces that empowered change in Mendocino mountaineering. All these transformations, for him, are contingent on globalization, a process that he defines as improvements in communications technology, but that also must be understood as one that facilitated and decentered movements, not only of information but of capital, people, and materials. The growth of neoliberal economic practices in the South is also very much connected to the worldwide merchandising of improved climbing gear and the expansion of the adventure tourism market. It was this juncture of diminishing distances (market, spatial, temporal, and knowledge) between the global and the local, on the one hand, and a national process of redemocratization and the local creation of the Aconcagua Provincial Park, on the other, that set the stage for Mendoza's mountaineering industry to flourish. It was twentieth-century globalization, then, as Rodríguez describes it, and in its more expansive sense, that became the underlying ideology for the new foundation of Mendocino mountaineering.

This new origin story that the Generation of the 80s was inscribing for mountaineering highlighted the hybrid nature of the sport in Mendoza by especially stressing the new primacy of its home-grown connections, both past and present. The daring protagonisms and feats of the Generation of the 80s set up an equation that linked them back to those first European scientist-explorers who came to Aconcagua in the late nineteenth century to discover and conquer. This, in itself, however, was merely a by-product of the integration of contemporaneous Northern mountaineering practices and philosophies by the Generation of the 80s who found themselves in a new, more globalized contact zone, often more virtual than geophysical, based on communication networks and economic flows. This transnational system of information, capital, and people was the successor to the worldview that allowed the 1934 Polish team to exclude Mendoza. Now Mendoza connected to the mountaineering network with Mendocino add-ons: a reinvention of the local origins of mountaineering that combined Incan heritage and San Martinian patriotic fervor to the modernist assumptions and globalized practices that defined contemporary Northern mountaineering. This hybrid, distinctively Mendocino understanding of its local activities in the high mountain zone would also be predicated on its relevance to international prestige, regional authority, and economic advantages.

Certainly the transculturative nature of Mendoza's mountaineering project responded to the impetus to capitalize on the growing international market for mountain climbing and the popularity of Aconcagua in the 1980s, which prompted a myriad of new undertakings for Mendoza, including the creation of a new civilian plan for managing Aconcagua, the formation of a mountaineering infrastructure, regulations for economic and ecological projects, and strategies for marketing. The Generation of the 80s would be protagonists at every level of this development. While this period of change responded to the flows of globalization, as Rodríguez pointed out, it was also anchored in the historical ideological values and practices of Western mountaineering and Argentine nation building. In this chapter I attempt to characterize the transculturated nature of Mendocino mountaineering that has vindicated and invented local elements to rewrite its origin story within a nexus of local-national-global cultural and tourism relations.

Military Beginnings

In keeping with the understanding of José de San Martín as founding father of Aconcagua mountaineering, and one that predates the European adventurer-explorers by many decades, *Historia del Aconcagua*, cowritten by Mario Punzi, with Major Valentín J. Ugarte, Mario L. de Biasey, and a prologue by President Juan Perón (Perón 1953), again proclaimed "San Martín, el primer montañés de América" (San Martín, America's first mountaineer). With San Martín as the first mountaineer of the continent, the origin of mountaineering in Mendoza and the Aconcagua zone is thus recast in the twentieth century to have a distinctly local and national, albeit military, beginning.

This locally based origin story that contradicts the narratives of European modernity and emphasizes national and regional military connections to Aconcagua was especially forged toward the middle of the twentieth century when Mendocino mountaineering gained momentum and prestige with the mountain exploits at home and abroad of the 8th Mountain Brigade, the army unit that has been stationed in Mendoza's high mountain since 1923. (The Brigade clearly still sees itself as the heir to the Army of the Andes and conservator of Sanmartinian principles, as it states on its website.)[2] This does not mean that there was no parallel civilian interest in mountaineering at that time. Quite the opposite was the case. In fact, the civilian Club Andinista de Mendoza, located in the city center, was established in 1935 and still functions as memory and archive of local mountain endeavors, both civilian and military. However, the 8th Mountain Brigade's location in Puente del Inca and its achievements in the midcentury afforded it primacy in inscribing a military veneer on national mountaineering in the zone. It would not be until the 1980s that local individual protagonisms in mountaineering and tourism enterprise would come to change the characterization of Mendocino activity on Aconcagua.

The Generation of the 80s owes much to the 8th Mountain Brigade, especially those members of the 16th Regiment and the Company of the Cazadores de los Andes who provided the first impetus for Mendocino-initiated mountaineering. The contemporary military legacy of Mendocino mountaineering dates back to the first Argentine ascent of Aconcagua in 1934 by Lieutenant Nicolás Plantamura and particularly to the activities coming out of the 1940s and peaking in the 1950s. This military era of Argentine mountaineering corresponds to the mid-twentieth-century nation-building directives of the country and to the first presidency of Juan Perón.[3]

In 1954 Argentina's first expedition to the Himalayas, the "Perón Expedition," was made under the leadership of First Lieutenant Francisco Ibáñez, who took a group including Alfredo Magnani and Fernando Grajales to Dhaulagiri. Perón's support of a national Argentine mountaineering effort at the international level was a symbolic complement to his 1947 nationalization of the railways that had first allowed foreign capital to develop the mountain area of Aconcagua. These bold moves by Perón (together with his investment in building hotels and retreats to spearhead a new high mountain tourism in Mendoza) promoted a sense of national pride and ownership in Argentine progress. Argentina's participation in extra-territorial mountaineering, in the imperial tradition of undertaking such a national endeavor in the West's "periphery," metaphorically aligned Argentina with the First World to spotlight its level of development and potential of influence. "Within a progressive version of Darwinist discourse, to control and dominate space conferred 'favored status upon' a nation and its peoples" (Bayers 2003, 5). Going to the Himalayas a year after the first summit on Everest would attest to the nation's superiority in the tradition of imperial national adventure and would broadcast to an international and national public Perón's haughty vision for Argentina.[4]

Perón's internationalization of mountaineering and nationalization of local economic interests, signs of modern status for its citizenry at home, as well as for the world community, coincided with the military's opening of new Argentine routes on Aconcagua. The exemplary symbol of this moment was Francisco Ibáñez. Touted as one of the heroic founders of Argentine mountaineering, Ibáñez left his name in the annals of Argentine history and on Aconcagua itself. In 1953, Ibáñez, along with Fernando Grajales and two Swiss climbers, Frédéric and Dorly Marmillod, opened up a new and difficult route along the southwest ridge to the south summit, which is now called the Ibáñez-Grajales-Marmillod Route, or the Ibáñez-Marmillod Route. If we understand the naming of a geographical site as an ideological possession of space (Bayers 2003, 145), the christening of this route marks a symbolic reappropriation of Aconcagua back into Argentine territory that recharts the map of Anglo-European mountaineering imagination. While the Ibáñez name did not give Argentina symbolic geographical exclusivity to the route or the mountain, as it was compounded with the name of the Swiss leader and his wife, Marmillod, it did, however, represent a new shared reterritorialization of Aconcagua where Argentina figured as equal to Europe in its claims to the area. However, the difficulty in consolidating an Argentine presence on Aconcagua is exemplified by the fact that in most English-language narrations and descriptions of this route on the Internet include statements like the following from *Mountaineering in the Andes* (Neate 1994): "In 1953 the Swiss couple Frédéric and Dorly Marmillod, with two companions, traversed across the western flanks from Plaza de Mulas and ascended to the south peak via the south-west-ridge" (Neate 1994).[5] Ibáñez and Grajales become only two nameless and nationless companions, witnesses of authentication for the exploits of the Swiss Marmillods. However, in a radio interview with Dorly Marmillod, soon after their completion of this route, she explicitly highlights the protagonisms of both Ibáñez and Grajales in the joint Argentine-Swiss endeavor.[6] The erasure of the Argentines in later mountaineering narratives speaks more to the hegemonic traditions of exclusion of the local participants in Anglo-European mountaineering discourses than to any personal or individual attempts by the Marmillods to claim recognition solely for themselves.

In the Anglo-European tradition of mountaineering, although Aconcagua lies entirely within Argentine soil, since the initiation of activities there in 1883 the mountain had been "colonized" by the practices and imaginings of Northern mountain climbing. In this paradigm Aconcagua figured as a vacant territory void of national deeds. Here Anglo-European exploration, development, and naming of the mountain symbolically superseded territorial rights of the Argentine state and annexed Aconcagua into

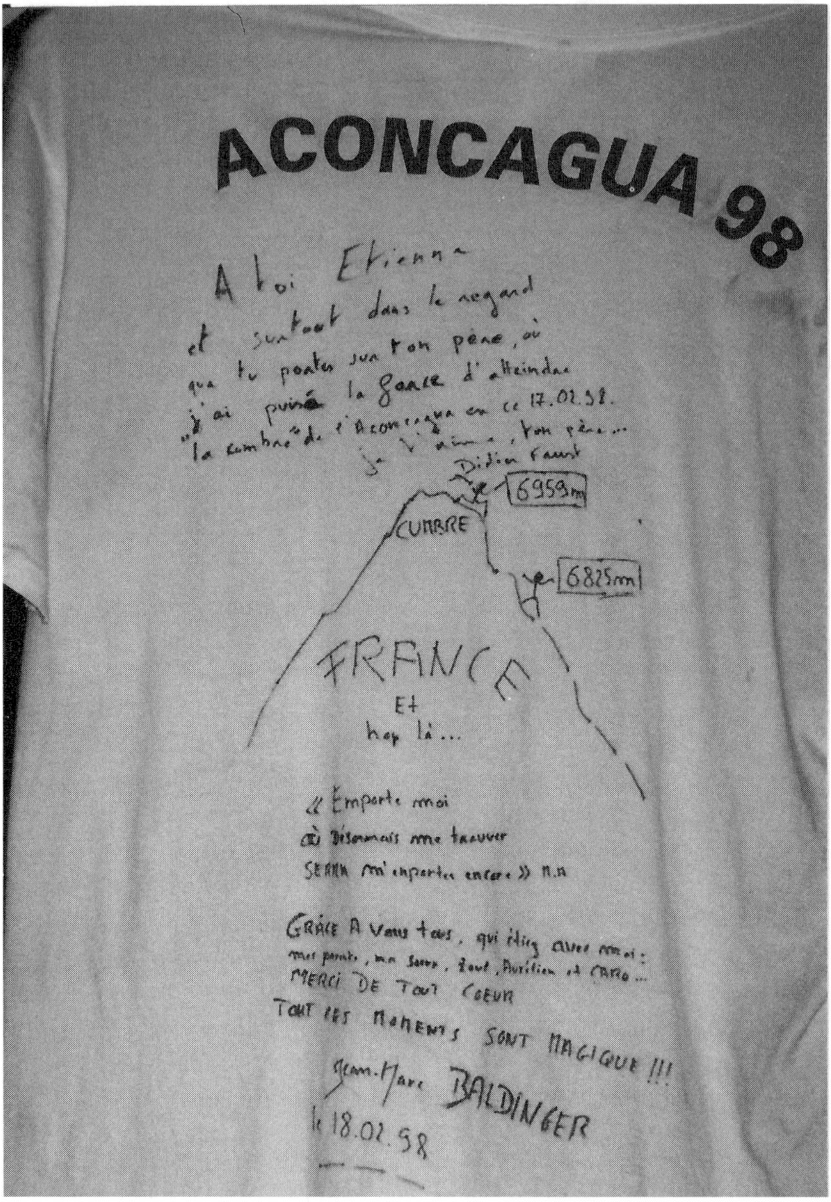

Figure 5.1. A t-shirt display, marking Aconcagua ascent as national conquest, in the Hotel Refugio Plaza de Mulas.

Anglo-European terrain in Western mountaineering's geographical imagination. The accomplishments of Ibáñez and Grajales and their names overlaid on Anglo-European mountain cartography would contest that mapping that erased Argentina. The highlighting of their participation, especially by Argentine-initiated narratives, can certainly be understood as the reinscription of a sense of national high-altitude heroism and nationhood following in the path of the patriotic legacy of San Martín.

Today, both Ibáñez and Grajales, sporadically present in international mountaineering histories and on Aconcagua maps, are ineradicably present on the geophysical Aconcagua. Theirs are names that most climbers both see and hear. Ibáñez is the name of a second site on the mountain, besides the 1953 route. On the North, or Normal, Route (the most traveled one), at the end of the Playa Ancha, Ibáñez is where most expeditions stop for lunch on the way up to base camp at Plaza de Mulas and again on the way down. The name of Fernando Grajales is also prominently visible and constantly invoked with regard to Mendocino mountaineering. For many, as one Mendocino guide told me, Grajales "inventó el Aconcagua" (invented Aconcagua). In addition to being a world-class climber, Grajales founded one of the first and most successful service-providing agencies for the Aconcagua industry. His name cannot be missed from the highway leading to the Horcones entrance of the Aconcagua Provincial Park (for the North Route), because it stands in huge bold letters on the building housing his agency's staging location near Puente del Inca. This remapping and reclaiming of Aconcagua topography not only makes visible the Mendocino impetus for control of the mountain, but also invokes the competing interests and imaginings that have prompted both past and present mountaineering initiatives.

The modernist narratives of mountaineering that were generated by the presence, writings, practices, and values of early European scientist-explorers and by the impulses of European imperial expansion that marked that era were first displaced by Argentine military national and international endeavors that prefigured globalization processes that would destabilize center-periphery positions. It was this displacement that opened a space for Mendoza mountaineering to articulate its own self-expression and, especially, with the coming of age of the Generation of the 80s, to allow that expression to form part of a critical dialogue that would challenge the univocal metanarrative of mountaineering by bringing to light the interests, desires, and the flux of national, international, and transnational economies of geography, culture, and capital that underwrite the mountaineering project.

Pioneering Enterprises

Grajales again teamed with Ibañez to pioneer Argentina's international mountaineering project. It was Ibáñez who led the first all-Argentine military expedition to the Himalayas to Dhaulagiri (8,167 meters) in 1954, in which Grajales participated. The expedition reached 8,000 meters and christened the course it followed the Argentine Route.[7] Tragically, Ibáñez died on his descent. His death, as ritual sacrifice for country and honor, has served to heighten his legendary status as national hero.

The memory of this period of mountaineering has especially been articulated to the public and preserved by another of the members of this first expedition to the Himalayas, Alfredo Magnani. Magnani has played a fundamental role in making Argentine mountaineering and Aconcagua more present in the national imagination through his mountaineering narratives and legal advocacy. As author of *Aconcagua, Argentina* (1981) with Rudy Parra, his eloquent and evocative descriptions of the mountains and chronicling of the history of Aconcagua became influential in forming and promoting a sense of personal and national admiration and respect for mountaineering.[8] In his work as a lawyer, Magnani's far-reaching vision, in terms of the importance of the mountain area for Mendoza, was especially influential in designing and establishing official plans for the preservation and administration of high-altitude areas. It was Magnani who drafted the project for a provincially run Aconcagua park in 1983 and spearheaded the creation of the Tupungato Provincial Park, which was approved in 1985 (García 2004, 2007). The province has recognized his service by naming the new visitors' center at the entrance to Aconcagua Park in his honor.

Other military mountain men of this period who blazed the trail for the Generation of the 80s are Emiliano Huerta and Valentín Ugarte. Huerta participated on the first all-Argentine military ascent of Aconcagua in 1942 via the Normal Route, and he was on the expedition to make the first successful winter ascent of the Normal Route in 1953. Huerta led Argentina's second expedition to Dhaulagiri in 1956, which ascended to 7,800 meters in its effort to reach the summit. Along with Valentín Ugarte he later formed part of a highly regarded military rescue squad on Aconcagua. Ugarte was the leader of early military expeditions to Aconcagua in 1945, 1946, and 1951, and one to Japan in 1953. His mountaineering activities on Aconcagua, which included establishing high-altitude refuges, leading the Aconcagua military rescue squad (on one of his expeditions he recovered the bodies of the German scientist Juan Jorge Link and his

French wife, Adriana Bance), working as a doctor for military mountain expeditions, and promoting mountain sports as a community leader, led to the Mendocino Mountain Guide School being named in his honor.

The military history of mountaineering in Mendoza is significant for providing the foundations of the industry today. The Ibáñez expedition to Dhaulagiri brought together three key figures who would set the stage for contemporary Mendocino mountaineering. Ibáñez, Grajales, and Magnani embody the roles of mythic leader, business pacesetter, and directing visionary. Ibáñez, as fallen hero, invokes the patriotic and valorous connotations associated with giving one's life for one's country. Grajales, in addition to the esteem in which he is held by the local community for his actual climbing activities, is venerated for developing the prosperous service-providing industry on Aconcagua. Magnani's highly regarded books and administrative plans set the tone for relating to the mountain, especially in terms of individual appreciation and provincial organization. Although not part of that first expedition, Huerta and Ugarte serve to supply a fourth originary corner for building the mountaineering industry. Their work at high mountain rescue personified those captains of responsibility who work to guide and protect the community. These four models representing patriotic and regional pride, business potential, leadership and safety, and the emotional and civilian appreciation of mountaineering became the cornerstones on which Mendoza's present-day narrative of mountaineering and its mountain adventure industry are based.

In essence, Mendoza's military mountain ventures signal the first transculturative moves in the development of Mendocino mountaineering. They pushed mountaineering in Mendoza to take for itself attributes belonging to the Anglo-European project, which it would have been denied within the traditional modernist paradigm where Mendoza was either absent or restricted to only providing transportation and strategic services like portering. In this way Mendocino mountaineering breaks the neocolonial bind in which its participation is assigned as subordinate, to appropriate for its own Anglo-European models of leadership; expectations about mountaineering for national, regional, and masculine identity construction; and attitudes toward personal transcendence. And it has tinged this appropriation with a nationalist, patriotic edge provided by its association with San Martín and the Argentine military that tie local mountaineering to an origin disassociated from Anglo-European imperial expansions.

Mendoza has also included in its configuration of mountaineering a focus on the service-providing business that modifies the modernist, epic, and heroic discourse of mountaineering. Paradoxically, at first glance, this focus invokes that traditional binary of foreign climber–national service worker. It is not that same old duality, however, as it is a lucrative Mendoza-based industry that was initiated by local climbing celebrities, like Grajales, whose international and national experience conferred status and authority to the enterprise. These first agencies were not run by businessmen or porters but by local climbers whose history in the mountains was most often superior to those international climbers that they outfitted and guided. These agencies, once the provincial park was established in 1983, took over much of the control of the movement of climbers up and down the mountains. Climbers were forced to adjust to the schedule, rates, and regulations of the muleteers, porters, and camp workers of the service-providing agencies, instead of setting up their own programs. Foreign climbers, despite their outlay of capital, in many ways then become dependent on the service providers. Of course, foreign climbers always have relied, to some degree, on service workers. What is different here is that the Mendoza industry has more power of control in the equation. Timetables, rates, amount of equipment carried by mules and porters, and the distances and hours that mules and porters will work are all determined by the service agencies, as well as the hour and substance of meals and number and brand of tent, if so contracted.

Thus, the practice of Mendocino mountaineering is hybrid by its very history and nature. Local mountaineering repositions itself within the Anglo-European ideological framework of the sport to take on traditionally hegemonic trappings, at the same time that, on another level, it seemingly maintains its traditionally subordinate place. However, this role is not one of "subservient" service provider but rather of "super-servient" participant in the mountaineering paradigm, one that takes economic and authoritative advantage of its "supposedly" inferior position within the traditional framework.

The groundwork for the mountaineering industry to develop in this way in Mendoza grew out of the accomplishments of the military mountain men of the midcentury and the indispensable work of the Mendocino arrieros. However, it is especially the achievements of the former that frame the educational formation, business sphere, guiding and rescue history, narrative traditions, and heroic myths of contemporary Mendocino mountaineering.

From these military beginnings sprang the motivating energies in the development of mountaineering in Mendoza in the second half of the twentieth century, which were to supply, initiate, and build. This triple initiative, driven by climbers from the midcentury generations, laid the foundation for the Generation of the 80s. They also were the first to recognize the economic benefits of increasing the mountaineering market and the necessity of publicizing Aconcagua to a wider international and local audience. Along with Grajales, it is Rudy Parra who especially stands out as a pioneer in imagining the economic potential of Aconcagua, as well as participating in a locally defined mountaineering program. Today, Fernando Grajales Expeditions (founded in 1976) and Rudy Parra's Aconcagua Trek (founded in 1979) are two of the best and most internationally known service-providing agencies for Aconcagua mountaineering, and they are emblematic of how the stage became set for the Generation of the 80s.[9]

Generation of the 80s

In discussing the relationship between modernity and globalization in Latin America, Linda Martín Alcoff (2002) argues that "it has actually been the displacement of 'modernist' narratives by globalization narratives that has opened up the possibility of rearranging the political, theoretical, and epistemological formations that rendered Latin America as a mere 'periphery'" (viii). It is this kind of formative metanarrative of modernity about mountaineering that fixed Mendoza's place in the mountains as peripheral that the local andinismo has come to rework through narratives of globalization invoked by the Generation of the 80s. Building from the traditions of the military climbers, the Generation of the 80s, praised as "transgressors and rebels" by some in the Mendocino climbing scene, made the greatest inroads in challenging the Anglo-European holds on local mountaineering.

Unlike the generation that preceded them, the Generation of the 80s was not part of a national institution or a project of nationalist impetus, so connotations of patriotic nationalism were never at the fore. The Generation of the 80s is made up of civilian individuals who may have reflected the newly redemocratized Argentina but who also clearly saw themselves as part of a globalized world. In fact, the Generation of the 80s based their connections to mountaineering on globalizing tendencies that tend to erase or make porous national boundaries and identity categories, thus rendering projects of nationalism problematic. Nevertheless, their endeavors created a high Mendocino profile for mountaineering that encouraged the retracing of local protagonisms back to the feats of San Martín and the 8th Mountain Brigade, which tied to two important nation-building moments, thus connecting the Generation of the 80s to the nation even as they projected themselves outward to a globalized community of mountaineering. In this way local Mendocino mountaineering identity was connected to the nation in the historical meanings associated with San Martín and the privileging of Mendoza in his legend of independence and with the international and national accomplishments of a Peronist-era nationalist project of mountaineering, as well as being linked to the global and the postmodern by its own contemporary accomplishments.

The Generation of the 80s followed in the footsteps of Ibañez, Grajales, Magnani, Huerta, Ugarte, and Parra in their passion for the mountain, the expanse of their ambition, and their initiative in the adventure tourism industry. However, the Generation of the 80s set their own course, which dramatically raised the profile of Mendocino-initiated mountaineering, not only in Mendoza, but across Argentina and internationally as well. They have set records, opened up new routes on Aconcagua, made the first Argentine summits in the Himalayas, received numerous awards, written books, made videos, founded the Valentín Ugarte Escuela de Guías de Alta Montãna y Trekking (EPGAMT) and the Park Ranger School, and served as consultants and members of regulatory boards dealing with the Aconcagua Provincial Park. In essence, they consolidated Mendoza's mountain adventure tourism industry through their focus on professionalization, business, and governance.

Leaders within this group include Daniel Alessio, Gabriel Cabrera, Antonio "Turco" Mir, Daniel Gonzalo "Danielón" Rodríguez, Alejandro Randis, Horacio Cunietti, Miguel "Lito" Sánchez, and Carlos Varela. The ambitions of these young Mendocino andinistas who came into their own in the 1980s coincided with the increase in the popularity of mountaineering worldwide, new availability of information and gear, and an Argentine peso (at least through the early 1980s and then again in the 1990s) that would make this expensive sport more accessible. During most of the military dictatorship (1976–1983), the Argentine economy's speculative and international borrowing habits kept the peso artificially strong and afforded many middle-class Argentines a material ease for foreign travel and purchases. Hyperinflation plagued Raúl Alfonsín's transition period (1983–1989), and the change to the austral was no answer to Argentina's burgeoning foreign debt. With the election of Carlos Menem in 1989 and the eventual return of the peso, Argentine buying power was buoyed again. The peso was fixed by the government at a one-to-one equivalency with the US dollar for over a decade, which supported Argentine travel and buying power, important elements in the development of a mountaineering tradition and industry.

The advent of the Generation of the 80s also parallels Argentina's redemocratization at the end of the military dictatorship, El Proceso de Reorganización Nacional (the Process of National Reorganization; 1976–1983). With a return to democracy for the nation, Mendoza also took the first step to democratize mountaineering on Aconcagua. The Aconcagua Provincial Park was established in 1983 with an open admissions policy and a civilian administration.

In complement to national circumstances that would facilitate their activities, the drive of the Generation of the 80s in the Mendocino mountaineering scene would also be secured through their international connections, not just in terms of information and gear, but in their own endeavors outside the country. The Generation of the 80s traveled beyond Mendoza, to Peru, Bolivia, the Alps, the Pyrenees, the Rockies, and the Himalayas, and changed the symbolic understanding of Mendocino mountaineering in significant ways.

Mendoza in the Himalayas

Lito Sánchez became the first Argentine, and first Latin American, to summit an 8,000-meter mountain, Dhaulagiri, in 1990.[10] There had been four previous failed attempts on Dhaulagiri by Argentines, including the first expedition in 1954. Unlike the Ibáñez expedition, which was supported by Perón, arguably to demonstrate Argentina's ability to compete with the First World, Lito's Himalayan experience was not tied to a national institutionalized project. He was the lone Argentine in an Andalusian climbing group. Both the Ibáñez expedition and Lito's summit disrupt the modern center-periphery mapping of the world of mountaineering. Nevertheless, within this decentered scheme the Himalayas still are positioned as the periphery and read, especially in 1954, the year of the first Argentine expedition, as that "empty" space in which Western subjectivities prove themselves. In 1990 no one could ignore the presence of the Sherpas in that same way (Ortner 1999), yet the Himalayas still remain a contested site in which national superiority can supposedly be measured. Although Lito is disconnected from an institutionalized patriotic mission of metaphorical imperial expansion, in what Bayers (2003) calls the postmodern condition of mountaineering, Lito's summit, heralded in websites and lists on the Internet and in climbing journals as the first Argentine and first Latin American summit of Dhaulagiri, illustrates that same impetus. With regard to national recognition, it seems that the imperial masculine ethos

(Bayers 2003) of earliest mountaineering does not dissipate in terms of establishing status for the climbing culture in the globalized, postmodern moment. (However, Bayers [2003] and Ortner [1999] have shown that the actual practice of mountaineering on Everest and international climbers' relationships with the Sherpas do challenge the supposed hierarchies fixed in modernist ideologies of mountaineering.)

A big year for the Generation of the 80s in the Himalayas was 1993–1994. Lito's fame was strengthened in 1993 when he summited Cho Oyu (8,201 meters) in February 1993. His was the first Argentine and first Latin American winter summit of the mountain. In that same year, Daniel Alessio and Mauricio Fernández also summited Cho Oyu. Alessio, working as a guide for an English expedition, summited Shishapangma (8,012 meters), another first for Argentines, in 1994. "First Argentine" became a source of pride for Mendocino mountaineering as local individuals met with great international success to represent the nation and the greater region of Latin America. This kind of international recognition of the caliber of Mendocino climbers is emblematic of the Generation of the 80s. This was underscored for me in 2006 when a Spanish climber came down from having summited Aconcagua and told me with a "groupie-like" excitement that she had met Lito Sánchez, and proclaimed, "Es una leyenda" (He's a legend).[11]

Travel and Return

The Generation of the 80s left the lowlands of Mendoza to return with skill, knowledge, and experience. As a group they found definition in their continued movements and flows in and out of Mendoza, unlike the monodirectional travel of earlier European immigrants who came to settle, or that of recent Argentine émigrés who have gone to Europe to make a living. Through this back-and-forth travel (not the traditional settlement associated with Mendoza), the Generation of the 80s was able to improve their climbing and the industry. While this travel model echoes the going out of those first scientist-explorers and mountaineering pioneers to "distant" places like Mendoza itself, it also ruptures this paradigm by the fact that they were participating as world-class climbers and not as service providers. Nevertheless, it does also reinscribe that same hierarchical paradigmatic Western binary of "modern" climbers and "nonmodern" destinations on which mountaineering is founded.

On one level, this travel out and back by the members of this generation loosened the neocolonial hold that had prevented Mendoza from forging its own mountaineering project, that same ideological (as well as informational and economic) grip that had justified the Polish team from not reporting its expedition to a Mendocino public in 1934. In attempting to develop its own mountaineering tradition, Mendoza found itself embroiled in an activity defined by European modern standards that would exclude locally based initiatives that might differ or patronize those that were more closely mimetic as immature and secondary. This is the neocolonial stalemate that Rodríguez was referring to in the beginning of this chapter when he talked about that "privileged secret" kept by the North that held the Mendocinos back. For the Generation of the 80s, it was not just the economic ability to travel out and return, but it was especially the communication revolution of the 1980s and 1990s, as a consequence of globalization, that afforded them an opportunity to move beyond the grasp of neocolonialism and take the lead in constructing a mountaineering culture in Mendoza. Much of the education of the Generation of the 80s came at home in Mendoza, through their own experience in Mendoza's Andes and with news about materials, techniques, and innovations in climbing tools that were more readily available in climbing magazines, books, catalogs, and through the greater influx of international climbers. Later the advent of the Internet made this exchange of knowledge even easier. Thus, the modernist narratives that constructed Mendoza in the periphery and imposed neocolonial status to the area and its mountaineering endeavors were displaced by a narrative of globalization based on access and communication. The juncture of these globalizing tendencies, Argentina's redemocratization, and periods of a strong national currency allowed the Generation of the 80s to take their position as the vanguard of Mendoza and to chart their own course in initiating huge changes in the practices and understandings of mountaineering in the region. For the subsequent generations of Mendocino climbers, the later economic and political crises of the twenty-first century would wrest from them much of the agency exercised by the Generation of the 80s and make them more reactive to extranational financial machinations and international tourism trends.

Firsts in Mendoza

Just as Ibáñez, Grajales, Huerta, and Magnani before them, the Generation of the 80s explored the mountainous zone of Mendoza, and especially Aconcagua. However, they moved well beyond their predecessors in opening up routes and leaving their mark on the highest peak in the

Americas. Recognition of their firsts, their new routes, and their overall accomplishments were benefits to Mendocino mountaineering. As one local andinista told me, "Firsts make it easier for everyone else, because now you know that it really is possible. They instill confidence." This is what the Generation of the 80s did. They made mountaineering feasible for other Mendocinos. As these world-class mountaineers continued to advance up the mountains, an exclusive Anglo-European or Argentine military activity was suddenly made to seem more accessible, or at least possible, for a new class and generation of civilian Mendocinos. The names of the Generation of the 80s now appear among the French, German, English, Swiss, Spanish, Italian, and countless other nationalities listed in the Aconcagua record book. Besides the opening of routes or firsts, many of the Generation also figure in early speed records for ascents: Daniel Alessio, Alejandro Randis, Horacio Cunietti, and Lito Sánchez figure in the list of fastest ascents via the Normal Route; Lito Sánchez and Gabriel Cabrera were among the first and fastest to summit in one day via the Polish Glacier.

The feats of the Generation of the 80s created a local celebration of mountaineering celebrity. Several members of this group have been awarded the military's highest civilian mountaineering award, the Cóndor Dorado. Members have also figured prominently at national and international media levels. They have participated in national video and TV documentaries as local experts and even as one of the principal guides in a Spanish TV reality show, *El cim*, which led Catalan participants who had trained for the ascent during the show's run to the Aconcagua northern summit.

The Generation also led the way in linking mountaineering into new areas for Mendocinos, that of the natural and social sciences. Gabriel Cabrera helped the archaeologist Juan Schobinger in the extraction and descent of the Incan mummy discovered on the West Face of the mountain in 1985. Danielón Rodríguez also assisted the archaeologist Roberto Bárcena further explore other Incan ruins held in the Aconcagua Provincial Park. In addition, Cabrera's collaboration with the Regional Center of Scientific and Technological Research (CRICYT) was instrumental in an international collaborative venture to put a GPS station on the summit of Aconcagua.

In a sociocultural sense, the Generation of the 80s has led in the democratization of mountaineering by taking Argentine mountaineering to new levels of civilian success and popularity above and beyond its previous military beginnings. They have spearheaded the development of the contemporary mountaineering industry in Mendoza, and they continue to direct its growth in the twenty-first century. Their influence on Aconcagua goes much further than their routes and firsts to the very core of the management and development of the park and its industry.

Aconcagua, the 1980s, and Beyond

Argentina's return to civilian government after the military dictatorship (1976–1983) coincided with the demilitarization of the mountain zone. With the passage of the statute 2807/83, Mendoza created the Aconcagua Provincial Park in 1983. The administration of mountaineering on Aconcagua then became a concern for the provincial government and a space for investment and development by tourism entrepreneurs as well as by Mendocino andinistas.

The fact that Aconcagua has remained under the jurisdiction of the province and not been commandeered by the system of national parks is somewhat surprising, as there has been much speculation about the federal system overriding provincial control and incorporating Aconcagua as a national park. Conversely, the province has pursued the conversion of the Tupungato Provincial Park to the national system, in a copartnership, with an eye on the federal funds that could be used to appropriate the lands surrounding the park and thus alleviate the standoff between mining, conservationist, military, touristic, and private interests that have made public access to the park difficult (García 2004). However, this is not the case for Aconcagua. Not only would its nationalization wrest administrative jurisdiction from Mendoza, but it would also remove economic supervision of the service-providing industry from local agencies. Currently, the Mendoza Chamber of Commerce of Service Providers works closely with the park administration and its members to jealously guard their favored status.[12] Provincial management of the park has reflected most favorably on the coffers of both Mendoza's tourism industry and its regional government, which uses park monies to support all provincial natural reserves.

Today, Aconcagua revenues and the park itself are administered by the Dirección de Recursos Naturales Renovables y Areas Protegidas (Department of Renewable Natural Resources and Protected Areas). Members of the Generation of the 80s have been fundamental in consulting and

Figure 5.2. Horcones Lagoon marks the entrance to Aconcagua Provincial Park, established in 1983. Climbers pass by Horcones and through the park area designated for tourism to access the route to Plaza de Mulas or Plaza Francia. Mountaineering routes are located in the restricted "sports" area of the park and require a trekking or ascension permit.

advising the government about the management of the park, often serving directly as consultants to the Park Administrative Commission. They also continue to participate as members of the Service Providers' Chamber of Commerce, a unit that, in its own right, regularly consults with the Department of Renewable Natural Resources. And ultimately, the influence of the Generation of the 80s in the local administration of the park is perhaps most significant at the personal and material level of mountaineering proper. They became leaders in the formation and development of the mountain-guiding profession in Mendoza that directs individualized and collective mountaineering practices as they are played out on Aconcagua.

Education and Mountaineering

¿Qué te gusta más de ser guía? (What do you like most about being a guide?)

Primero, la cantidad de años que llevo un poco siguiendo una especie de pasión por la montaña. Junto con la gente que me toque, tratar de compartir una experiencia positiva y valiosa entre todos. (First, the number of years that I have spent following a kind of passion for the mountain. Together with the people that I meet, to try to share a positive and valuable experience with them all.)

—LITO SÁNCHEZ, PLAZA DE MULAS

When I asked Lito Sánchez about his life as a mountain guide, he expressed what I believe are two of the most entrenched values regarding mountaineering coming from the Generation of the 80s: that mountaineering is a passion and that it should be shared with others. The members of this Generation have been extremely generous in giving their time and expertise to promote mountaineering in Mendoza. They have a long history of offering training classes to the public on basic and technical andinismo, safety, rescue and orienteering, and survival. Their greatest accomplishment in the area of education and training is the founding and running of the Valentín Ugarte Escuela de Guías de Alta Montaña y Trekking (EPGAMT). In 1990–91, Danielón Rodríguez began working with an unofficial group of interested young mountain enthusiasts who met informally and for free to learn about mountain guiding. Three years later, with the help of an instructor of educational psychology to create the curriculum, EPGAMT offered an officially approved, two-year, postsecondary course of study. The degree focuses especially on the technical mountaineering skills involved in guiding and includes required classes in foreign languages, the environment, marketing, and what Rodríguez calls "formación humana," or communications psychology dealing with leadership and constructing and maintaining group cohesiveness.

In large part thanks to the efforts of Rodríguez and others like Lito Sánchez and Alejandro Randis who teach, or have taught, at the EPGAMT, guiding has become a viable profession for Mendoza, and the guide school is an established institution with local, national, and international connections. Today, most Argentine guides on Aconcagua, as well as base-camp workers, porters, and members of the rescue squad, have passed through EPGAMT. The school also offers services to the wider Mendocino community by providing training sessions for the army and the police, and technical advising for the national parks. In addition, it has collaborated on international educational and training projects with mountain guide schools in Europe.

The prominence of the school and its dominance on Aconcagua logically reflect the authority of the province in running the park, but it also evokes those same tensions that underlie the situation inherent in Aconcagua being part of a provincial, rather than national, system. The fact that Mendoza has its own distinct guide school disrupts the sense of a nationally defined mountaineering project and pits province against province in forging international connections. The Asociación Argentina de Guías de Montaña, or AAGM, in Bariloche was founded nearly five years before the guide school in Mendoza. Therefore, the Bariloche academy is the official Argentine school recognized by the Union of International Associations of Mountain Guides (UIAMG), which acknowledges only one institution per country. There is much controversy in the Mendocino industry about the EPGAMT and AAGM competition for international accreditation. Although the Mendocinos uphold the validity of their degree at a national and international level, the Bariloche school, for its seniority, is considered to confer Argentine accreditation by UIAMG. The Aconcagua Provincial Park thwarts both national and international assumptions of control by awarding guiding privileges and credentials to graduates of both institutions. Therefore, Mendocino-instructed guides remain the majority on Aconcagua, which is the best-known Argentine peak and the one most visited by international climbers. This makes Mendocino guides those most important in generating the image of Argentine guides to an international mountaineering public. This conflict between the two Argentine schools and their vying for international recognition—one through documentation, the other through practice—is illustrative of a tendency in globalization to fracture the national and promote non-nationally defined institutions to create and regulate international networks.

Mountain Attitudes

El montañista es alguien que está dispuesto a hacer mucho esfuerzo, a someterse a situaciones de riesgo, de gran molestia y soledad. . . . Es una persona que ama hacer, moverse, exigirse. (The mountaineer is someone who is willing to expend a lot of effort, to submit to situations of risk, discomfort and solitude. . . . It's a person who loves to do, to move, to test himself.)

—LUIS JAIT (2004, 33)

The achievements of the Generation of the 80s, the increased visibility of mountaineering, and the economic possibilities it has provided the province have meant that, as one andinista told me, "Mendoza now understands this activity as a way of life." For many, the view of mountaineering as a life choice is especially derived from the professional nature, in terms of educational degree and status, that is attributed to the work done by those who have chosen to guide on Aconcagua.

The Generation of the 80s, as mountain guide icons, have contributed to both professional and philosophical interpretations of mountaineering. Alejandro Randis is especially significant for creating and popularizing images of mountaineering that evoke a more personal and spiritual, rather than just a professional, relationship with mountaineering. A front cover of his book *El Aconcagua: El Centinela de Piedra* (1991), an artistic portrayal of a single man struggling valiantly against the white and the wind of the mountain, was sold as a poster of Aconcagua, not just as a publicity addendum to his book. The text and artwork of the book, especially the poster that was plastered on windows and kiosks for several years after the book's first publication, have become engraved in the Mendocino imaginary as representative of Aconcagua. The composition of Randis's book, his romantic meanderings about Aconcagua, and the impressionistic color sketchings created by Marta Lavoisier (his girlfriend at the time) tell us that mountaineering is not just a skill, but also an art. This interpretation ties into a common understanding of mountaineering, where, according to Richard Mitchell (1983), "Mountaineering is not like Russian roulette, craps, or coin-flipping, in which outcomes are unalterable through the player's skill. Rather it is more like painting or musical composition, in which skill and imagination determine the outcome within the broad known limits of the qualities of canvas and paints, the sounds producible by various instruments" (157).

Mountaineering as beauty and danger conjoined, for Randis, is not just about technique but about the way you interpret the experience and how you appreciate the splendor and the perils of life at a higher altitude. Randis's book implies that mountaineering deals with the transcendence of spirit and, like art, the need to express those sentiments and revelations. There is, of course, the implication that the receptor of those feelings would either realize the unique superiority of those expressions, or respond to shared understandings it would find therein about the self, the mountain, and adventure. Both of these receptions insinuate an extraordinary bonding of exclusivity in the vision of mountaineering, and in this case, Aconcagua, as an esteemed world in which to test individual limits. This is one of the pervading perceptions among Mendocinos guiding on Aconcagua today. Several have spoken to me at length about the testing of physical and personal limits and its ability to create new and shared understandings about self and other. According to one guide, "You have to break limits—your patience, the limits of the clients, try to get them to break their own limits, to share everything completely, within the frame of security that they need. That's what's good about the mountains, limits don't exist." Another echoes those ideas and states that mountaineering is especially a test of self-understanding "in general when one is pushed to the limit. When one is physically totally exhausted and disassociated your perception is right at the surface. It's incredible. A virile, very masculine figure, suddenly, on arriving at the summit, begins to cry like a child, he's afraid, he's cold." This heightened sense of feeling and understanding that one gains by pushing physical and mental limits is the message of Randis's book about Aconcagua. It tells us that this is what makes Aconcagua attractive, in terms of self-identification, for those who already participate in this singular world and recognize a kindred spirit, as well as to those who dream about being part of something "bigger."

Randis's book served to promote mountaineering, not through education, or by suggesting it as a possible way to earn a living, but as a way to self-realization on spiritual, physical, and cultural levels. *El Aconcagua: El Centinela de Piedra* expresses the infatuation with mountain climbing as the quest for an aesthetic and mystical experience linked to the extremes of physical exertion. As in the case of Lito, there is an understanding of mountaineering as a passion, in whatever expression, that informs the decision to make it a way of life. Many Mendocino mountaineers have told me that both inspirational and professional motivations and desires aroused their initial interest in andinismo.

Guides and Reputation

It is the reputation of the Generation of the 80s, more than the seasonal routines of current Aconcagua guides, that props up a local understanding of mountain guides as superlative professionals and inspirational leaders. Luis Jait, in his book about the experience of his two attempts at summiting Aconcagua (1990 and 1991), *Elogio de la desmesura: Una aventura de autosuperación en el Aconcagua* (Praise of Excess: An Adventure of Self-Betterment on Aconcagua; 2004), explains how the image of the Generation of the 80s as Mendocino guides motivated potential mountaineers in the early 1990s: "Uní al montañismo una historia profesional muy ambiciosa y fui relacionándome con los mejores, con aquéllos que trabajan como guías del Aconcagua" (I joined a [my] very ambitious professional history to mountaineering and started dealing with the best, those who work as guides on Aconcagua) (33). Jait, who set out to train for Aconcagua under the advice of well-known Mendocino mountain man Ulises Vitale, equates his sense of ambitious professionalism in his personal life with the level of proficiency that he sees in the guides in the mountains, who were considered as standards of determination and success. His description of Alejandro Randis is a case in point: "es un aristócrata que 'se hizo a sí mismo,' en él sobresale su convicción, su decisión de ser 'el mejor.' Alejandro Randis ya es una marca, pero no se la usa en una remera o en una vincha, se la usa para incorpararse a este mundo de montañas y de ambiciones" (he is an aristocrat, self-made, in him his conviction, his decision to be the best, stands out. Alejandro Randis is a brand name, but not the kind that is worn on a t-shirt or a headband, it's worn as a way of incorporating yourself into this world of mountains and ambitions; 57–58). Elite competitiveness is at the basis of Jait's description of Randis. The drive to be the best, and to be branded visibly so, as mountain guide, is what the Generation of the 80s stands for in Mendoza. It is that allure to be tested and to be counted among the finest that drew Jait into seeking entrance into the game of mountaineering and underscores the prestige of the Generation of the 80s and their drawing power to attract new enthusiasts. Paradoxically, it is the very exclusivity of mountaineering (which the educational and training work of the Generation of the 80s helps to undo), that draws in novices like

Jait, with no previous experience, which then effectively diminishes its exclusive nature.[13]

Debriefs: Toward the Twenty-first Century

The Generation of the 80s and the narratives of globalization that their protagonisms, together with the development of Aconcagua mountaineering since 1983, have generated, serve to shatter the hegemonic discourse of mountaineering as a Western modern project that sanctioned the actions of the 1934 Polish team to restrict Mendocino access to mountaineering. The actions and entrepreneurship of this Generation, while they connect themselves back to these modernist beginnings, and along with it some of the problematics of regional, national, ethnic, and gendered identity hierarchies that are inherent within, have served to battle the neocolonial legacy of mountaineering that fixed Mendoza as subaltern within the paradigm of Western modernity.

The Generation of the 80s popularized and professionalized mountaineering while helping to instill new ways of understanding and of practicing a sport heretofore primarily thought of as foreign or institutionally military. They took mountaineering beyond the mountains into the mainstream of Mendocino life. They became administrators, businessmen, and educators in the mountaineering industry. They cooperated with scientific and conservation efforts and became the protagonists of local mountain celebrity. The boom of international mountaineering that they have managed has changed the face of Mendoza itself. The downtown area is now populated with adventure tourism agencies that offer guide and other support services for Aconcagua and with technical clothing and gear shops.

The current state of twenty-first-century mountaineering in Mendoza owes much to its local pioneers—the arrieros and the mountain men of the military—but it is especially indebted to the continued presence and leadership of the Generation of the 80s. Mendocino mountaineering grew from its roles as service providers for Anglo-European expeditions, to national military protagonism beyond Argentine borders, to civilian achievements in mountaineering proper and in the adventure tourism industry. The multiple and diverse components of local development signal the transculturated nature of Mendocino mountaineering and how its hybridity reflects changing world relationships and dynamics, from modernity's binaries through globalization's networking. It reflects Mendoza's alignment with national militarizations and nationalisms and the promotion of a national project to undo Western modernity's hierarchies in which Argentina is located as subaltern. It also represents Mendoza's positioning for autonomy over its own resources and territories within both a national and international paradigm. Mendoza's endeavors to engage more fully and autonomously in a globalized network of tourist capital, images, and adventure will also echo the crisis of the national that characterized Argentina at the beginning of the twenty-first century.

Mendoza's Generation of the 80s has promoted mountaineering as an activity to be shared and has emphasized through their education and training programs the importance of group dynamics. Yet their celebrity and inspirational images tend to reinforce the traditional exclusivity attributed to mountaineering. Within these changing attitudes it remains to be seen how local twenty-first-century mountaineering integrates the imperial masculine ethos of mountaineering with concerns about gender, ethnicity, and regional, national, and international relationships and the globalized tourist economy.

CHAPTER SIX

Matters of Life and Death

Mountain Guides, Nation, and Memorialization

Our organization is not merely seeking monetary profit from the exploitation of the mountain. WE ARE MOUNTAINEERS who know the needs and preferences of those coming to America's highest peak.

—INTRODUCTION TO ACONCAGUA TREK WEBSITE, CIRCA 2006 (www.rudyparra.com)

Our abilities to organize expeditions will place us as your best choice as you decide to hand responsibility over to the TRUE PROFESSIONALS.

—AYMARÁ ADVENTURES AND EXPEDITIONS BROCHURE

The responsibilities of mountain guiding sometimes concern very real issues of safety and health, and most clients who hire guides expect that their outlay of capital will safeguard their lives on the mountain. It is with some irony, then, at least to me, that one of the sites to visit most often suggested by Mendocino guides to their clients when they spend the afternoon in Puente del Inca or Penitentes before starting the expedition deals specifically with death: the Cementerio de los Andinistas. Of course, a visit to the Cementerio serves to heighten the idea of risk and increase the excitement quotient for the expeditioners, as life is never felt so preciously as when it is seen to be acutely threatened. But more than just a "thrill-inducing" or "fear" factor that might persuade clients to respect the guide's authority, I have found that the Cementerio also narrates the many and diverse histories of people and nations and the processes of modernity and globalization that have constructed Aconcagua as a contemporary mountaineering site. On the other end of the spectrum, guides, who symbolize life on the mountain—life can be interpreted in varying ways here, as a way to earn a living, as a manner of living, and as safeguarding the lives of others—are representative, through the social functions and values ascribed to them, of how these same processes and the mountain itself have materialized in Mendoza society.

Nation and Masculinities

Dura es la montaña. Duro es el trabajo en la montaña. Duros son los hombres de la montaña. Lo que no quita que sean unos señores.
(Hard is the mountain. Hard is work on the mountain. Hard are mountain men. Which doesn't keep them from being gentlemen.)

—MENDOCINO RESCUE SQUAD MEMBER

Ortner (1996) offers a description of mountaineering in the Himalayas that is apt for understanding it on Aconcagua: "It is built on male styles of interaction derived from other all-male institutions, especially the army: and while it was about many things—nature and nation, materiality and spirituality, the moral quality of the inner self and the meaning of life—it was always in part about masculinity and manhood" (184). The Mendocino mountain guide as both supreme professional and mountaineer, then, is thrust into a game that is inherently motivated by the playing out of masculinities. This legacy, conjoined to the acceptance in Mendoza of guiding as a "way of life," contours the image of the Mendocino mountain guide according to the drives of international mountaineering, as well as to the negotiations of regional and national gendered identities.

As Mendocino guides insert Mendoza's presence into the international mountaineering sphere on Aconcagua, their representation of Mendoza in this realm is emblematic of the province's redefining its position with reference to the nation and the global. The freedom, unrestricted movement, and restless nature generally associated with mountain guiding unsettle Mendoza's own image. As an immigrant-based, sedentary, and agricultural region, Mendoza has been anchored in its marginal and provincial, subordinate status with regard to Buenos Aires. On a more global level, Mendoza traditionally has seen itself as a destination to "travel to" rather than an as an origin to "travel from." In contrast, mountain guides, instead of planting roots, continuously pull up stakes to leave Mendoza, traveling out from the lowlands of the city and the vineyards (that land of sun and good wine) to the danger zones of high altitude, thereby disrupting and contradicting social assumptions of Mendocino behavior and identity. Their travel takes them to Aconcagua, mimicking the route of nineteenth-century modern travel whereby adventurers journeyed to distant zones to explore and bring back new knowledge about the world and self (Pratt 2008). However, Mendoza's mountain guides' travel is a parody of the earliest scientist-explorers' journeys because the Mendocinos do not travel great distances but in fact remain in Mendoza province. Yet, Aconcagua, in its multinational mixings and international histories, is one of the most cosmopolitan and globalized areas of the country. Mendocino guides who travel up and down Aconcagua are marked with a kind of regional-global identity status that undermines time-honored Mendocino self-conceptualizations based on agricultural traditions, national models, and patterns of immigration, as well as through more traditional Latin American travel by the upper and middle classes to European centers for study or work.

The Mendocino mountain guides' constant comings and goings and the interruption of Mendoza's settled nature also reflect many of the attributes and functions of the Argentine masculine archetypes that Eduardo P. Archetti (1999) theorizes in *Masculinities: Football, Polo and Tango in Argentina*. The perceptions of Mendocino mountain guides by Mendocinos exemplify the traits of Archetti's models of Argentine manhood, which he claims are hybrid, free, active, risk taking, individualistic, physically strong, willing to sacrifice for honor, and having no room for family. Using these characteristics, Archetti has theorized national models of masculinity as the *tanguero* (tango dancer), the polo player, and the *futbolista* (soccer player) as representative of Argentine modernity and its presence in the international sphere. In many respects all the characteristics that he finds salient in these figures are similar to ones that define mountaineering subjectivities and that reflect the way Mendocino mountain guides function within Mendocino society.

In writing of late twentieth-century Argentina, Archetti (1999) looked for those hegemonic images of manhood that developed out of the turn of the last century and that have provided a sense of the national in contemporary masculinities. Following this precept, Archetti has tapped into those official regional and period-specific icons and foundational myths that have traditionally undergirded a generalized sense of Argentineity.

Despite provincial complaints that the dominant understanding of Argentina, outside of the country, is essentially tied to icons of the port-city capital, Buenos Aires, and of the east-central plains, Archetti (1999) invokes just these images in his characterization of national masculine commonalities that he posits transcend regional differences. I find that Archetti's figures, while linked to hegemonic representations of Argentina tied to specific localities, are also closely associated to modern national historical transformations. The tanguero as logo of Buenos Aires points to European immigration at the turn of the last century. The polo player, as emblem of the rural oligarchy of the cattle-ranching pampas, and the soccer player, as an urban cross-class model spearheaded by the Buenos Aires clubs and linking to the dominion of British interests in Argentina in the early twentieth century, are both sports icons of modernity. In other words, Archetti (1999) elides regional icons into national symbols of historical transitions. This process reminds us that the construction of national identities and national cultures has always been done by selecting, excluding, and articulating those historical elements that would provide coherency to the state in terms of its present and future projects (Sáenz 2002, 24; García Canclini 2000, 85).

With the exception of their geographical specificity, Mendocino guides fit many of the parameters of national masculinities that Archetti derives principally from Buenos Aires and the pampas, but the guides correspond to another place and a very different epoch. The twenty-first-century economic crisis that nearly bankrupted Argentina financially, politically, and in terms of trust in national institutions and the hopes for a better tomorrow also destabilized the traditional notions of what it means to be Argentine. At the turn of the millennium, Argentine political instability and corruption, bank closings, the devaluation of the peso, personal losses of savings and pensions, reduction in buying power, and the mass emigration of young trained professionals to Europe and North America all served to challenge the validity of what those well-worn symbols of nationhood represented or projected as a national project.

Argentine belief in a cohesive Argentina had already been on the wane before the 2001–2003 economic and political crises came to a head with the stepping down of President Fernando de la Rua, the devaluation of the peso to a third of its former value in international markets, and the institution of the *corralito*, or restriction of access to personal savings and banking accounts. Leading up to this, María Sáenz Quesada (2001) finds that the political, moral, economic, and ethical struggles of the late twentieth century had already served to provoke in Argentina the breakdown of its national myths and ideologies (717).

In contemporary Argentina those founding myths fell to the toll of globalization, defined to me by many Mendocinos as the external pressures from the world market and transnational financial institutions like the IMF and World Bank, which weakened the authority of the Argentine state to manage national concerns and protect the rights of its citizens. This ultimately undermined established beliefs about nationhood, citizenship, and the future.[1] Thus, in thinking about Argentina's questioning of its history and national self, it might not seem out of line to propose adding a contemporary regional figure to Archetti's traditional ones in considering national masculinities. As the effects of globalization have particularly marked Argentina in the first decade of the twenty-first century, it might prove meaningful to take into account a figure from within this newest world order, one that reflects the relative advantages of the international tourism market that were created with the devaluation of the peso and the driving forces of globalization.

The Mendocino mountain guide, while tied to those traditional characteristics that Archetti postulates, is also representative of the present forces of globalization. The image and work of the guides symbolically allude to a global connectivity, as well as to the fracturing of the nation-state in the sense that the hegemony of Buenos Aires and the pampas to represent nationhood is no longer convincing. The mountain guide, in the abstract, is a globalized figure that transcends national boundaries and is also uniquely illustrative of a specific geographical area of the Argentine nation. How overly determined by region the figure of the guide may seem, it is no more so than those Archetti has chosen for speaking of national male identities. It reconfigures Archetti's paradigm to begin to address Argentina's cultural and geographical diversity and the flux inherent in national identity construction within a globalized world that tends to homogenize and, paradoxically, to highlight the particular (García Canclini 2000, 24).

Besides the absence of the contemporary period of globalization, in Archetti's archetypes there are no masculine figures associated specifically with the mountainous regions of Argentina. Traditionally, the Andes have not been seen as personifying characteristics of the Argentine nation, which is usually defined in terms of two movements and two geographical areas: (1) Spanish colonization and independence and (2) European immigration and settlement, as expressed in (1) the pampas and (2) Buenos Aires. At a great distance from the capital, the Andes have served to mark the "extremes" of the state, the national frontier, its indigenous peoples, folkloric traditions, and natural threats to state stability (i.e., earthquakes). The Andes' distance from the hegemonic characteristics of Argentine national identity is not just measured in kilometers and topography but also in ethnicity, time, and risk. The figure of the Mendocino guide might add another facet to the representation of the Argentine Andes and provide a model for mountain masculinities that connects closely, in terms of characteristics, to those of national features theorized by Archetti. However, it is still problematic in other ways. Although this model would redress the traditional absence of the mountain zone from figuring in national identity construction, the image of the Mendocino guide, in general, is complicit with the masculine prototypes that Archetti configures by continuing to exclude Argentina's native identities in representing the face of the nation. For example, although Daniel Pizarro, an Uspallata guide, may be identified as "el Indio" and as a descendant of the Huarpes for the 2008 Argentine Channel 9 docu-reality show *6962 Desafío Aconcagua* ("El regreso" 2008), on his agency's website he and his brother do not openly claim such heritage and instead explain the area's indigenous traditions by highlighting the Incas and the disappearance of the Huarpes from the zone in the seventeenth century.[2]

Mountain and Home

Si quiere tener familia, no puede trabajar en la montaña. (If you want to have a family, you can't work on the mountain.)

—MENDOCINO BASE-CAMP WORKER

Archetti's types share several salient features that correspond to the understandings Mendocinos hold of their mountain guides. One of these seems to be the guides' rejection of a committed relationship and steady home life. According to Archetti, his archetypes of national masculinities inhabit a traditional and complex masculine world in which "there is no room for the family, work and fatherhood" (1999, 189). While Mendocino guides do certainly have time for work, as by their very definition as guides they are employed, there is the perception by many that guiding on the mountain is not really work at all. Thus, all their comings and goings are seen as consequences of an uncontrollable need for freedom rather than a commitment to a job.

Certainly the expectation that guides put the mountain above marriage and family is a common belief among Mendocinos. While exceptions to this perception do indeed seem to be the rule, as I have met many working mountain guides who have stable and established family lives, Mendocinos still tend to suspect that mountaineers go to the mountain only to escape responsibilities. "She should stop going out with andinistas. With them, we're going nowhere," was what a Mendocino woman in her twenties said to me in regard to a relative who was dating a guide against the advice of friends and family. Although the literal meaning of this struck me as humorous, to suggest that you'll go nowhere with the very persons who are accused of always going somewhere, it clearly underscored the idea that for her a settled married life should be the final destination for dating and that mountain guides would probably never quite arrive there. Others in Mendoza have voiced similar opinions to me, saying that "andinistas are just passing through here, they belong up there." They explain that mountain guides have no reason to stay below, have a higher rate of divorce and broken relationships, and, as one put it, have no need for female companionship because even their sexual needs are satisfied by their relationship with the mountain: "they go up to screw the mountain." In addition, they cite one or two of the most famous members of the Generation of the 80s and their string of divorces to prove their points.

This perception of domestic inconstancy goes against the grain of early twentieth-century Mendocino incursions into mountain tourism at the luxury hotels in Cacheuta and Puente del Inca that promoted romance, pairing up, and marriage. In contrast, the seemingly unfettered movement, inability to commit, and freedom-loving nature of mountain guides negate established Mendoza social patterns and contradict and destabilize historical models of Mendocino identity. In this way, mountain guides, as representative of regional masculinities, function similarly to how Archetti sees the tanguero, polo player, and futbolista: "This national male imagery is not the official one. All these liminal figures become signs of the nation because they are, in many and dissimilar ways, ambivalent and ambiguous, and they threaten well-established moral codes" (1999, 189).

The mountain guide as an icon of regional masculinity, following Archetti's guidelines, is risk taking, free-spirited, active, physically strong, and hybrid by the nature of his inhabiting both the urban sphere of Mendoza as well as the mountain, representing Mendoza's past and its future tourist-focused plans. His hybridity is also marked by his proximity to international subjectivities, which distances him from Mendoza's provincialism. Immigration to and settlement in Mendoza has been the norm that the region has traditionally used for self-identification (Campana et al. 2004; Lacoste 2003; Ponte 1987). The mountain guide disrupts this story of settlement by adding one of unsettled movement, that of international tourism and Mendoza's evolution in a globalized world. Like Archetti's models, mountain guides are clearly liminal figures functioning, if you will, as an outlaw model of masculinity and regional Mendocino identity that in its ambiguous and ambivalent nature reveals the limits, constraints, and expectations of society just as it transgresses them.

Regional Identities

This reading of the figure of the mountain guide as representative of the province seems to stand in opposition to Pablo Lacoste's (2003) view of Mendocino identity that he derives from official history and traditional Mendoza. In this essay for *Los Andes*, Lacoste, a Mendocino historian, discusses the direction Mendoza's future should take and argues the importance of continuing to distance Mendoza from Buenos Aires. He posits three images as reflective of Mendocino identity that also offer viable bases for continued growth. For Lacoste, it is the arriero of transport, not the gaucho; the wine producer, not the tanguero; and the chess champion, rather than the soccer star or the polo player, who best typify Mendocino regional identity. Two of the models that Lacoste posits—the vintner and the chess player—are sedentary and emphasize intellectual abilities. While it is true that the arriero insinuates the mountain into Lacoste's model, the mountain as traditional adventure is absent in Lacoste's triptych. Lacoste invokes the arriero as a long-standing historical mode of transportation tied to agro-industries and not specifically linked to mountaineering. Nor does Lacoste address the issue of the association of indigeneity with the arriero, reflecting again how Mendoza's indigenous peoples have historically been subsumed by social and labor categories that erase ethnic difference (Escolar 2007).

Even within the realm of mountaineering, the differences between guides and arrieros in terms of their symbolic relationship to adventure and the mountain mean that they offer differing and complementary readings for regional identity construction. The arriero has not enjoyed the same "supposed" freedom of movement as the mountain guide.[3] There is not the assumption that the arriero is looking for the unknown frontiers of self or quest, which the category of guide inherently contains. And while travel in the mountain for both is a way of earning a living, for the arriero it is explicitly so, while the guide's economic gain is mitigated and subsumed by the risks he takes for his clients and by the expectation of his searching for self-realization or new routes or new extremes. The class difference, with its underlying ethnic division, between the two figures also conditions the way that the mountain is perceived within the scheme of Mendoza's social relationships. In Lacoste's paradigm, the mountain as terrain of the arriero of agricultural transport disconnects this work of physical challenge from middle-class endeavors and implicitly relegates indigeneity to the provincial underclass. Adding mountain guides, who are generally middle-class, educated professionals, to Lacoste's framework allows for that traditional class divide to be bridged so that the mountain becomes both a working-class and middle-class territory, but this addition does not explicitly mark it as multiethnic.

Similar to the connections that Lacoste's other figures offer, the Mendocino guide, as an explicit symbol of mountaineering, also links international and national histories. The Mendocino guide dialogues with Anglo-European practices and also invokes Argentine military traditions. Mountain guides, as symbolic of the province, project a Mendoza that is connected to the outside world, one that would function on equal terms within an international forum yet still remain tied to Mendoza's own history and traditions. The multiple national and transnational relationships and connotations attributed to Mendocino guides would add another trajectory to Lacoste's regional model that would include Mendoza's undeniable dependence on the development of its tourism industry and thus provide a more complete view of the region's unique identity and present and future potential.

Women and Guiding

Ya no voy con la novia. No uno mi objetivo deportivo con mi novia.
(I don't go with my girlfriend anymore. I don't link my sports goals to my girlfriend.)

—MENDOCINO MOUNTAIN GUIDE

Connecting Archetti's ideas about national masculinities and Lacoste's regional identity models to the role of the mountain guide may reflect touristic movements of Mendoza in the twenty-first century that update its traditional self-representation as settled and agricultural, but it is not entirely satisfactory. In addition to erasing ethnic difference from the province, envisioning the symbolic value of mountain guides in these ways offers a gender-restricted sense of both regional and national citizenship. It begs the question of how women are to embody these roles that are taken to epitomize national and regional identities based on models of masculinity.

While women indeed graduate from the EPGAMT, they have usually either been designated to women's domestic territories, such as the base-camp cook tents, or have been subsumed under the masculinization of mountaineering in which they are still often found wanting because of perceived gender difference. Common statements about women not being strong enough or restricted by motherhood are argued by both men and women on the mountain. Catherine Palmer (2002), in a discussion of the media's negative treatment of Alison Hargreaves, the second person, male or female, to summit Everest without supplemental oxygen, theorizes that the morality of risk taking in mountaineering is heavily gendered and that culturally embedded ideas about maternity and motherhood are the most salient in denying social acceptance of women as mountain protagonists (333–334).

In a discussion with two Mendocino-trained guides who graduated in the same year (the male graduate had worked several years as a guide, and the female had only worked at base camp, cooking during that same period), they explained that "la montaña es netamente de hombres" (the mountain is clearly a man's place). Within this man's world women are seen as inherently subordinate and dependent on men's assistance in gaining the experience and knowledge about mountaineering necessary for entrance into it. The woman rationalized that "muchas mujeres se interesan por el novio. Si vas con el novio estás mejor—seguís su ritmo—caminan más rápido—pasás tiempo con el novio . . . te presta equipo, sabe adónde ir" (Many women get interested [in mountaineering] because of their boyfriends. If you go with your boyfriend, you're better off—you follow his rhythm—they walk faster—you spend time with your boyfriend . . . he loans you equipment. He knows where to go). But this dependence had its cost too, as she clarified that this perception informed the excuses that men gave to exclude them—" 'no venís porque es demasiado peligroso' o no te invitan, hombres no llaman a mí para subir . . . piensan 'tenemos que esperarlas' " ("you're not coming because it's too dangerous," or they don't invite you, men don't call me to go to the mountain . . . they think "we'll have to wait for them"). Inclusion in the masculine group that would facilitate outings and offer the necessary experience in the formation of guides depends on women's ability to exceed masculine standards and expectations. The female guide confessed to having heard on numerous occasions the following sentiment: " 'Mirá vos, che, cómo se lo banca, cómo anda' como si para una mujer fuera raro que llegue a ese nivel" ("Hey, look how she holds up, how she's going," as if it were odd for a woman to be at that level).

Both guides agreed on the reasonings behind the gender divisions and women's inferior positions within mountaineering activity on Aconcagua as being dictated by client preference, but their reasons were contradicted by their own perceptions of the actual practices of mountaineering on Aconcagua. In terms of employing women as guides, they pointed toward the service agencies, who tended not to hire women in that capacity but actually preferred them in the base camp, allegedly as a concession to the foreigners. "Los dueños prefieren tener mujeres en sus campamentos: desarrollan actividades de mujeres—cocinar, limpiar, poner buena cara, que venga un gringo que no vea un tipo de cara de mugre" (Owners prefer to have women in the base camps: they carry out women's activities—cook, clean, put on a nice face, so that when a gringo comes he doesn't see a grimy-faced guy). Although I have recounted here the opinions of only two guides, I heard the same ideas repeated almost verbatim over a period of six years, confirmed by guides and service agencies alike. Rudy Parra was quoted in *Los Andes* as expressing the same sentiments: "La mujer es lo mejor que le pasó al Aconcagua. . . . Estás perdido en la montaña, saturado de hombres y de riesgos y una chica te sirve la comida, es maravilloso . . . a los gringos les encanta" (Women are the best thing that has happened to Aconcagua. You're lost in the mountain saturated with men and risks and a girl serves you a meal, it's marvelous, the gringos love it) (Walker 2003).

While these attitudes defer blame to the "gringos" who are buying services, spending money, and apparently in need of the gentle appearance of a woman back home at base camp, the two guides also admitted that in terms of accepting women as guides "argentinos mantienen la división, gringos, sí aceptan mejor a las mujeres" (Argentines maintain the division, gringos do accept women better), and they offered examples of a Mendocino woman who worked in the United States as a principal guide. This was not the usual case for Mendocino women on Aconcagua.

However, there are very visible nontypical cases of women guiding and excelling on Aconcagua. Ortner (1996) uses the concept of "gender radical" to describe women who participated in Himalayan mountaineering, defining the term as "someone who is questioning or breaking gender rule" (184). Although it can be argued that just engaging in mountaineering at any level is a challenge to tradition, for most women on Aconcagua there is no questioning of Mendocino gender rules: they remain in the places that Western patriarchy has assigned them, in domestic or domestic-like spheres (the cook tents in the base camp). More recently, due to an increase in the number of entrants to Aconcagua Provincial Park and increased demand for Aconcagua guides, a handful of Mendocino women have found their way into the profession, but almost consistently in subordinate, inferior roles, in terms of power and pay, as assistant guides (Logan 2006).

There are several Mendocino women, however, who have garnered respect among the contemporary climbing community, and they have been highlighted as role models for women on Aconcagua. Adriana Domínguez and Popi Spognuoli are two such examples. Adriana's multiple summits of Aconcagua and her strength as an andinista have been pointed out to me as testimony of women's capacities in mountaineering. In a similar vein, Popi's 2005 winter summit of Aconcagua has also been highly touted as signifying women's potential in the field. However, neither Adriana nor Popi have been working regularly as guides; both primarily have worked in those more-accepted "feminine" domestic spheres of base-camp support. They may have jostled, but have not broken through, established gender-based roles in Mendocino mountaineering.

This is not to say that no women have acted as gender radicals in Mendocino mountaineering. There have been, and none is so obvious as Nancy Silvestrini.[4] I met Nancy on Aconcagua in December 2001 as she was guiding an expedition of foreigners to base camp at Plaza de Mulas. She was the first and only Mendocino woman I have seen at work as a principal guide, although by 2006 there was at least one employed by a local agency as a principal guide, and there were several women who generally served as assistant guides but who were occasionally asked to take the lead with small groups. In 2001 Nancy was a pathbreaker, not only as a guide on Aconcagua, but in the entrepreneurial sense, as she had also started her own mountain shop. And Nancy was the first woman from Mendoza to attempt and summit an 8,000-meter mountain, Gasherbrum I (8,080). She accompanied a group of climbers from Spain to the Himalayas and was successful in reaching the summit, but she fell to her death on the descent on July 5, 2003. Nancy's initiative, ambition, and protagonism in all aspects of mountaineering exceeded the level of many of her male contemporaries. Her contributions to Mendocino mountaineering and to women in mountaineering are important. Although her record is perceived by most Mendocino andinistas as an exception to the "natural" rule, it also marks the kinds of firsts that allow others to follow more easily, to know that it is, after all, possible. Those possibilities were reflected in the Mendocino-based 2005 climbing project "Argentinos al Himalaya" that was dedicated to Silvestrini's memory. This expedition attempted to send two teams, one consisting of three women, to the tops of Gasherbrum I and II.[5]

The New Generation

Un buen guía de alta montaña: Un profesional formado, capacitado, que se entrena, que estudia y es capaz de conducir un grupo de personas en cualquier condición en la montaña. Además da un servicio adecuado, servicio a nivel humano, honesto, gentil. (A good high mountain guide: A formed and trained professional, who practices, studies and is capable of leading a group of people in the mountains under any kind of circumstances. Besides providing (this kind of) appropriate service, also giving service at a human level, honest and genteel.)

—FACULTY MEMBER AND ADMINISTRATOR OF EPGAMT

There has been an assumption by some leaders of Mendocino mountaineering that after the firsts and records of the Generation of the 80s in the late 1980s and early 1990s there has been little advancement locally in the sport or in its technical level. They have criticized the newer generations for a "lack of ambition to take the initiative to pass from trekking guide to high altitude guide" or a "lack of initiative in forging new or difficult routes" by "focusing on three-months work on Aconcagua and not going outside Argentina to guide on other mountains."[6] According to Danielón Rodríguez, these deficits are most self-evident in the makeup of the EPGAMT. He states that while the first graduates had come to the school because of their experience and love of the mountains, subsequent students have entered the program with much less experience, primarily motivated by the work possibilities, which are almost always exclusively linked to Aconcagua. For Rodríguez this marks a clear difference between his generation and those newer graduates who dedicate themselves exclusively to Aconcagua. It also brings us back to how traditional understandings of mountain adventure grapple with the new reality of economic motivation that is often primary for most Mendocinos who are now engaged in mountain guiding on Aconcagua.

While the popularity of Aconcagua and the increased number of non-mountaineers with the economic capacity to undertake an expedition to Aconcagua since the 1980s has meant a more lucrative business for the Mendocino guide community, it has also required a reworking of mountain adventure that integrates the risk of capital on both sides of the equation, for the amateur sportsmen who pay to climb and for the guides who are paid to lead. It is this recharacterization that has inspired some of the criticism of the newer generation of Mendocino guides for not loosening their ties to Aconcagua business and returning to a more traditional performance of mountain adventure as challenge, travel, self-realization, and metaphorical conquest.

However, while the Generation of the 80s first found their footing along this historical ideological path, many of them subsequently turned toward blazing the trail in initiating and developing the money-making enterprises of Aconcagua mountaineering. Their engagement of mountaineering

Figure 6.1. Mendocino mountain guides relaxing in Hotel Refugio Plaza de Mulas.

functioned to connect traditional mountaineering styles with the economics of mountaineering. Their trajectory in the aspects of business follows an international trend, especially since the 1980s, of professional climbers "selling their expertise," as Johnston and Edwards (1994, 467) put it. To this end, one of the courses in EPGAMT, founded by a member of the Generation of the 80s, deals with the commercial aspects of tourism management. Ironically, however, the criticisms of the Generation of the 80s toward the new generations are based on the former's perception that economics is becoming the defining feature of Mendocino mountaineering. They would prefer to see an equilibrium maintained between traditional idealistic and technical expectations and current practices motivated by the business of mountaineering.

Current Mendocino guiding on Aconcagua has a tenuous foothold on the scale balancing the ideals of mountaineering adventure and its commodification. While the responsibility of weighing the challenges of weather, fulfilling client demands, and meeting the exigencies of the climb make every expedition a unique, unexpected, and risky endeavor, the leading of groups up the same routes, expedition after expedition, calls into question whether daily rhythms and activities start to verge on the familiarly routine for the guides. If the guides' activities are no longer seen as a symbolic exploration of the unknown to meet uncertainty and challenge themselves physically, mentally, and spiritually, then the traditional sense of adventure and mountaineering diminishes. Mountaineering of this kind, no longer extraordinary for the guides, becomes more a job than an adventure. In other words, guiding as a way to earn a living supersedes mountaineering as the path to self-knowledge.

It is difficult to ignore that the living provided by guiding on Aconcagua is a good one. As a principal guide during a four-month season, one can earn nearly three to four times the normal salary for a teacher or a tourism agency employee in the city during that same period. And, fortunately, the work is plentiful. Both guides and park administrators have spoken about their desire to institute a new future requirement so that a locally accredited guide would accompany every foreign expedition. This is not currently feasible because there are not enough local guides to handle all the mountaineering activity permitted at this time by the park authorities.[7] With demand outpacing supply, the prospect of guiding now and for the foreseeable future seems very promising. But profit margin undermines the romantic and idealized notion of mountaineering. The negative connotation of practicing andinismo for pay, and not for the "love" of adventure, still unsettles the Mendocino mountaineering community.

The consequences of globalization that supported the emergence of the Generation of the 80s and the shortening of distances with regard to information, gear, and capital, have made Aconcagua a magnet for international mountaineering and have also been at the root of the cleavages between the generations of Mendocino andinistas. The creation of a profitable mountaineering market is what keeps Mendocino guides at home, relatively speaking. It is this lack of travel outward to greater distances, one of the foundational elements in the origins of mountaineering, that some members of the Generation of the 80s have criticized. And it is true that the majority of younger Mendocino guides do not work outside of Argentina. But many of them have indeed traveled outside the country to scale peaks in Bolivia, Peru, Ecuador, the United States, France, Italy, and the Himalayas, as did those in the Generation of the 80s. And similar to the Generation of the 80s, a great majority of guides work during the off-season in Mendoza in teaching roles or for adventure tourism agencies.

Changing Access

The newer generation of guides has followed the paths laid out by the Generation of the 80s in continuing to form andinistas. Several work in *polideportivos* (state-supported sports clubs) and routinely sponsor their students for training positions such as porter or base-camp assistant on Aconcagua. In order to work officially as guides, students must graduate from the EPGAMT, but the polideportivos are significant in spurring interest and providing training and experience that makes their students more successful in the guide school. This is important because there is a high dropout rate for the EPGAMT as both physical and academic standards are strict. Approximately 20 percent of the students leave after the first three months, and 30 percent leave by the end of the first year.[8]

This new generation of guides promotes andinismo not only in specialized courses in the polideportivos but also across the general secondary school populace. The guide school uses the facilities of the Instituto de Educación Física. "Dr. Jorge Coll 9–016" and many graduates of the guide school hold degrees from both institutions. This means that they are licensed to teach physical education at the secondary level, which some do. Trekking excursions are regularly part of the secondary physical education curriculum and andinistas within the school system serve to heighten the interest, not only in these introductory excursions to the mountain area, but in mountaineering itself.

The post–Generation of the 80s guides are important participants in the experience and perception of mountaineering in Mendoza. Some work in adventure tourism agencies during the off-season, and some have started their own guiding agencies. Freelance mountain photography has also become an outlet, and many of the postcards and posters of Aconcagua and surrounding mountains have been taken by Mendocino guides.[9] Like their predecessors, this new generation of guides has worked to increase visibility and popularize mountaineering, both for the passion of mountain adventure and for economic opportunities within Mendoza.

Nevertheless, there still exists in Mendoza today the belief that mountaineering remains an exclusive and unique practice that does not resonate for most Mendocinos. As one Mendocino guide told me, "Andinismo cannot really be compared to any other kind of activity," so most Mendocinos have no real frame of reference. This assumption coincides with a generalized consensus that the majority of Mendocinos are simply not interested in mountaineering. Another guide reported that the average Mendocino is not going to think about heading up to the mountains or spending vacation time on an expedition on Aconcagua. According to a letter to the editor in *Los Andes*, "Para la mayoría de los mendocinos, los que vivimos en la llanura, el desierto, los oasis o centros urbanos, la montaña es un mero accidente geográfico más o menos pintoresco" (For the majority of us Mendocinos who live in the flatlands, the desert, the oasis, or the urban centers, the mountains are merely a more or less picturesque geographical accident) (Triviño 2004).

Traditionally, Mendocino vacations have meant going to the Chilean seaside or to the eastern Argentinian coast. If the mountains have figured at all in terms of leisure activities, it has been as the location of a vacation chalet to escape the summer heat or as the backdrop to a Sunday picnic. I've been told repeatedly that "on weekends the furthest Mendocinos go is a few meters' distance from the side of the highway to have an *asado* [barbecue]." There has been an additional lament by some of the guides who say that even if Mendocinos are interested in mountaineering, they would not think to hire a guide: "A Mendocino will go alone. He won't pay a guide." They contrast this with the much longer mountaineering tradition that they imagine in Europe where they assume (usually with no substantiated knowledge or experience on their part) that on the other side of the Atlantic a novice mountaineer would look first to a trained professional for instruction and guidance. In Mendoza and its mountaineering community, there still remains an internalized belief that a "mountain culture" is intrinsically Anglo-European, especially when it comes to mountaineering practices and attitudes.

Mountaineering, for these Mendocino guides, is fundamentally seen as an exclusive activity restricted first by skill levels, which can be taught, and also by attitudes that reflect traditional assumptions about North-South hierarchies in mountaineering, which is much more difficult to reconfigure. Both guides and nonandinistas have expressed to me that only a select few Mendocinos have "broken the code" of mountaineering. For Mendocino guides, their training and experience have helped them to overcome any regional or national attitudinal barriers prejudicial to their full enjoyment of the sport. Despite attempts to open mountaineering up to a wider public, Mendocino andinistas continue to see themselves, and are seen by others, as a special group, "a kind of Mafia" according to one guide, that guards entrance into its tight circle with an elitist zeal.

There are also economic considerations that certainly must also contribute to the way Mendocinos in general perceive the exclusivity of mountaineering and their distance from it. While schools and clubs may provide relatively inexpensive, or free, workshops and excursions, the appropriate gear and climbing tools necessary for mountaineering are very costly. Most of the equipment that beginners would need is available in Mendoza sporting goods stores, but often at prices targeted to international tourists. (The North Face now has a facility in nearby Santiago, and what cannot be found in Mendoza shops is surely to be found on a weekend drive to Chile.) In addition, although Aconcagua has reduced entrance fees for nationals, the price of support services on the mountain and that of a guided expedition is the same for all climbers. While not anywhere near the prices of Everest, Aconcagua expeditions are still costly for most Argentines.[10]

Entrance figures to the Aconcagua Provincial Park seem to support some of these suppositions by Mendocino guides about the state of mountaineering's popularity as a pastime in Mendoza. However, the figures do not prove a lack of interest in the mountains by local Mendocinos, quite the contrary. While the numbers of climbers who enter the park to summit Aconcagua are overwhelmingly foreign (between 80–90 percent every year over the last decade), the great majority of backpackers and hikers who enter the park for one-, three-, or seven-day treks are indeed Argentine. (There is no breakdown for regional numbers, only national.)

The discrepancy in these numbers seems to imply that trekking in the mountains is quite attractive to the average Mendocino, but that high-altitude mountaineering is seen as something beyond their grasp. Perhaps the intention to rectify the disproportionately low percentage of local participation in mountaineering, and the continued emphasis on integrating the sport into the mainstream of Mendoza by local professionals, is what brought about a program called Aconcagua Para Todos (Aconcagua for All). The program was originally organized in 2003 by Professor Sergio Furlán and Viviana Araya to help local nature enthusiasts to prepare for Aconcagua over the course of a year. The importance of this project, according to the *Los Andes* reporter Fabián Galdi, is that for people with no previous experience in andinismo the taking on of Aconcagua is to break taboos and prejudices (2003). This program was continued briefly with the support of Danielón Rodríguez and Heber Orona, the most highly acclaimed member of the new generation. Orona, the only Mendocino to complete the Seven Summits Route, in 2006, was the Mendocino sportsman of the year in 2000 after his successful summit of Everest.[11] Orona's successes align him with the career paths of the Generation of the 80s who excelled at both international and national levels. Like members of the Generation of the 80s, he also founded his own guiding and adventure tourism agency in Mendoza, which was known for programming expeditions to other local mountains as well as Aconcagua. In 2006 he merged his enterprise with Rudy Parra's Aconcagua Trek and now is a partner in Parra's more than thirty-year-old business.

It is significant that Orona, who is seen as a leader of the new generation, teamed up with Danielón Rodríguez, one of the "founding fathers," to disclaim the exclusivity of Aconcagua mountaineering and reclaim it as a territory for all Mendocinos in Aconcagua Para Todos. The program was intended to attract a wider audience by inviting all to participate, and the invitation was made infinitely more attractive by extending it from two of the most prominent andinistas in Mendoza today. Aconcagua Para Todos announced that mountaineering was no longer just for the Anglo-European scientist or adventurer-explorer, the military hero, the economically advantaged international novice, or the professional guide. It was for common Mendocino folk as well. On one level, however, it always had been. Since 1935, the Club Andinista de Mendoza (CAM) and other mountaineering groups that developed over the years have offered opportunities to "hacer montaña" for those Mendocinos who were so inclined. Work opportunities in the Aconcagua Provincial Park, such as those for park rangers, the police rescue squad, porters, base-camp workers, and arrieros, also continue to promote the practice of andinismo across a broad cross-section of Mendocino society. What was different about Aconcagua para Todos was that it sought new enthusiasts from among the noninitiated, from those outside the group of the already interested or knowledgeable. It opened the sport to those Mendocinos who might never think to seek membership in CAM or to regard the mountain as anything more than a "geographical accident."

Programs such as Aconcagua Para Todos provide a different outlet for those not interested in professional mountaineering, but who would rather enjoy the mountains in their leisure time. It breaks the opposition inherent in world tourism where "traditionally First World countries send out and Third World countries receive." With Aconcagua Para Todos, local Mendocinos were partaking in the experience at a relatively equal position to international climbers. Now Mendoza no longer just receives mountain tourism, but it also practices it, to a degree.

The professionalization of the sport by educational and training programs, the expanded labor market due to increased international popularity, the new achievements and levels of participation by local women, and the reconfiguration of the activity by programs that offer Aconcagua as a leisure location for all Mendocinos have changed the face of mountaineering adventure in Mendoza and highlighted the social and economic significance of its adventure tourism industries. This linking of mountain adventure with Mendoza positions Mendoza to question its traditional gender and labor roles and to reevaluate its own history, its relationship to the mountains, to the nation, to international tourism, and to the process of globalization. This complicated and complex weaving of histories, peoples, places, roles, desires, and practices that have come together in the development of the Mendocino mountaineering industry on Aconcagua is perhaps no better illustrated than in a site in Puente del Inca, the staging area for the most heavily traveled route to the summit, the Cementerio de los Andinistas.

Bodies of Memory

El Cementerio de los Andinistas: la antesala de la gloria y la muerte (The Cemetery of the Andinistas: the waiting room of glory and death).
—RAYMUNDO LUNA RANGEL (1996, XCVIII)

In the Cementerio de los Andinistas, a place of death and memory, the transnational and local understandings of mountaineering flow together to narrate the modern and contemporary histories of the occupation of the mountain area by the practices of tourism and mountaineering. As a complement to the presence and movements of Mendoza's mountain guides, the traces or vestiges of corporeal presence on Aconcagua, or the memory of the absent body held in the Cementerio, have been especially informative for considering the history and politics of mountaineering there and the hybrid, fluid, postmodern identities of nation and self that Aconcagua mountaineering constructs.

The Cementerio de los Andinistas lies five kilometers from the entrance to the Aconcagua Provincial Park. One of the most prominent and unusual grave markers, in the form of a soaring condor, pays tribute to General Nicolás Plantamura, the first Argentine to summit Aconcagua. As a metaphor for the Argentine mountaineer's accomplishments, the condor, which is endemic to the high altitudes of the Andes, serves as a geospecific symbol of unbounded freedom. Caught in an eternal moment of flight, symbolically intuited as unrestricted by earthly, political, and cultural borders, the condor not only commemorates Plantamura's crossing over, but also celebrates Argentina's crossing into the terrain of international mountaineering. Although Aconcagua as national Argentine territory has been the destination of international mountaineers since the 1880s, until Plantamura's successful summit on March 8, 1934, Argentines themselves had figured only marginally. Plantamura's feat is commemorated as a symbolic remapping of Aconcagua from an Anglo-European peripheral space of exploration to a sign of Argentine modernity. The overlappings of national imagination on international claims over national territory have been the legacy of the development of mountain climbing on Aconcagua, and they are nowhere more evident than in the Cementerio.

The Cementerio as a tourist destination figures as a stop on many general tours of the "alta montaña" run by Mendocino travel agencies, and it figures prominently in the best-known, most sold, and locally produced video on Aconcagua, *Aconcagua: Techo de América* (1998). In addition, the Cementerio is regularly pointed out to climbers by guides as they drive by on their way to the entrance of the Aconcagua Provincial Park. Guides often suggest it to climbers as an option for a recreational trek on their day or afternoon off before starting the expedition. The memory it holds of danger and death seems to have a perverse appeal to andinistas and mountain tourists alike.

The Cementerio's recent "rehabilitation" by the Las Heras council to make it more attractive, or to distinguish it as a destination, was certainly motivated in part by the fact that it is thought of as a local tourist draw. The plaque that the Las Heras council erected serves to inform tourists of the uniqueness of the spot and to direct their interpretation of the site. As a tourist destination the Cementerio functions as a museum of memory for Aconcagua, and the plaques, markers, and epitaphs chart a graveyard tour of the past and present of the mountain.

The Cementerio is not just the burial ground, or place of memorialization (some are buried elsewhere or are still on the mountain), for those lost on Aconcagua. It honors not only those who died tragically on Aconcagua, but also local protagonists in the development of the high mountain area who died peacefully in their beds. The cemetery was originally set aside in 1887 as the resting place for those local workers who lost their lives during the construction of the FCBAP, or trans-Andean railway. It was not until approximately 1928 that it became known as the resting place of mountaineers, or andinistas (Campana et al. 2004, 5:94). Its location is about one kilometer away from the ruins of the Puente del Inca Hotel, the site of Mendoza's first incursion into mountain tourism, which, along with the cemetery's original purpose, serves as a reminder of the range of local social classes involved in early mountain tourism in the area. The Cementerio location also marks it as a witness to the comings and goings of Aconcagua mountaineering because it falls between two main staging areas, Penitentes and Puente del Inca, and is directly across from the third, Los Puquios, on the international highway to Chile.

The Cementerio, in its memorialization of sacrificed bodies, offers a diachronic and synchronic reading of the highest mountain outside of Asia.

A walk in this hallowed ground takes you through the stages of development of andinismo. On the one hand, it celebrates the heroic, individual endeavors of early foreign activities. On the other, the Cementerio juxtaposes this early European exploration and British investment with the presence of Argentina on the mountain from the building of the trans-Andean railway and early mountain tourism, through the militarization along the Chilean border and the history of the 8th Mountain Brigade, through redemocratization and civilian governance, to the explosion of adventure tourism in the last thirty years that has occurred during a period of significant sociopolitical changes in Argentina. The graves and commemorative markers of the Cementerio register these adjustments in focus, authority, control, and use of the area as well as reflect the contemporary, postmodern pastiche of Aconcagua today.

The Cementerio is laid out in rather uneven concentric circles on a small hill with an ecumenical cross situated at the top. Other than a stone-marked pathway, there is no strict order to the Cementerio, and visitors may walk up, down, on the diagonal, or around the site with ease. Memorials to European, Asian, North American, and South American climbers, as well as to climbers from the past and present, lie side by side. Various religions and nationalities are displayed. The dedications on the headstones are in many languages, and often English rather than Spanish is used, regardless of the origin of the climber. The layout of the Cementerio and its recording of Mendoza's development of the mountaineering industry reflect the process of globalization there. Its approximately one hundred sites connect moments of British investment in the area (a Mr. Cotton who was a supervisor for the railway's early hostelry endeavors in Puente del Inca whom FitzGerald [1899] mentions in his account of the first summit on Aconcagua [see fig. 6.2]), early foreign exploration (e.g., the Austrian Juan Stepanek, the first fatality in 1926 whose body was not recovered until 1946 by a group led by Valentín Ugarte) and Euro-Anglo scientific expeditions (e.g., the German Juan Jorge Link and his French wife, Adriana Bance, the first woman to summit in 1942, who died, with their dog, on the mountain in 1944, also recovered by Ugarte). Other sites commemorate Plantamura's first summit, the Argentine military presence (e.g., Jorge Nelson Juárez, an Argentine military pilot lost in a rescue attempt), the recent surge in international popularity (e.g., the Korean Sang Suk Park and the American Janet Mae Johnson), Latin American undertakings (the flashy memorial in memory of the Brazilian Mozart Catão [see fig. I.2], who died in an avalanche with his two climbing companions on the South Face in 1998), and local participation in andinismo, from the namesake of the Mendocino High Altitude Mountain Guide School, Lt. Col. Valentín Ugarte, to the father of the mountaineering industry in Mendoza, Fernando Grajales (who died of natural causes in 2004). People of all backgrounds are represented, from service providers (the porter Gustavo Lo Re, who fell returning from Plaza de Mulas in 2002) to sportsmen (Walter Sergio Tocona, Germán Brena, Gustavo Martín, Daniel Mario Morales, four young Mendocino andinistas lost together in a tragic accident on the Polish Glacier in 2000).

The five memorials to the young Mendocinos killed in 2000 and 2002 are very telling about the evolution of Mendoza's role on Aconcagua. Gustavo Lo Re brings attention back to Mendocinos as service providers, a role that falls naturally into the dominant Anglo-European discourses of travel and adventure and that has usually been excluded or ignored. The Cementerio, however, marks the contributions of these service workers on an equal footing with those of more internationally renowned figures. Memorials to service providers, whether porters or railway workers, alongside those of international sportsmen and military heroes, reintegrate and revalue their stories in the history of mountaineering. In the same way, those memorials to four Mendocinos who enjoyed mountaineering as sportsmen, rather than as service workers or military men or guides for pay, incorporate their presence as protagonists into the traditional "heroics" of mountaineering in an equal, rather than subordinate, role. In some ways, the presence in the Cementerio of all five young men tends to heighten their status, as family members and friends care for the sites and leave flowers and other mementos that make the headstones stand out from many of the others. In this way the Cementerio elevates Mendoza's presence in the mountain region and illustrates a change in the value and functions of Mendocinos' roles in mountaineering on Aconcagua.

While the cemetery is inclusive of distinct and specific economic, political, and social references to the local Mendocino mountaineering industry and juxtaposes them to the transnational and national histories of Aconcagua, none of these are salient issues for local marketing promotions of the Cementerio, which by extension is a promotion of Aconcagua. The global, transnational, modern, and postmodern aspects of the Cementerio contrast with the rhetoric most employed by local Mendocino travel writers or video makers who romanticize the cemetery as a symbol of the transcendence of the self, the self ennobled by supreme and perilous danger, risk, and the ultimate sacrifice of life.

A Mendocino touristic video, *Aconcagua: Techo de América*, describes scenes of the Cementerio with just such an attitude, telling us that "these

Figure 6.2. The memorial to Edward Joseph Cotton, who was employed by the Puente del Inca Hotel during the time of Edward A. FitzGerald's expedition (1896–97), in Cementerio de los Andinistas.

headstones, on which are inscribed names from all the latitudes of the world, are not sad. . . . Instead we find a resplendent aura, a breath that comes from the determination of mountaineers." The video narration evokes the assumed universality of the romantic self, manifested in the proud, determined, nonvictimized mountaineering spirit. It subsumes the imperialistic and Eurocentric connotations that understand travel as a transformative act stemming from Western, humanistic, masculine, and middle-class valuings (Clifford 1997, 33; Kaplan 1998, 50).

Although the cemetery elicits the particular romantic and imperialist legacy of the video, especially through the rhetoric of the epitaphs and the markers of early European explorers and scientists, it nonetheless disrupts it as it displays alternative and other mountaineering subjectivities, those of women, non-European, and nonexpeditionary members. In a similar vein the Cementerio also documents the unromantic pragmatics of implementing and developing a local tourist industry by making visible the participation and sacrifice of workers, guides, and rescue team members.

In contrast to the video description, the Cementerio itself creates a more egalitarian discursive field in its haphazard layout that disrupts hierarchical, patriarchal narratives of the mountaineering self. Here, the absent hero of Aconcagua is represented by the juxtaposition of varied nationalities, professions, genders, ages, chronologies, and histories that both contradict and invoke romantic universality and imperialist overtones of mountaineering. It is not just a "cemetery of the vanquished," of "those who gave their lives to reach the highest summit of the Americas" (Campana et al. 2004, 5:94), but a monumental and geographical text that commemorates all those who have participated in mountain activities since the arrival of the trans-Andean railway. In this inclusive way, the Cementerio narrates transnational and national history, sociology, economics, anthropology, science, and politics in an unstable text of porous and overlapping boundaries that metaphorically represents Aconcagua.

As a narrative of memory on Aconcagua, the Cementerio offers a rich and complex reading of local, national, and global interactions that include images of non-Western, nonmale, and nonheroic subjectivities. The visible narratives of nation, adventure, gender, class, modernity, tourism, and capital held in the tombstones, as well as the indigenous history of the mountain notable by its very absence, combine in the Cementerio to reflect a globalized Aconcagua where the contemporary practice of international mountaineering has become an important economic resource and a way of life for Mendoza.

Debriefs

The heterogeneous, hybrid, and fractured nature of the Cementerio provides a counternarrative of Aconcagua, one that encompasses the very different histories, functions, and attitudes that have evolved to define Aconcagua but that also disrupts, through its nonhierarchical, nonchronological, and nonexclusionary layout or syntax, the traditional interpretations given to Aconcagua mountaineering. The Cementerio especially provides a post-modern reading of Aconcagua that draws attentions to the global and regional aspects of its contemporary character. Markers of other local subjects and heroes of Aconcagua mountaineering give prominence to the regional over the national, putting recollections of Mendoza on equal footing with international and global memories.

The Cementerio's disparate, varied, and often conflicting discourses about Aconcagua that address issues of globalization, tourism, gender, and class hierarchies are the same ones that Mendocino society has grappled with through transculturative moves in coming to terms with the roles and functions of mountaineering in everyday life. The spiritual assumptions about the nature of mountaineering, the historical subordination of Mendoza in the modernist legacy of the sport, the newfound tensions between gender and class labor divisions, the commodification of adventure, and the restructuring of a sense of the national to reflect contemporary issues of global economic pressures and regional needs, as seen in the Cementerio, are also all embodied in the perceptions Mendoza has of its local mountain guides. Similar to the Cementerio's more egalitarian view of mountaineering, the practices of mountain guides in Mendoza, especially through education and other training initiatives, are opening up and democratizing the sport, as well as provoking an incipient uneasiness about Mendoza's gender-based and class-based labor hierarchies. The guides' endeavors also show us how Mendoza, with respect to mountaineering, is reevaluating its own history and its relationship to the nation to focus on the economic advantages of international tourism for the region. The memory practices held in the memorialization of life in that site of death, the Cementerio de los Andinistas, and the social messages and understandings projected through the ways of living of Mendocino mountain guides provide complementary texts for understanding how entrenched notions of adventure, nation, and Mendoza's own self-articulated identity have come to adjust and adapt to twenty-first-century economic and global pressures.

CHAPTER SEVEN

The Dream Weaver

Performing Gender, Adventure, and Mountaineering

It has now become something of a truism that we are functioning in a world fundamentally characterized by objects in motion.

—ARJUN APPADURAI (2000, 5)

Mountaineering on Aconcagua is always about movement, the constant going up and coming down the mountain of people, mules, information, gossip, and materials. It is also about the flow of capitalism articulated through the narrative of adventure. How do these movements and flows constitute and plot Aconcagua? How do the differing natures of these bodies in motion reconfigure the ideological, affective, and economic understandings of mountaineering there? How do the presence and practices of international and local mountaineering bodies chart the topographies of gender, nation, adventure, tourism, and memory on the Americas' highest peak? Where do these corporeal and discursive flows intersect with environmental concerns, indigenous rights, and tourism management within the Aconcagua Provincial Park? These were the queries that guided the ethnographic research that I carried out on Aconcagua during four climbing seasons and five trips to base camp over a period of six years, from 2000 to 2006, to consider twenty-first-century mountaineering and the dynamic mobility of the global, local, and national nexus it constructs every year in the central Andes of western Argentina.

Dual Purposes

Of the seven summits, Aconcagua offers the climber the best value in terms of altitude gained for effort expended.

—RYAN (2004, 19)

As part of the Seven Summits Route, Aconcagua has been touted as a "walk up," a categorization that reworks its designation as one of seven prestigious peaks into one that is also technically available to novice enthusiasts. In terms of both experience and capital Aconcagua is taken to be extremely cost-effective. A guided expedition to Everest can cost from $35,000 to $75,000. The permit from the Nepalese government for a team with up to seven members can cost around $50,000. An Everest expedition requires a time expenditure of at least eight to nine weeks. From this comparative standard, Aconcagua, the second highest of the seven summits, would clearly be the budget-basement mountain. Expeditions on Aconcagua, after entering the park, generally take 15–20 days for a summit attempt and return. Aconcagua summit permits for foreign nationals during the high seasons of 2006 to 2008 were approximately $300 and by 2010–2011 a permit was approximately $1,000. The cost of a locally based expedition, which included airport transfers, overnight accommodation in Mendoza pre- and postexpedition, transfers to and from the Aconcagua Provincial Park, mule support, food during the expedition, tents, access to toilet facilities, and locally trained guides, was approximately $3,000–$6,000. With airfare from North America, Europe, Asia, or Australia, the approximate time of an Aconcagua trip is 28 days and the cost could range from $5,000–$9,000, quite a difference from the outlays of money and time that a sojourn to the Himalayas would incur.

Aconcagua's availability makes both the marketing and the practices of mountaineering on Aconcagua appear to be at cross purposes. Aconcagua's draw hinges on both its attractiveness as an elite mountaineering destination, as well as on its appeal to a wider, nonspecialized audience. The practices of mountaineering on Aconcagua also tend to both invoke and be in dissonance with traditional expectations about mountaineering adventure. In this sense Aconcagua mountaineering seems to be skirting a fine line between what might be considered mountaineering proper and adventure tourism. It reflects what Bayers (2003) calls postmodern adventure, in which mountaineering subjects are "feminized" by the subordinate position of preplanned and guided expeditions, and it illustrates the philosophical cleavages that Houston (2006) sees between the old school "with its circumspect notion of pilgrimage," or escape from civilization, and the new school of mountaineering that expects all the conveniences and assistance that "civilization" can offer (153).

Mendoza's mountaineering industry has designed promotional strategies, whether it be through videos, pamphlets, posters, or websites, that represent Aconcagua as distant from the materiality of the everyday and steeped in the latest mountain safety and techno jargon. Beedie (2003) finds that this kind of paradox in advertising that pits the idea of the extraordinary against the safety net of conveniences and technology associated with our daily urban sphere is a generalized result of the commodification of adventure. Within this paradoxical duality, Aconcagua is projected as premodern, pristine, grandiose, remote, and Incan to engage traditional suppositions about mountaineering adventure, while its infrastructure and guiding support are often highlighted for their cutting-edge modernity. While these two narrative modes seem to negate each other, they function together by linking adventure-ness to questions of modernity.

In the promotion of mountaineering the economics of tourism and cultural identity become indelibly entwined. To sell adventure on Aconcagua, local Mendocino tourism marketing practices have drawn heavily on traditional narratives of international mountaineering that would be familiar to climbers across the globe. If tourism, and especially mountaineering, is to get away from it all, then marketing strategies must focus on that difference from the assumed universality of a daily routine, which is always already included in traditional mountaineering narratives as the exotic landscape, the uncivilized, the less modern, the "empty" space. This preordained difference erases the modern and up-to-date Mendoza that is more similar than different to Anglo-European mountaineering practices and practitioners and which protagonizes the other touristic discourse about Aconcagua. This balancing act between familiarity and difference becomes tricky for the Mendoza mountaineering industry as it seeks to rupture entrenched hierarchies of North-South identity politics, but also to take advantage of them.

The Adventurous Spirit

Celador de los sueños, déjame entrar. (Guardian of dreams, let me in.)

—MENDOZA GOVERNMENT'S ACONCAGUA WEBSITE, CIRCA 2007 (www.aconcagua.mendoza.gov.ar)

The guitar-strumming crooner who sang greetings on the official Mendocino government Aconcagua website alluded to the dreamscape of Aconcagua, a realm outside the real, contoured by the ideals of adventure and not by the mountain's economic and technical accessibility. That otherworldly place of Aconcagua mountaineering is remote from the quotidian and foremost in the imagination, founded on a complex process of reconceptualizing space, time, and self that envisions Aconcagua as a far-flung, dangerous locale for testing personal limits of endurance and fortitude. It is in this kind of invented area where Gregory Crouch believes that mountaineers "ride the limits of . . . human potential" (2002, 211). For Crouch, and those many others who have written about it, mountaineering has been defined as a physical and spiritual quest to go beyond the possible, to challenge whims of fate, and to defy peril. This notion is commonly interpreted visually in magazines, catalogs, pictures, and websites through the juxtaposition of the physical magnificence of the mountain to the fragile and diminutive human form. Postcards, pamphlets, and adventure agency websites abound of Aconcagua depicted in such a fashion: that solitary (masculine) figure looking out toward the horizon or perched perilously on a steep grade. These images project the mountain as a proving ground, a blank stage, if you will, to "make great history, to try to be magnificent or seriously romantic" as Luis Jait envisions mountaineering on Aconcagua (2004, 14).

The magnificence of self that Jait would realize draws from a romantic reading of nature as sublime and awe-inspiring, wherein the subjectivity that beholds and experiences this wonder is transformed. What constructs Jait's "seriously romantic self" is the imposing Aconcagua landscape that creates in him a newfound affinity for the notions of freedom, challenge, danger, courage, and conquest that underlie the concept of mountaineering adventure. Crouch's pronouncement that in the mountain "our lives are victories, for we do not live like slaves" (2002, 211) is the fundamental mantra of this kind of sentiment that harkens back to a romantic conceptualization of mountaineering, one that still drives the fantasy of contemporary mountain adventurers. It presupposes the illusive and seductive power of absolute freedom and the exertion of individual will, an important narrative trope of mountaineering gleaned from the tales and feats of the earliest explorers. According to Houston's (2006) reading of the "old school" of mountaineering of the 1950s that held "a reverence for the majesty and remoteness, the setting and the wildness of it all," even in the mid-twentieth-century there was still the assumption that the solitary grandeur of the mountains served as a proving ground for self-transformation (153). These are the kinds of traditional and romantic narrations of mountaineering—as the actualization of the independent spirit in communion with the majestic wildness of the mountains—that contemporary publicity images of Aconcagua especially invoke.

Dreams versus Practice

The expression of independence and boldness of spirit to meet and master the unforeseen obstacles of mountain ascent does not always translate into the actual experience that most international climbers have on Aconcagua. In a Mendocino-guided open expedition, one that is prescheduled and programmed by the service-providing agency and that includes participants from all over the world, the time, food, activities, body, and gear of the mountaineering client are supervised and constrained by the agency's guides, the schedules of the support teams, and the time limit of the park entrance permit. Private groups who make the trek alone or those who hire Mendocino guides still find their schedule contingent on the time and service restrictions that the agency sets and on the supervisory roles of the guides, park rangers, and doctors. Those international expeditions that bring along their own guides also follow this same kind of preorganized plan set up in advance by their home agencies. Once in the park, they too must conform to the controls and checks of the park's regulatory bodies, as well as to the schedules and restrictions set by the providers of those services they hire locally (generally mules and porters). All entrants are under a time constraint of twenty days, which is set by the park. If additional time on the mountain is desired, a second twenty-day permit must be purchased.

At the first expedition meeting in Mendoza, the guide does a mandatory check of clothing and equipment and determines if the gear meets the required standards. Most Mendocino agencies provide a list of necessary apparel, technical gear, documentation, a map of the route, a description of the expedition and timeline, and even training suggestions on their websites that potential clients are urged to review before booking the trip. If needed, guides will later lead group members to one of several local sporting goods stores to either rent or buy the materials they need. During this first briefing session, usually held in a room, lobby, or bar of a local hotel, the guides detail the expedition schedule, discuss the use of gear, and answer client questions. Houston (2006, 153) and Beedie (2003, 206) believe that this reliance on packaged information, descriptions, lists, brochures, and maps to prepare beforehand is the principal way in the current mountaineering scene that a sense of anticipation and adventure is created. Houston cites this phenomenon as one of the major differences that today's mountaineering has with the old school, which preferred to distance itself from these "trappings of civilization" and the allure of technological advances that agencies use to market their expeditions (2006, 153).

If adventure on Aconcagua expeditions relies on imagining adventure through anticipation, the sense of team that Houston sees as defining old-school mountaineering (2006, 153) now depends on artificially constructing a group identity among clients of differing nationalities and ages who have just met. Mendocino guides nurture a sense of teamwork from the first by doing all the informational and administrative tasks together. Generally, expedition members spend the night in Mendoza in the same hotel, sometimes as roommates, and the following morning go as a group to buy the entrance permits in downtown Mendoza, at the Ministry of Tourism building on the main street, San Martín. Clients are then transported to the staging areas of Penitentes, Los Puquios, or Puente del Inca (2,700 meters). There the guides supervise the team members in the separating and repacking of the gear destined for the mules and the gear for their personal carry. The afternoon at the staging area is free for climbers to take short walks, to visit the Puente del Inca site, which consists of the natural bridge over the Mendoza River and the ruins of the Puente del Inca hotel, or to tour the Cementerio de los Andinistas. After spending the night at the staging area, the expedition begins the following morning. On the most-traveled Normal Route, all expeditions must enter at Horcones

Figure 7.1. This sign in Aconcagua Provincial Park marks the entrance into the trekking and mountaineering areas and the trailhead to Plaza de Mulas. The South Face is visible in the distance.

and register at the park's ranger station. At the park the entrance date and permit number are recorded and each expeditioner receives a numbered trash bag for personal litter and waste that must be returned by them or by their agency on the day of their exit.

Expeditioners, or clients, as they are called by the guides, all check in at each park station on the route (Horcones, Confluencia, Plaza de Mulas, and Nido de Cóndores) and are all asked to see the doctors at the last three camps to have their blood pressure and their oxygenation percentages noted. Those clients on Mendocino-led expeditions are required to do so by their guides. Individuals or groups without local guides are often remiss about visiting the doctors, although the doctors and park rangers, on their walks through the camps, do actively try to recruit those mountaineers who have not reported for checks. Doctors may recommend to the park rangers that clients not be permitted to ascend, or should be evacuated, according to the results of the check-ups. Usually a person is required to have an 80 percent oxygenation level at Plaza de Mulas in order to be cleared to continue higher.

The expeditionary members eat the meals prepared for them at the same time, use specific assigned agency-controlled toilet facilities at lower camps, make their high camps in the same places, and can mail a letter, make a phone call, send an email, or shop for souvenirs at the makeshift *shopping* (mall) from Mulas. The North, or Normal, Route as romantic exploration has become a facsimile, a simulation, a touristic and hyper-real version of the Swiss guide Matthias Zürbriggen's arduous and solitary claim of the first summit in 1897. There is, then, a disconnect between the imagination of adventure stemming from early mountaineering narratives, romantic notions, and contemporary publicity, and the present-day planning and practice of mountaineering on the North Route of Aconcagua.

As a social construct, there is a general understanding of adventure as an activity that entails an intense engagement with, or heightened emotional response to, an experience outside the routine of daily life that has personal significance for the adventurer. For cultural theorists it is the manner of both experiencing and understanding the activity that have been seen to be crucial in identifying its adventure-ness. According to Gordon (2006), one's awareness of danger and the freedom to challenge it are fundamental elements of an adventure (4–5). Gordon echoes Georg Simmel (1972), who, in his 1911 seminal essay "The Adventurer," argued that an adventure, while taking place outside the routine of life holds meaning for it, and that it is defined by the subject's capacity to freely accept ambiguity and the unknown while taking definitive action. Simmel summarized this kind of experiencing of the autonomous synthesizing of chance/necessity, activity/passivity, certainty/uncertainty, as an adventure.

The ability to work out Simmel's oppositions freely, for most expeditioners on the Normal Route, is severely limited by the presence and actions of the guides and by the restrictions and regulations of the park. In this sense their adventure-ness is subordinate to those others who make the decisions and take the responsibility of negotiating those dualities for them. From this perspective, Aconcagua mountaineering on the Normal Route crosses over into that hybrid zone of adventure tourism where someone else structures and defines the experience (Gordon 2006, 7). This lack of independence and initiative, or deference to the will of another, prevents the experiencing of "real" adventure and is one of the underlying assumptions in much of the criticism surrounding Dick Bass's being led up Everest to be the first to complete the Seven Summits Route. Bass's financial ability to pay someone to lessen his opportunities for dealing with Simmel's oppositions, but heighten his chance of summiting, corrupts his experience of "authentic" adventure. His money buys the appearance of adventure but not the "true" feeling of it. "Those that buy their way to the top are, by implication, 'impure' and unworthy. If the means by which climbers undertake the summit is somehow 'corrupt,' then meaning is lost" (Houston 2006, 158).

In light of its history one would be hard put to think about mountaineering adventure in any sort of egalitarian terms. Mountaineering adventure already holds within itself the legacy of imperialism and modernist hierarchies concerning nation, class, and gender. So most international clients, Anglo-Europeans and especially North Americans, who are the majority, who hire a local Mendocino guide, have already turned the North-South historical hierarchy of mountaineering on its head. Their subordinate experience of adventure on Simmel's terms is what Bayers (2003) sees in contemporary Himalayan mountaineering as the "postmodern adventurous" where "masculinity is no longer construed as 'naturally virile,' nor . . . particularly heroic" but rather as a "decentered postmodern masculinity feminized by dependence on a guide or Sherpa" (128). Nevertheless, commodified and feminized postmodern adventure still harbors within itself the traces of its imperial history. It is this conflict between practice and memory that is navigated along the Normal Route to base camp.

The problematic of contemporary mountain adventure is doubled for women if traditional understandings are held as standards. Simmel, as a product of his time and place, naturalizes adventure as masculine by suggesting that women's "naturally" passive nature precludes them from "true" experience (1972, 195). Within this scheme and out of the legacy of mountaineering as a masculine competition (Ortner 1999; Bayers 2003), both money and gender then are real complications for experiencing mountaineering adventure as it has been dreamed by many who eventually make their way to Aconcagua.

The push and pull between a traditional understanding of mountain adventure and the invasive presence of socializing practices and structures is negotiated both discursively and materially throughout the course of the expedition. The first day for climbers accessing the North Route is a three- or four-hour trek from the park entrance in Horcones to the camp at Confluencia, where they will usually spend two nights. After spending the first night in Confluencia, the following morning guides usually lead the group on a day hike (approximately seven hours from start to finish) to view the South Face, an ascent of 900 meters that helps acclimatization. From a spot called El Mirador, expeditions eat lunch and rest for about an hour (see fig. I.3). Here, guides frequently discuss the history of the South Face, Aconcagua's most dangerous and most technical ascent. They usually mention the base camp, Plaza Francia, named for the expedition that made the first summit (a French team in 1954), Reinhold Messner's feats, the accomplishments of the Generation of the 80s, and other kinds of records on the southern wall.

Discursive control of the contact zone that is formed daily at El Mirador is in the hands of the Mendocinos, albeit predominantly in the default language of international mixed expeditions, which is English. This contact zone is forged within a folkloric mode, as it is steeped in oral tradition and performativity, over and against technology. At El Mirador, guides function as modern-day troubadours, entertaining and informing their clients who gather around them and listen attentively, as they tell their stories and answer questions about the history of the South Face and Aconcagua. Sometimes the guides stand and point to distant areas on the South Face as they narrate, commanding the attention of the expeditioners. The telling of the histories and stories of the South Face serve as a performative act that marks the knowledge, rank, and authority of the guides.

Equally as important as the narrative performances of the guides is the visual cue, or backdrop, the view of the South Face itself, which sets the stage for the performance. As the expeditioners listen, they engage in a contemplative act, in which nature, the massive wall of the South Face, serves as spectacle. Mountaineering history is steeped in romantic notions of nature as the sublime, in which idealized nature "became not only a mirror but an extension of the soul" (Pimentel 2004, 159). And as Luz Aurora Pimentel reminds us, "Direct observation does not mean unmediated perception of reality" (2004, 165); thus, we can argue that the contemplation of the South Face holds within it the historical legacy of mountaineering on Aconcagua that emerged from a nineteenth-century modern system of hierarchical relationships between nations and masculinities, in other words, an Anglo-Eurocentric imagined geography of high adventure.

Somewhere during these discussions there usually surfaces the story of Brazil's three leading climbers—Mozart Catão, Alexandre Oliveira, and Othon Leonardos—who, in 1998, were hit by an avalanche while attempting a summit of the South Face and subsequently died. The bodies of the Brazilian climbers were irretrievable and are still on the side of the mountain. Depending on the eloquence of the guides and the degree of interest of the clients, the story may be brief or it may include the details of how one of the Brazilians, Othon Leonardos, who suffered two broken legs, reported the accident, described the fate of his two companions, and spoke to his base-camp team for several hours as he waited to die. In other words, while gazing at the most spectacularly steep and glacier-covered view of Aconcagua, discussions of the heroic and tragic dominate. Both discourse and image here are more in line with constructing the kind of mountain adventure that many clients have fantasized. And as a fantasy, unseen but projected against the white, icy screen of the South Face, death, or the specter and illusion of death, is invoked and imagined. It is a death steeped in all the values of conquest and adventure traditionally associated with mountaineering—glorious, sacrificial, patriotic, noble, and otherworldly. As expeditioners sit and eat their lunch they can envision that idea of the adventure that lifts you out of the ordinary, to the extraordinary, to another sacred level. Gordon explains that "adventures are fueled in the imagination but grounded in perceived and real risk, that were it not for the adventure, could be avoided" (2006, 3). The stories of the Brazilian tragedy and other mishaps on the South Face serve to heighten both the perception and the materiality of the dangers of Aconcagua and thus confirm the expedition's location well within the realm of adventure.

This memory of heroic adventure held on the South Face that the guides invoke for their clients serves as a counterweight to the image of purveyors of safety and knowledge that marketing practices bestow on the guides. Adventure is most commonly marketed, according to Catherine Palmer, through a discourse of extremity that characterizes guides as "fearless adventurers, capable of meeting any challenge" but that also "runs the line that anyone can do it" (2002, 329). In other words, by minimizing the danger of a traditionally high-risk activity, you maximize the market. These oppositional discourses of marketing and the stories told at El Mirador are illustrative of a historical ambivalence to risk taking illustrated by both its glorification and attempts to eliminate it (Davidson 2008; Beedie and Bourne 2005). Certainly the imagined risk invoked in the expeditions by their viewing of the South Face contrasts with the actual routine practices of the North Route expeditions and the atmosphere of the camp where they will return to spend their second night at Confluencia.

Women Reign

Estamos acá porque queremos tocar el cielo, como dice la canción.
(We're here because we want to touch heaven, as the song says.)
—CONFLUENCIA CAMP WORKER (VILLAFAÑE 2006)

Confluencia has been labeled the "kingdom where women rule" for it is primarily women who run the base-camp operations there (Villafañe 2006). It is the first stop on the Normal Route and the route to the South Face, and it takes its name from its original location at the confluence of the Superior and Inferior Horcones Rivers. This first location was moved for the 2001–2 season for ecological reasons, when the increase in numbers of mountaineers at the camp threatened the destruction of its several ecosystems. (The park has registered sixty species of birds and mammals, such as the gray fox and guanacos.) The second location, on higher terrain on the opposite bank, was soon found to be in a precarious situation when, during the 2003–4 season, glacier movements threatened to flood the area. The third Confluencia sits on the plain well above the rivers and has proven to be the most accessible and best suited for improvements in sanitation and waste disposal. The lower altitude of Confluencia (3,300 meters) also translates to a lower degree of mountain adventure. It's "safer" for women and more appropriate for receiving an influx of new kinds of travelers, trekkers, and day tourists, in addition to the andinistas stopping over before making their way higher. While the third Confluencia no longer marks the joining of the two rivers, it now signals a different mountain mix: a confluence of tourists and mountaineers under the auspices of feminine control.

Confluencia is the overnight rest stop for many who enter the park as a one-day or three-day trek, and it has become a very popular destination. The new location for entrance permits to the park has been moved to downtown Mendoza, on the ground floor of the Turismo building, in the heart of the city center and the tourist district, at Calle San Martín and

Sarmiento. This optimal site for publicity offers the park to tourists right off the street who may have had no intention of visiting the mountain area but who are intrigued by the possibility of hiking into the park of the highest mountain in the Americas and spending the night. Trekkers, those who do not intend to attempt the summit, have shown the greatest increase in admissions to the Provincial Park in recent years.[1] And, interestingly, Argentines form the greatest percentage of trekkers, while approximately 80–90 percent of those who come to summit have been foreign nationals.[2] Access to Confluencia is relatively easy and recent additions to accommodation options to the camp have made it possible for tourists and locals to spend time there without any backpacking equipment. Aconcagua-Xtrem set up its dome in Confluencia and fully stocked it with cots and blankets for the unequipped. The atmosphere in Confluencia is generally more relaxed than in Mulas. The mix of tourists and andinistas, the lower altitude, vegetation, small mountain flowers, bird songs, and flush toilets make Confluencia more comfortable and more festive.

As the "little sister" of Mulas, Confluencia combines general tourism with mountaineering and has become a site that is controlled primarily by women as camp managers, although local institutional authority figures, park rangers, doctors, and guides are almost entirely male. While both men and women work at the campsites in Mulas, few men work in the same positions in Confluencia. It has been designated in practice and by the local media as a feminine space, subordinate to Mulas in altitude, in its degree of risk and difficulty of access, and in its hybrid tourism-mountaineering nature. In this sense it can be seen as a zone of "feminized" and postmodern adventure.

At every turn, women's participation in mountaineering adventure, this would-be game of masculinity, is a prickly, complicated matter. If we go back to Ortner's interpretation of mountaineering as a game of defining the masculine self, it seems fitting, or almost overdetermined, that Viagra, a drug that increases male potency, would also be found to benefit mountaineers' performance at altitude. It is, after all, the heterosexual dynamic of the erotic that Simmel uses as supreme metaphor to explain how adventure functions. Simmel argues that it is in the erotic relationship where adventure is most easily delineated by those syntheses of forces that "can, perhaps, be found only in the man" (1972, 195). However, Mendocino women's adventure on the mountain cannot be taken as simply facilitating a quest, symbolic or real, for erotic fulfillment at altitude. Although I have been privy to gossip about some of the romantic liaisons in the base camps, infidelities, as well as proposals of marriage, I have found that

Mendocino women understand their mountaineering adventures especially as the travails of managing the modern and orderly industry that Mendoza is striving to produce. Their understandings and experiencing of Aconcagua suggest that as a social construct mountain adventure mutates and reformulates itself according to the social constraints and desires of the subjectivities experiencing it.

It was in Confluencia where I first heard women openly debate their presence and sense of adventure in Aconcagua mountaineering. On my second trip to base camp, I spent an evening listening to Chilean women working as mountain guides (on Aconcagua at that time with an expedition) and Mendocino women with guiding credentials, but working in cook tents, speak at length about women's roles on the mountain. The Argentine women reported that they felt that Mendocinas' emphasis on fashion, flirting, and modesty made them less likely to become interested in mountaineering and that foreign women were more practical in their approach to the mountain. While the Chileans reported that they had found little difference between men's work and women's work in the labors of guiding, the Argentine women noted clear differences in employment practices. Work on the mountain was indeed available to them, but it was specifically designated to campsite management. However, the Mendocinas were quick to highlight the high degree of responsibility and the complexity and difficulty of their jobs, as well as the positive support from the men working with them. They also noted the respect and admiration they felt from friends and families in Mendoza for their daring to work on Aconcagua. In other words, they recognized the danger and risk of their activities and felt proud of themselves for freely entering into them. In this sense, Argentine women believe themselves to be both adventurous and privileged to take part in the overall project of mountaineering on Aconcagua, even though they do not fully participate in what would be deemed the more traditionally "adventurous" activities, like guiding. As one Confluencia worker reported in a *Los Andes* article in 2006, "Es un trabajo redituable, porque no cualquiera se banca estar en medio de la montaña, sin medios de comunicación ni comodidades" (it's a rewarding job, because not everyone can stand being in the middle of the mountains without means of communication or comforts) (Villafañe 2006). The women of Confluencia hold an elite and exclusive position, one that they consider adventurous, especially when compared to the routine of daily life in the urban capital of Mendoza and the proclivities of what they deem the "typical" Mendocina. However, their adventure is still a restrictive one limited by the gender-based roles applied to them in the park that do not reflect the freedom of movement of international women mountaineers coming to Aconcagua either to summit or to guide. Nevertheless, while "this feminization of adventure, in terms of [Mendocino] women's activities on Aconcagua, may still tend to follow patriarchal patterns of gender-based territories and labor, . . . it also, paradoxically, disputes a single definition of adventure grounded in the competition for masculine supremacy" (Logan 2006, 177).

Confluencia to Plaza de Mulas

¿Cuándo subís? ¿Cuándo bajás? (When are you going up? When are you going down?)

—TRADITIONAL MENDOCINO GREETINGS ON ACONCAGUA

After two nights in Confluencia the group makes its way to base camp at Plaza de Mulas, approximately an eight-hour march with a 1,000-meter altitude gain. After crossing the bridge over the Inferior Horcones River and making a short ascent, expeditioners follow the trail to the Playa Ancha, that high plain bounded on both sides by mountains that the Bass and Taplin expeditions of 1983 and 1990, respectively, referred to as "Afghanistan." It is perhaps the lack of vegetation and birds that mark the desolation of Playa Ancha that would spur the imagination, but now, in the twenty-first century, not necessarily the absence of people.[3]

On an open expedition, Mendocino guides regulate the pace of the expedition according to their experience with acclimatization and their knowledge of the route, which is the most strenuous at the very end of the day when climbers are already tired. Guides closely monitor their clients along the route because some expeditioners try to hide symptoms of altitude sickness. Guides tend to be proactive in safeguarding the health of the members of their group by constantly reminding expeditioners to drink and drink again, by making sure the group takes the scheduled breaks, and by setting a steady, moderate rhythm.

There is really only one route to follow from Confluencia through the Horcones Valley to Plaza de Mulas. While groups may either stay closer to the river or follow a trail a bit farther to the right that skirts the mountain, it is the same route that all expeditions and arrieros use to approach Playa Ancha. On entering Playa Ancha, teams may spread out, but if different groups are ascending they are usually within eyesight of each other for the nearly three hours that it takes to cross the river plain. Once Playa Ancha ends, some parts of the trail become very winding and narrow, affording only single-file progress and faster groups disappear to reappear in the distance as the day goes on.

Within this expeditionary grid, timepieces are not needed to gauge the hour. The movements across the plain and up and down the mountain mark the day. Arrieros have a specific schedule to follow in transporting expedition materials and foodstuffs to and from base camp. They ascend to Mulas at dawn with equipment and supplies and start their descent from Mulas with equipment and trash in the early afternoon. The helicopter, if the weather permits, makes its runs to Confluencia and Mulas in the early morning, and it tends not to fly as much in the afternoon because of wind currents and atmospheric conditions. The helicopter transports the rotation teams of the park rangers, doctors, and the rescue squad. It also flies in provisions to service agencies who have contracted its service, and it flies out trash and biological refuse. It is also essential in evacuating climbers who need immediate medical attention beyond the base-camp facilities. Expeditions that descend from Mulas generally cross with those ascending from Confluencia at lunchtime or shortly thereafter.

Guides can easily assess the progress of the group based on when and where they intersect with these other flows of people, materials, machinery, and mules. Besides time and the status of the expedition, guides often exchange information, gossip, weather reports, and news with the arrieros and the other guides they meet going up or coming down, especially if they are approaching from opposite directions. Although Mendocino-guided expeditions all carry radios, communication on the trek from Confluencia and Mulas is generally through the reading of their position on the space-time grids that chart currents of movement on the mountainside itself or through those points of intersection where the different flows of climbers, materials, and arrieros meet.

All Mendocino-led expeditions—in fact, all expeditions in general—tend to make the same rest stops. The first is at Piedra Grande, after the ascent from Confluencia and the trek to the mouth of Playa Ancha. Lunch is usually taken at Ibañez, at the end of Playa Ancha, after crossing the river, which may mean several crossings depending on the water flow. Two hours later (depending on the pace of the group), there is another rest at Colombia, before attempting the Cuesta Brava, the portion of the route with the steepest grade and where most of the 1,000-meter altitude gain from Confluencia to Mulas takes place. From the top of the Cuesta Brava it is a short 15–30 minute trek to Mulas. (Those expeditions staying in the Hotel Refugio Plaza de Mulas start the ascent of Cuesta Brava and then veer to the left, up the Cuesta Amarilla that leads directly to the Refugio.)

It is especially on this part of the expedition, from Confluencia to Mulas, when team members and guides begin to form opinions about the expedition, the other members, and their own performances. There is often a great deal of jostling for position and authority among the group as it moves to base camp. Those with more experience, as well as those in better physical shape, often compete to set the pace and rhythm of the trek. Some vie to always be next to the lead guide, some try to outpace the guide, and others race each other across Playa Ancha; no one wants to be last. In this testosterone-inspired competition, some members have been known to complain when the guides require breaks at Piedra Grande and at Ibáñez. The masculine nature of the competition is undeniable and with it comes the assumption that women, if there are any in the group, will be slower, bring up the rear, and not be engaged in the game of "who will be first." This is not always the case, of course. In 2006 one Mendocino guide mentioned to me that in making his way to Mulas with a group of eight very tall, strapping gringos (both Americans and Europeans; "gringo" is often used in Argentina to denote foreigner) to his surprise and delight he found that his two strongest members were petite women. His degree of surprise at feminine strength underscores the assumed naturalness of the masculine nature of the mountaineering project.

Although this part of the expedition is not technically difficult, it is arduous and dependent on the climber's process of acclimatization. For those unaccustomed to altitude or to the rigors of hiking, it can be difficult and even deadly. I have seen expeditions take more than thirteen hours from Confluencia to Mulas, on what is generally done in seven to nine hours, because of persons whose fitness levels put the whole expedition at risk. As Aconcagua is technically and economically "easy," some people think that it must not be very physically challenging, and many do not prepare as they should. Johnston and Edwards argued in 1994 that the commodification of mountaineering, with its easier access and reduced levels of risk for novice climbers, could serve to put more people on the mountain and more in harm's way (1994, 464), which is often the case on Aconcagua's Normal Route.

Physical fitness and stamina are not the only determinant elements in a client's capacity to reach Mulas safely on this approach. I have seen guides have to return the fittest of clients back to Confluencia from Playa Ancha because of advanced symptoms of altitude sickness. Although novice climbers assume the problem of altitude will only affect them later, it becomes a problem for many early on. In 2006 a Spanish climber never reached Mulas at all and died at the foot of the Cuesta Brava at Colombia, at about 3,800 meters. Some expeditioners who, in arrogance or ignorance, have rushed to reach base camp, have not hydrated properly, and have paid little attention to suggestions of how to acclimatize, arrive at Mulas and become incapacitated. There are many cases every year where climbers make it to Mulas only to be sent down or evacuated by helicopter or mule the following day. During the time I was on the mountain in the 2005–6 season there were three fatalities (all Europeans) that were not the result of accidents or falls but due to the effects of altitude sickness or underlying physical conditions. One of the complaints that park doctors have is that many novices will rationalize or even lie about their physical conditions or their medications so that they can continue to ascend, which is what authorities believe led to the lone fatality that occurred in 2008. Inexperienced climbers often refuse to believe the severity of altitude's effects on the body, and they will disregard the need to monitor symptoms carefully.

The purchasing of adventure by some inexperienced expeditioners extends beyond its replication in performance (the traveling to an exotic locale, purchasing a guided expedition, and wearing and possessing the right gear) into attempts to replicate adventure biophysically. Guides and park doctors have expressed to me their concern for climbers' health with regard to the rampant self-medication by many climbers who choose to take drugs like Diamox and neglect to inform the park doctors during the checkups. Diamox, or "liquid courage," as one guide sarcastically put it, is a diuretic that helps the body raise its blood oxygenation levels. There is the perception among some guides that many novices who rush to buy an experience also buy this medication as an alternative to the acclimatization process. There is the fear among park doctors and guides that the medication may mask other physical symptoms that could affect clients' health on the mountain. Most Mendocino guides do not take Diamox and believe that with the proper acclimatization program it is not necessary for Aconcagua. But issues of money and time often override the advice of professionals. Many climbers merely want to take all precautions available, but some purchase the help of modern technology and science without making the investment in the time necessary for physical training before the trip and for the acclimatization process on the mountain.

According to many of the Mendocino guides I have spoken with, it is on the Confluencia to Mulas trek where they start to assess their clients' ability to acclimatize, their level of competitiveness, fitness, and the degree to which the expeditioners will accept the authority of the guides. There is sometimes a reluctance by expeditioners to trust their guides. Although I have been assured by guides that this is infrequent, they did bring it up regularly by discussing how it makes the sense of a "team" difficult. Guides interpret this mistrust on language difficulties, expeditioners' inexperience with mountaineering or altitude, or on suppositions made by clients who have previous experience but not under the conditions that Aconcagua presents. (What I have heard numerous times from climbers is that while they believed that Kilimanjaro and Aconcagua would be comparable because of their similar lack of technical difficulty and moderate difference in height, they were amazed, and often dismayed, by how much more demanding Aconcagua was because of wind, climate, and humidity differences just on the approach to base camp.) In a prepackaged and highly controlled adventure activity, such as an open expedition ascent via Aconcagua's Normal Route, it becomes possible that "notions of trust, as well as of risk" break down (Palmer 2002, 330). The commodification of adventure and the manipulation of the discourse of risk through marketing practices that advertise safety and diminish the concept of danger (Palmer 2002) subsequently can also serve to reduce the expeditioners' sense of urgency in following the advice of their guides. A further complicating component in this relationship of power and authority between guide and client on Aconcagua is that entrenched notions of Northern superiority are not always overridden by trust in local qualifications, authority, and knowledge.

There is also, however, the opposite case that occurs in some expeditions when the group becomes ultradependent on guides and elevates them to a "super human" status. Mendocino guides tell me that neither position benefits the cohesiveness of the group and that they work hard to find the right balance. Their formation in the EPGAMT stresses the psychological underpinnings of group behavior, and many of them discuss the necessity of *contención*, or the creation and supporting of a group identity. Gordon (2006) explains that "one of the attractions of adventure has been the camaraderie of the small group," but nowadays the constraints of time and structure no longer foment *communitas*, but rather construct "peg communities," which unite them by a common hook (Gordon 2006, 20). In terms of Aconcagua adventure, this temporary "peg" that connects the group, the desire to summit, is not always strong enough to create real cohesiveness and community. In fact, it often serves as the very factor that divides the group because individual members sometimes resent or rebel against changes to pace and schedule that the guides make to accommodate the slower members of the group. The regulation, observation, and contención of expedition members by the guides are tied to the latter's understanding of the tenuous and contradictory nature of the "peg" that defines the team but that also can divide it, the desire of summiting. However, when that individual desire is expressed as freely exerting one's will within the realm of adventure, it can make it difficult for guides to reign in clients to ensure everyone's safety and to increase the chances for summiting for all.

The regulation of the expedition, which harkens back to the military underpinnings of mountaineering in general, problematizes the experience of adventure in terms of actively navigating the unknown. This is also true of the regularity of the time and route from Confluencia to Mulas that prescribe periods of activity and rest and marks where expeditioners can and cannot tred and camp. This scheduled precision of the expedition exemplifies Beedie's (2003) argument that "the more detailed, planned, and logistically smooth an adventure tourist itinerary becomes, the more removed the experience is from the notion of adventure" (206). Besides providing the relative safety of numbers and schedules and facilitating information exchange, such expeditionary routines also exacerbate problems that are direct consequences of mountaineering's incursion into Aconcagua Provincial Park. Of critical concern on the Normal Route is the ecological damage caused by the intrusion of climbers and mules to the zone. In addition to whatever seeds and contamination that might be spread by the boots and hooves of people and animals, the waste products of both litter the area. Human waste is a real problem in the regularly visited rest areas of Piedra Grande, Ibañez, and Colombia. Yet the park has not sought to ameliorate the situation by providing toilet facilities or strictly enforcing that all waste be packed out of these areas.[4] Other problems that have surged because of the increased numbers and mountaineering movements include international criticism of the treatment of the mules and the noise pollution caused by helicopters.

Movements to and from Mulas narrate time, the status and nature of the expedition, the business and administration of the mountain, ecological issues, animal rights, and gossip. Within the grid is interpolated the discourse of danger. Peril, real or perceived, contradicts the practical and modern nature of the mountaineering enterprise and allows expeditioners to return to their imaginings of adventure. Along this line, it is hard to ignore that the Normal Route is spattered with mule carcasses, the most common *memento mori* of Aconcagua mountaineering. On my way to base camp in 2006 there were three sets of remains. One was lodged by the bridge over the rushing waters of the Horcones River near Confluencia; another lay at the bottom of a small scree slope beyond Playa Ancha;

and a third, which had obviously fallen recently, lay at the bottom of the Cuesta Brava.

In addition to the symbols of risk and death that the unlucky mules provide (one expedition member said the Normal Route should be called "the mule cemetery route"), news of climber deaths reach all expeditions with alarming alacrity. As guides and arrieros meet on the way up or down, they pass on news of accidents, romances, robberies, weather, and summits. The death count is always at the forefront of the updates. Houston reports that in today's mountaineering world, "in climbing as adventure, a brush with death is now expected" (2006, 156). On the Normal Route, except for those with acclimatization problems, it is more a brush with the image and imagination of death through symbols and discourse than the actual encounter with mortality. However, these imaginings serve to provide a sense of "uncertainty and potential for personal harm that generate excitement by setting such undertakings in a context of challenge and adventure" (Beedie 2003, 205).

As a complement to reminders of mountaineering's fatalities, some guides stir the danger pot and invoke the otherworldly idea of mountain adventure by telling stories of the *futre*, a kind of headless horseman who roams the mountain area, or of the *corredor* de Playa Ancha, the "Runner," a gringo dressed in shorts, who approaches climbers walking through Playa Ancha and asks how to get to Confluencia. It is often within this frame that the discovery of the Incan mummy is proudly recounted. The exotic nature and aura of sacrificial ritual and spirituality associated with the mummy add to the dream of adventure.

Guides invoke these stories of danger, death, the mystic, and the supernatural to re-infuse peril and risk back into the Aconcagua expedition. On the one hand, these stories fulfill the expectations of clients about adventure and the exotic, and they counter the diminution of traditional mountaineering adventure caused by the inversion of power and control and the subsequent authority of the "subaltern." On the other hand, the telling of these stories keeps alive folkloric traditions, legends, and tales of the mountain zone. All of these fantastical and mystical tales also tie into the rhetoric of magical realism, perhaps the most common discursive tradition that the world holds of Latin America. Later these stories, facts, and legends find themselves reprinted on clients' websites, blogs, and in expedition stories and books, and these tales certainly form part of the daily conversations of international clients.

Mule skeletons, death reports, ghost stories, and the Incan mummy all counter the regularity and regulations of safety measures and modernity that diminish the ability to experience adventure in the way that many of the expeditioners have imagined it but do not experience on Aconcagua. Certainly, on the march from Confluencia to Mulas expeditioners are not "touching the void,"[5] so to speak. In fact, in an ironic turn of events, it is their very presence as would-be adventurers on the mountains and the infrastructure necessary to support them that will "tame the landscape" (Mathers and Hubbard 2006, 203) and contaminate it with the vestiges and waste of their passage.

Status of Place

Of course the ultimate experience is to climb a virgin peak, where there are no prior standards to guide one.

—SUTTLES (1983, x)

While postcards and website pictures show solitary figures and lonely places, most expeditioners are constantly surrounded by people from their own teams and other expeditions who tend to follow the same schedules. This conflicts with how many in the expedition assume mountain adventure should be played out: that they should be in a pristine, timeless, and unrestricted medium in which to realize their feats of strength, endurance, and glory. However, for many expeditioners that illusion is destroyed by the reality of mountaineering on Aconcagua, in the same way that Norman (2000) describes his first view of Plaza de Mulas: "And if the terrain here was inhospitable in its natural state, the presence of humans made it worse. . . . There were clusters of tents all over base camp and the vivid colors of Mountain Hardware, the North Face, and Marmot looked gaudily out of place in the bleakly monochromatic setting" (218–219). The vacant space of the mountaineering imagination quickly fades as the neon billboard of the Anglo-European mountain gear industry that decorates Plaza de Mulas advertises familiarity, relative comfort, safety, and the look and feel of a community. As a result of the commodification of the mountain that has turned heterogeneous space, defined as freedom of movement and expression, into enclavic space of constraint and convention (Beedie 2003), Plaza de Mulas no longer fits the mountaineering profile of a base camp but instead it acutely conforms to the dictates of the adventure tourism industry that needs to manage and control efficiently larger and larger numbers of adventurers.

Over several years of fieldwork at Plaza de Mulas, I have heard from mountaineers from various countries that while they do enjoy the social nature of Mulas and the expedition as a whole, it really isn't the wilderness experience that they had in mind. One expeditioner who voiced this opinion to me was later diagnosed by base-camp doctors with a severe health condition that might have proved fatal at a higher altitude. For obvious reasons this climber chose to abort his summit attempt. Had he been in the kind of uninhabited, solitary wilderness that he said he would have preferred, he might not have lived to tell about it. Nevertheless, the idea of risk, danger, and challenge is part of what sells mountaineering. At the same time, these elements are exactly what the province tries to minimize in the name of safety.

There are other mountaineering options on Aconcagua and in and around Mendoza for those who prefer a less "social" atmosphere. For this reason, on Aconcagua more and more expeditions are avoiding the Normal Route and the Plaza de Mulas base camp in order to enter through Punta de Vacas. The Polish Glacier Route, the Polish Glacier Traverse, and the Guanacos Route all emanate from there.[6] The Polish Glacier and the Polish Glacier Traverse follow the Relinchos Valley to take an eastern approach to the summit from the base camp at Plaza Argentina. The Polish Glacier is a technical route and not appropriate for novices; the Traverse takes longer than the Normal Route but does not require more mountaineering experience. There are fewer expeditions that take the Punta de Vacas routes, although their numbers have increased dramatically over the last few years. With regard to what expeditioners have labeled "social," in terms of numbers of people, established campsites, and regulatory supervisions, the sociability quotient may be lower, but it is still not that unspoiled landscape of individual freedom that many expect. The province still maintains park rangers at Pampa de Leñas and park rangers and doctors at Plaza Argentina, and service providers have base-camp facilities in place all season long.

To continue to attract climbers seeking the "wilderness" quotient, Aconcagua Park officials have opened up the nonmountaineering, or "area intangible," section of the park for climbers to follow the Guanacos Route, also nontechnical, and agencies like Aconcagua-Express highlight the section's "virginal" terrain: "Our route via the Guanacos valley is a wild and pristine alternative to the heavily traveled routes of the Horcones and Relinchos valleys. Only recently explored, this route promises you freedom from crowds, clean trails and camp areas, breath-taking views of the neighboring peaks and glaciers, and abundant wildlife."[7] There is an extra fee of up to 500 pesos for a permit to follow the Guanacos Route, but conservationists have complained about this breach of the park's supposedly protected areas merely to satisfy the hunger of the mountaineering industry. Although the park may limit access to this route in the future, it has not offered to close it altogether. The lucrative results of its attractiveness to climbers may override the concern of conservationists. This balance between the park's capacity to make money for the province and the need to protect the flora and fauna of the reserve is one of the major and most criticized issues in Mendoza concerning Aconcagua Provincial Park.

Besides Aconcagua, there are other excellent possibilities in Mendoza province and western Argentina that might take some of the pressure off the park. These sites offer more primitive high-altitude mountaineering experiences with no social or safety infrastructure that requires everything to be brought in and out by the mountaineers themselves. Tupungato (6,800 meters), El Plata (6,100 meters), and Maipo (5,800 meters) are in Mendoza province.[8] Mercedario (6,770 meters) is located in the next province to the north, San Juan. Further north are Ojos de Salado (6,865 meters) on the border with Chile, Pissis (6,882 meters) in Catamarca, and Bonete (6,759) in La Rioja. All of these mountains approximate Aconcagua (6,962) in height, and while local mountaineers may frequent them, the peaks receive relatively little interest from international climbers. Although they might approximate the image of a "virgin" peak, they do not have the notoriety of being the "Roof of the Americas," as does Aconcagua. So despite complaints from some expeditioners on Aconcagua about there being too many people, most would still choose the "Mecca of the mountains of America," as Jait calls it (2004, 33), over unpopulated and "wild" mountains in order to have bragging rights about conquering one of the Seven Summits and the highest peak outside the Himalayas.

Tourism or Adventure

No es un lugar de turismo. (This is not a tourist site.)

—LUIS JAIT (2004, 59)

The expeditionary group usually spends three to four nights in Mulas for acclimatization purposes. They have two to three days of rest and scheduled activities, such as carrying gear to a higher camp or practicing with crampons. The expeditioners also have free time between the scheduled meals to explore the camp on their own. A typical timeline for ascent after the acclimatization period at Mulas is to spend four nights, divided between three higher camps: one at Canada, two at Nido de Cóndores, and one at Berlin or Cólera.[9] The attempt at the summit is usually made on the fifth day. There are two extra days factored in for adverse weather, but generally this still means that each expedition has only one summit attempt, not two. Expeditioners may wait an extra day for the weather to clear, but normally they will not try a second summit if the first was turned back because of weather. The return from the summit may require another night at one of the high camps, usually Nido (or Berlin), but if possible, guides prefer to return the expedition directly to Mulas for the night. Regardless of a descent night in Nido, all expeditions returning from the high camps have a night in Mulas to regroup, celebrate, or commiserate on the way back. The following morning the team walks out to Horcones.

In terms of the adventure of mountaineering, the North Route is not a great technical challenge. In addition, the schedule and practices of the guided expeditions and park regulations have made a concerted effort to reduce the elements of chance and uncertainty. In fact, the number of deaths on Aconcagua continued to fall each year until 2009 when there were extreme weather conditions during the first two months of the season. In the first decade of the twenty-first century, the largest number of fatalities during a climbing season was six. This first occurred in 2000. There were three deaths respectively in 2004, in 2005, and in 2006. In 2007 there were two; in 2008 only one; then in 2009 there were again six. There was one in 2010; and in 2011 there were five. There is always great risk involved at such altitude and the threat of pulmonary and cerebral edema is real for everyone, as is exhaustion, frostbite, and the possibility of accidents or falls. And despite its being a walk-up, Aconcagua's North Face regularly takes its fatal toll from among both experienced and novice climbers.

There is a very generalized and often voiced critique of the adventure industry on Aconcagua in the way in which the mountain is advertised as accessible and convenient to nonmountaineering clientele. Because the Normal Route is not a technical one, for some like Richard Mitchell, who has written about the social aspects of mountaineering, it would not even be classified as mountaineering because of this lack of a technical component (1983, 1). *Seven Summits* calls it an easy (perhaps too easy) training ground for Everest (Bass et al. 1986, 34), and a more recent Aconcagua mountaineering guide book is entitled *Aconcagua: Highest Trek in the World* (Ryan 2004). Even local newspapers have reported on the negative reception by many in Plaza de Mulas of the practices of adventure agencies that capitalize on those clients who buy a trekking package and make their way to base camp as a tourist excursion, to eat on fine china, to go shopping, and to enjoy late disco nights at "Geo-Trek" that disturb the "serious"

Figure 7.2. This "pub" is one of the dining and socializing options at Plaza de Mulas.

climbers. At the heart of this criticism is the fact that the exclusive nature of mountain climbing on Aconcagua has been opened by the adventure tourism industry to amateurs who can afford to buy "travel-adventure-heroic" status and enter the ranks of the mountain elite through simple consumerism—the purchase of an expedition package and gear.

Gear

For some, mountaineering symbolizes certain quintessential human qualities—plucky striving and courage in the face of adversity and danger; achievement, conquest, self-actualization.

—MITCHELL (1983, 2)

In his study of mountaineering as a social construct, Mitchell tells us that "the seven components of mountaineering endeavors are: planning, equipment, companions, conditioning, travel, technical climbing, talk and debriefing" (1983, 1). Gear, then, second on Mitchell's list, is an essential element in the nature of mountaineering. Accordingly, the acquisition of gear and its display contribute to the social meanings conferred to the activity. Among those would be connotations of adventure, status, and membership in an exclusive group.

The exclusivity of mountaineering is represented by both the cost of equipment and clothing and its specificity, in terms of where it can be bought and its designated use. In discussing his preparation in 1990 for Aconcagua, Jait (2004) describes his difficulty in finding the appropriate gear in Mendoza. He ordered some things from the United States, traveled to a factory in San Juan, and bought other items from andinistas returning from the mountain. Although access is easier today, because there are several mountain adventure-sporting goods stores in Mendoza, the specialized nature of this kind of store and the high cost of its merchandise (this is true in the northern hemisphere as well) imply a special status to those who can afford to buy in these shops and, it is assumed, know how to use its products.

The cachet of gear is especially increased by the prestige of those labels that connote the uniqueness of its technologically advanced and costly materials designated for the extraordinary, not for the everyday. Jait explains that "Las marcas Ansilta y Patagonia no son de las que se usan a diario" (Ansilta and Patagonia are not brands for daily use) (2004, 39). The labels he mentions are the top Argentine maker of adventure wear,

Ansilta, and one of the top US producers, Patagonia. Owning these labels implies a sense of superior national and transnational knowledge of mountaineering, and by extension, engages the underlying ideological notions of the sport found in the playing out of heroic imperial masculinity (Bayers 2003) and modernity (Ortner 1999). It also serves as a visible sign of belonging to an elite group. Once he finds himself on the mountain, Jait offers a corporeal reading of mountaineering identity: "Ya soy uno más de los de allí. He usado mi equipo" (Now I'm one more of those from (up) there. I've used my gear) (2004, 59). This is a body apparently unmarked by nation, gender, race, ethnicity (although all these are implied by the very nature of mountaineering), or even skill level. Of the identifying signifiers that the wearing and using of mountaineering gear carries (which are many in terms of the above-mentioned categories, First World–Third World production, distribution and profit relationships, globalization and nationalism), one of the most distinctive is the commodification and performance of adventure. It is this "degradation," or externalization, of the mountain experience that Suttles warns against: "Mountaineering is also subject to a substantial degree of commercialization with clothing, equipment, and color slides serving to advertise products as well as awe the masses. Its own stratification system and audience appeal threaten to turn it into only a performance, something done rather than felt" (1983, x).

The performativity of the mountaineering experience undermines the idea of adventure as a test of personal limits. Ownership of gear now competes with characteristics of individual strength and will, heroism, and sacrifice that formerly were the exclusive means to mountaineering status. A telling story that I have heard from at least four different sources concerns a man from Buenos Aires who was found by two Mendocino guides; he was collapsed by the trailside on the way to Confluencia (a four-hour and not especially demanding trek). Reportedly, his first words to the guides offering him help were "¿Por qué esto me pasa a mí si tengo todo el equipo?" (Why is this happening to me if I have all the gear?). In holding this account up to mirthful ridicule, local guides illustrate their disfavor with the way that Aconcagua is being sold, and they justify their disapproval by using the tale of the hapless porteño to punctuate, as does Beedie (2003), the safety risks involved in opening up the adventure market to those well equipped, but ill-trained, for the rigors of the mountain.[10]

I surmise that an outgrowth of regional tensions also underlies the critical attitude found in the gleeful relish that the Mendocino guides took in reporting the absurdity of the porteño's belief that his gear would carry him up the mountain, and not the other way around. Within the traditional valuing of mountaineering as a First World modern practice, the presence of weekend hikers and base-camp groupies, the majority of whom are Argentines, who only reach Confluencia (that kingdom of women), places the national image of Argentina on a lower rung in the international hierarchy of climbing as it is traditionally understood. In other words, national Argentine expeditioners are only trekkers, while international expeditioners come to climb or summit, a more challenging and more prestigious endeavor. However, national here translates to porteños, and Mendocinos, who tend to distance themselves at every turn from Buenos Aires' reflection, reject their inclusion in this grouping. Their work as mountain guides for those expeditions headed to the summit, as well as their efforts in supporting such expeditions, which are generally international, at base camp, make them members of this more prestigious mountaineering category. Their privilege contrasts with the status of other Argentines, predominantly porteños, and reflects the capital-provincial tensions that exist on a more general level. One Mendocino guide explained that relationships with other Argentines on Aconcagua, those from places like San Juan, Catamarca, Jujuy, or Rio Negro were much less conflictive than those with porteños, "as the provinces understand each other better." This illustrates again how, on Aconcagua, Mendoza's ties to international interests and its sense of itself within Argentina tend to override concepts of nation based on nineteenth- and twentieth-century understandings of a Buenos Aires–dominant nationhood.

I do not want to insinuate with the story of the porteño that the brands, fashions, and labels of gear hold no merit or prestige on the mountain except among the "uninitiated." The rescue squad has told me of the frustration they feel when seeing people enter Mulas "in cowboy boots and denim jackets," sure that they were looking at future "clients" for rescue. The fashions and trends of clothing and gear certainly do hold sway in assigning status and also serve to demonstrate the underlying consumerism of mountaineering that reinforces Anglo-European hegemony in the sport as the climbing gear market is dominated by initiatives from the northern hemisphere.

The US-based status brands of mountaineering are not just used by North American climbers, but by many international expeditioners as well. Many of the local Mendocino service-providing agencies regularly use North Face tents for all the clients on their expeditions. The North Face, Mountain Hardware, Columbia, Black Diamond, and Patagonia visibly dominate the bodies and the topography of Aconcagua. This point was never more clearly made to me than during a New Year's Eve celebration at the Hotel Refugio Plaza de Mulas. That evening in the dining hall there were representatives of six of the seven continents and mountaineers from at least fifteen different countries. One of the Mendocino guides looked around the room at the similarity of style of the celebrants, cocooned in their down jackets as they toasted with sparkling cider, to pronounce that someone should film the scene for a North Face commercial, because the room was a rainbow of North Face jackets (see fig. 6.1). Indeed, the vast majority of the international climbers at the dinner party, regardless of nationality, age, gender, or ethnicity, were decked out in North Face down jackets. Tellingly, on their website, The North Face explains that the north face of a peak in the northern hemisphere tends to be the coldest, the iciest, and the most difficult.[11] Thus, the reason behind the brand name is self-evident. In the southern hemisphere, however, it is, of course, the south face that is most demanding. Therefore, just the name of the gear is a reminder that the South is still an outsider in the climbing game. Nevertheless, possession of brand-name gear is often seen as the price of admission to this elite winners' circle.

This North-South hierarchy was reiterated in a Sahalie catalog (2006), an outdoor clothing company that has been "getting off the beaten track since 1972," according to the slogan accompanying the company name. In advertising its "Furnace Shirt," Sahalie explains that it was "field-tested on Argentina's Mt. Aconcagua," obviously quite off its regularly beaten track, probably located near that other outdoor clothing kingdom of Patagonia, which is, as they tell us, not quite on the map.[12] Sahalie's commentary reads, "Our Furnace Shirts were warm, comfortable and the envy of our guides and mountain staff! We really had no option but to leave these wonderful garments with our guides . . . the delight on their faces was heartwarming" (2006, 31). Sahalie's "fashioning" of adventure replicates the modern origins of mountaineering where Anglo-European selves sought personal transcendence in those untamed and nonmodern locales far from home where they would be aided by unnamed helpers and servants. Today ownership of the latest and most up-to-date mountain clothing and gear allow Northern expeditioners, who are subordinate to Mendocino guides on the expedition and thus experience a diminished degree of adventure, to reinsert this paradigm and to reestablish their primacy, control, and "natural" position of superiority in the mountaineering endeavor. In leaving their shirts to the "grateful" and delighted guides (2006, 31), the Sahalie expeditioners not so subtlely remind readers that they were the economically superior, as well as the more technologically advanced, members of the expedition. The guides may have taken the responsibilities and the risks associated with the idea of "real" adventure, but their status was now diminished both by their inferior economic standing (already present in the fact that they were being paid by the expeditioners) and their distance from modernity, as their assumed delight in receiving modern adventure fashionwear illustrated.

Debriefs

The performativity of gear-laden bodies on Aconcagua both support and destabilize entrenched notions of North-South hierarchies present in the mountaineering tradition. While a transnational mountaineering subjectivity may be one that embodies a North Face jacket, its fashion statement is still heavily accessorized by the primacy of the First World. Brand names like Ansilta (Argentine) and Doite (Chilean) may ascribe nationality and an elevated mountaineering status to its wearers; however, they still are subordinate to the transnational capital and reputation of the big players, such as Patagonia, The North Face, Black Diamond, and Mountain Hardware, all from the North.

Within the ever-shifting global, local, and national nexus that is Aconcagua, the performativity of gear-laden mountaineering bodies represent its complexity and the multiplicity of its meanings and functions. As mountaineers and the materials they use and bring with them move up and down the mountainside, they narrate the histories of modernity, safety, industry, administration, authority, ecology, gender, and the differing constructions of adventure that come together to characterize Aconcagua mountaineering. In them we see how safety-oriented and social practices of a modern-minded Mendoza mountaineering industry are counterbalanced by romanticized dreams of adventure, solitude, transcendence, and the physical and discursive reminders of the danger and perils of the mountain. Their movements and schedules also reflect women in the Mendocino-based mountaineering project as still primarily a marginalized minority but nevertheless essential to Mendoza's industry and instrumental in revealing the mutable nature of mountaineering adventure.

The reality of Aconcagua is not its stationary location in the central Andes of Mendoza but rather the itineraries and flows of people, capital, and information that trace and traverse it. This fluid and mobile Aconcagua that Mendoza administers shakes up the province, grounded in its traditional sense of history and relationship to the nation, to reposition focus toward the twenty-first-century tourism market and globalization.

CHAPTER EIGHT

Plaza de Mulas

Memory, Musealization, and the Global

La fantasía de vivir en la majestuosidad del Aconcagua se convierte en realidad sin levantarse del sillón. (The fantasy of living in the majesty of Aconcagua is converted into reality without even getting up from your armchair.)

—DESCRIPTION ON THE BACK COVER OF *ACONCAGUA: UNA MANERA DE VIVIR* (GILARDONE 1990)

The Normal Route is the most traveled and least technical way to the summit of Aconcagua, and approximately 80 percent of all expeditioners choose to follow it.[1] On a daily basis it is traversed by adventurers from all over the world who converge for a few days of rest and acclimatization, in Plaza de Mulas, a meeting place for mountain enthusiasts from more than sixty countries. The international nature of Mulas, as it is commonly known, is perhaps epitomized by the way I spent downtime in 2006, playing a Vietnamese card game taught by a Dutch man to me and a group consisting of a Swede, a Finn, a Spaniard, and an Argentine. The international mix of peoples such as this in a place designated as national territory has been characterized in the local Mendoza media as the global nature of Aconcagua. However, the global temperament of the base camp is much more than just this convergence of nationalities. Mulas also functions as a global transportation hub, receiving bodies, materials, and information, and sending out people, goods, and images. As a communications network Mulas is not exclusive to the daily endeavors of mountaineering but also branches out into the business of international media. This became particularly evident to me when, during my first season in Mulas, at every turn, I ran into film crews from Korea, Chile, Japan, and Argentina as they crossed paths and shot footage for their own local TV shows. What may best express the idea of a globalized Aconcagua, however, especially in terms of the time-space compression that has come to characterize the process, is the live action webcam at base camp that allows a worldwide audience to view the daily comings and goings of mountaineers at 4,300 meters of altitude. The webcam and cyber forum at www.aconcaguanow.com.ar function as forms of self-narrative of Mulas that enable expeditioners, friends, families, and interested parties around the world to dialogue in a variety of languages with the Plazamuleros and keep up to date with the daily details of an expedition. No longer is Aconcagua a faraway and distant locale as described by those first European scientist-explorers of the late nineteenth century. Nor is its characterization and significance only available to the nonclimbing public through travel books, expedition journals, and articles in specialized magazines. Today, more so than ever, if you have access to the Internet, you don't even need to leave your home to experience Aconcagua adventure!

Deterritorialized by cyberspace, Aconcagua remains territorially bound to Argentina, controlled and administered by the provincial Mendocino government and adventure tourism industry, and primarily inhabited by international climbers. The global nature of Aconcagua, obviously, is much more than the mere sum of countries represented by its international mountaineers. Globalization on Aconcagua concerns questions of capital, technology, cultural autonomy, ideology, narrative authority, territory, and nation.

The globalization of Aconcagua corresponds to the rise of adventure travel since the 1980s, the commercialization of mountaineering, and the advent and easier access to worldwide communications, all of which have subsequently fostered different kinds of narrativizations of Aconcagua in new media forms. Just as the genre of travel writing both shaped and conveyed the message of European imperial expansion in earlier centuries, these new discourses of Aconcagua hold meaning in their very structure. As Janet Wolff (2000) argues, "the very codes of art and literature, the narrative structures of the text, are part of the ongoing process of the construction of meaning and, hence, of the social world" (171). Therefore, narratives of Aconcagua articulated through cyberspace discourses, via the mountaineering memory constructed by the Hotel Refugio Plaza de Mulas climbers' museum, and by the everyday practices on the mountain all provide meaning themselves for Mulas "society" as they serve to construct the social order of global Aconcagua. Although these alternative new tellings (as opposed to traditional travel and mountaineering narratives) still connect a line back to the discourse of Anglo-European modernist and imperialist projects, they also, at times, counter the elitist and intellectual connotations most often associated with those nineteenth- and early twentieth-century accounts.

Cyber Territories

The highest mountain in the western hemisphere, located in the Andes Mountains of western Argentina, near the border with Chile, coast of Pacific Ocean, Santiago de Chile, incredible people, one of the kind native environment, unique culture.

—THE POLISH ALPINE CLUB (http://expeditions.net.pl/?skin=01&lang=en&sub=aconcagua)

As a tool of marketing and memory practices and emblematic of globalization, cyberspace locates Aconcagua within the same modern romantic topography of tourism publicity that situates it in a borderless global sphere to nonetheless accentuate "natural" understandings of national identities and hierarchies. Alternately, the temporal-spatial conflation of the Internet is analogous to the way that the Cementerio de los Andinistas undoes these "naturalized" hierarchies by juxtaposing and equating various and disconnected subjectivities, narratives, and timelines of mountaineering endeavors. In terms of touristic marketing that would characterize Mendoza as modern, as opposed to the premodern and unexplored domain projected by Northern modernity, the Internet has been perhaps the most important tool for inserting the province and Mendocino-based services into a transnational imaginary. Nonetheless, in general, Mendoza still barely registers in most internationally initiated cyber representations of Aconcagua, which tend to deal with personal histories of expeditions and to rearticulate traditional characterizations of North-South identity politics. The webbed reach of the Internet that takes Aconcagua into the nooks and crannies of homes, cafés, institutions, and iPhones across the globe also tends to leave Mendoza behind.

The scope and range of the Internet can insert this Aconcagua disconnected from Mendoza into other conceptual and cultural realms in which traditional meanings of the mountain may be renegotiated according to its functioning within a particular discursive economy. This was explicitly illustrated to me when the deterritorialized Aconcagua was reterritorialized into North American academia by the show of solidarity and support given to the Ecuadorian climber Santiago Quintero Sylva, via an email message generated by a regional interest group of the Latin American

Studies Association (LASA), a US-based international association, in February 2002. Quintero Sylva, reported to be Ecuador's best extreme climber, ascended Aconcagua's daunting South Face in one day, according to the LASA message: "en medio de condiciones ambientales sumamente adversas a las que se sobrepuso con un enorme valor, . . . y logró la tan ansiada meta, conseguida anteriormente sólo por 3 montañistas a nivel mundial. Esta conquista lo ubicaba ya entre los mejores escaladores extremos del mundo" (in extremely adverse climactic conditions which he overcame with enormous courage, . . . he reached his long sought goal, previously only achieved by three world-class mountaineers. This conquest placed him among the best extreme climbers in the world). In the process, Quintero Sylva suffered frostbite on both feet, and as a result, his parents' letter asking for contributions to help pay for his treatment was forwarded in an act of solidarity by the LASA group to its members. It is Quintero Sylva's Ecuadorian identity, located simultaneously on Aconcagua, within a transnational circle of worldwide climbers, and among Latin Americanists of LASA, and which is constructed through an "ennobling and courageous sacrifice in the face of adversity," that is offered up as validation for the request to LASA's Andean research group. This is problematic, on the one hand, because one can read into the request a fixing of Quintero Sylva's Ecuadorian identity (implicitly understood as indigenous, subaltern, Third World) that would erase all notions of fluidity, ethnicity, and class. On the other hand, by imagining this fixed Ecuadorianess as a disruption of the "universalized" romantic notion of the climber-hero, the letter also plays on the assumption of the request as an act of postcolonial resistance to Anglo-European hegemony. This notion legitimizes the petition for donations as something more than collective compassion for a sports accident and registers it as an appropriate plea for academic solidarity. It is ultimately a First World valuing of mountaineering on Aconcagua as colonialist project, which an Ecuadorian disrupts and which might validate the LASA group's asking financial support from its members for Quintero Sylva. This reading of mountaineering on Aconcagua stems from the history of mountaineering itself, as well as from the understanding, as Mowforth and Munt (2003) explain it, "[of] the uneven and unequal nature of tourism development . . . [or] the inequality of First World and Third World tourism . . . in which tourism is owned and controlled largely from the First World" (156). This academic, primarily US-based interpretation of Aconcagua ignores the significance of Mendocino governance, its agencies, park rangers, and the rescue squad; the role of Aconcagua mountaineering in Mendocino economics and conservation; and Mendoza's own heroic climbing history on the South Face that broaden and disrupt the context in which LASA's plea locates the Ecuadorian hero and Aconcagua. Tellingly, there was no parallel movement of solidarity by LASA to help better equip and compensate the notoriously underpaid and underequipped protagonists of the Mendocino Patrulla de Rescate (or rescue squad) and the Mendoza park rangers who were all called on to evacuate the Ecuadorian climber when he chose to put himself and them in danger by climbing "in extremely adverse climactic conditions."

Cyber Reality

¡Visc el CEP y visc Catalunya! (Long live CEP and long live Catalonia!)

—MESSAGE BOARD (www.aconcaguanow.com)

The erasure of Mendoza from Aconcagua and Aconcagua from its local social, political, and economic context is common. Indeed, the dislocation of Aconcagua is, perhaps, its most salient global representation, by academics, interest groups, individual climbing narratives, and the mass media. A case in point was the multimedia program *El cim*, a Catalan TV-3 reality show from Barcelona, Spain. In September 2002 six participants, with no prior mountaineering experience, were chosen to go to Aconcagua. *El cim*, which constructed a totally controlled space for the participants providing training, guides, and all expenses, set up no other competitive situations or prize other than the opportunity to summit Aconcagua. Every night Catalunya's TV-3 gave an update on TV, and there were Internet video clips, Internet narrative updates, an online photo gallery, and an online discussion forum.

In the *El cim* forum, the Internet conversations constructed the Catalan hero explorer in the tradition of the imperialistic tendencies of exploration narratives and displaced the formation of Catalan identity to the cyber territory of Aconcagua where national and regional identity politics were to be worked out. Discussion participants highlighted how the Catalan flag and Catalan bodies, carriers of Catalan identity on the summit, symbolized a moment of pride and national Catalan achievement (metaphorical conquest), especially within the realm of contemporary Spanish regional autonomous politics. Caren Kaplan (1998) has detailed that traditionally in Western modernity these kinds of discursive constructions of self and nation are displaced to distant nonnational locations (27–64). This displacement stems from the imperialist tradition in mountaineering that allows Catalunya to read the accomplishment of the three *El cim* participants who summited as a patriotic act of Catalan nationalism in the context of contemporary Spanish regional politics. While the online forum questioned such thinking, it did so only in terms of Catalonian identity politics, not in terms of the context of mountaineering on Aconcagua in January 2003.[2] In *El cim,* Aconcagua served as the muse and catalyst for discussions of group solidarity, gender bias, and the individual personalities, histories, and daily actions of the show participants and support staff of Catalan guides and doctors. However, the show gave very little coverage or focus to the accompanying Mendocino guides, Danielón Rodríguez and Heber Orona, who are iconic figures in Mendocino mountaineering history, or to the development and contemporary practice of Aconcagua's mountaineering industry. Mendoza always remained invisible, or on the margin, and Aconcagua was reterritorialized as Catalunya's "cim," or pinnacle, of self-exploration.

Cyber Domains

In contrast to the representations of a program like *El cim,* Mendocino-initiated use of the Internet for marketing purposes renationalizes, or better, reregionalizes the "Centinela de Piedra" and puts Mendoza back on the cyberspace Aconcagua map. While Mendocino institutions and agencies acknowledge and invoke the opposition of transformative travel and modern convenience to market Aconcagua, they also engage local Mendocino identity politics in the context of Aconcagua's relationship to the nation, the extra-national, and modernity, in a more complex way, demonstrating clearly how, as Michael Fischer asserts, "cyberspace reconfigures knowledge-power nexi" (1999, 246). This reconfiguration has been advantageous to Mendocino adventure tourism agencies by giving them greater access to information and to international markets through cyberspace's networking of communication and information. Most climbers heading for the summit are not Mendocino or even Argentine; therefore, local European, American, Asian, and Australian agencies previously maintained a privilege based on geographical proximity to potential clients. The Internet has greatly reduced this geographical advantage based on the material location of an agency, as well as that held by big travel companies who can afford high-priced ads in elitist international climbing magazines.

The Internet inserts Mendoza into the international mountaineering network of communications and histories of Aconcagua and allows Mendoza to jockey for position within a Mendoza-Argentina-global nexus. There are two primary Mendoza-based Aconcagua.com websites, although some local agencies have added Aconcagua to their domain name to capitalize on search engine results. The site www.aconcagua.com.ar, with links to local Mendocino agencies that are service providers to Aconcagua, has been highlighted in local newspaper accounts for its service to both Mendoza's mountaineering industry and as a true gateway to Mendoza province as well. In an industry where many agencies now transact nearly 90 percent of their business through the Internet,[3] direct access to international markets, as well as the creation and recognition of a Mendocino-based Aconcagua, in both geophysical and virtual space, separate regional from national concerns. This move, reflective of the tendencies of globalization to fracture the nation, also speaks to the current Argentine situation in which confidence in national guidance and economics has been greatly undermined.

Dis/Locating Aconcagua

Against the dislocating impetus of the Internet that floats Aconcagua histories and timelines through cyberspace, the need to ground Aconcagua in Mendoza and to regulate and control its virtual displacement seems to underlie local government's drive to restrict Mendoza-based Internet mountaineering providers to only those agencies that are registered as full-service tourist agencies. Several mountaineering agencies have spoken against this measure that favors the bigger, already established agencies that maintain year-long physical business locales. They see this as restricting the growth of the industry within Mendoza and prejudicing Mendoza-based agencies' competitiveness abroad, as international agencies, not each other, are their biggest competitors.

Playing to both of these locating and dislocating tendencies is the webcam at www.aconcaguanow.com.ar, which is located in Plaza de Mulas. The webcam and its Internet access and related forum, all maintained by Miguel Doura, in residence throughout the season in Mulas, provide visual and textual narrations of Aconcagua that are bound to the geographical space of Plaza de Mulas but are always in dialogue with the interpretations and chartings of its participants from Mulas and sites around the globe. While the webcam and forum provide a multivoiced and imaged narrative that puts Aconcagua and the daily activities of expeditioners at reach from your armchair, they also undo the distant, exotic aura of the mountain's remoteness assumed by mountaineering tradition. This cyber narrative creates a story of the accessibility and modernity of Aconcagua in which most of the postings convey messages of celebratory tenor, or supportive accolades, or queries of concern about the dangers and hardships being faced by expeditioners. The extrinsic rewards of public recognition, fame, and glory, once derived from national and official institutions after a lapse of time to journey back to the homeland, are now received immediately from individuals, family, and friends from home and are displayed for a global audience that includes Mulas. The Internet's conflation of time and space and the change in relationship of mountaineering subjectivities to national institutions and projects epitomize the postmodern state of mountaineering on the globalized Aconcagua.

Musealization

There's a lot of ego on that wall.

—CLIMBER IN HOTEL REFUGIO PLAZA DE MULAS

Even within its postmodern scheme, the modern concept of Aconcagua as a stage for enacting national identity seems to remain paramount, regardless of the mode of narration. Historically, Aconcagua has had its share of travel narratives in the form of histories of particular expeditions, personal memoirs, guidebooks, documentaries, marketing videos, websites, and even reality-based TV-internet extravaganzas. From FitzGerald's *The Highest Andes* in 1899 to Catalan TV-3's *El cim* in 2003, these accounts have embodied Anglo-European traditional narrations of heroic travel. As disparate as the media employed to articulate these narrations, and as different as the genres are themselves, there is an underlying ideological legacy that connects them. "As powerful masculinist discourses, adventure and exploration writing," Kaplan (1998) tells us, "proved to be instrumental in the construction of rationales for imperialism" (53). These same gendered and imperialist discourses are reflected in narrativizations of Aconcagua by the Hotel Refugio at Plaza de Mulas, as a postmodern museum of site. This unofficial climbers' museum is a space of self-musealization that also chronicles the contemporary history of mountaineering on Aconcagua since the early 1990s. The Hotel Refugio, constructed through private and provincial cooperation (1990–1995), is an indication of the initial indecision on the part of the province on how to capitalize on Aconcagua's draw. Critics argued against its construction based on the lack of a comprehensive assessment of the environmental consequences. Criticism continued even after construction was completed, as just the idea of a hotel in Plaza de Mulas was offsetting to some who saw it as a "touristic" incursion into elite mountaineering terrain. There was an expectation that the hotel might create a tourist route wherein nonmountaineers could visit Plaza de Mulas as a tourist destination and not as a mountaineering base. There is an apocryphal story that this idea to capitalize on general tourism was thwarted when an Austrian couple rode up to the hotel on mules and the woman dropped dead as she dismounted. (Supposedly, her ghost still haunts the building.) The story of her untimely demise points out that acclimatization difficulties in the rapid ascent on muleback make mass tourism impractical. It also evokes the fissure between how a capitalist view of the tourist potential of Aconcagua conflicts with environmental concerns and the traditional elitism of the sport that sees mountaineering as a dangerous activity that should not be bought by someone without the "right stuff." Johnston and Edwards (1994) used the example of Hotel Refugio, which they mistakenly characterized as a tourist infrastructure with "private bath, satellite TV, a restaurant, bottled oxygen, and a helicopter pad" that allowed clients to fly directly to base camp avoiding acclimatization, to argue that enhanced convenience and security have compromised commitment, "the very backbone of mountaineering" (1994, 464). Today, that kind of "purist" resentment against the Hotel Refugio has greatly diminished (perhaps because there has been no satellite TV, and helicopter service is used only for park officials, rescue operations, and refuse removal), yet the managers still make a special effort to point out that its official name and designation is Refugio although everyone continues to refer to it as "the hotel."[4] The Hotel Refugio has become a local attraction for everyone in the Mulas base camp due to its local telephone (not satellite), mail and Internet services, café and restaurant offerings, souvenir and postcard sales, activity rooms, indoor showers, and its role as the "institutional" memory for Mulas.

The Hotel Refugio entranceway, dining hall, passageways, Ping-Pong room, and campers' kitchen function as sites of exhibits of individual and group mountaineering activities.[5] Expeditionary, regional, national, and institutional banners, flags, decals, emblems, posters, drawings, and articles of clothing (principally inexpensive t-shirts) are displayed on walls, beams, door frames, and from a series of clotheslines that crisscross the largest open space, the dining hall, to form a climbers' museum. The first flag was hung by a group in 1997, which subsequently sparked other climbers, in a competitive game of self-expression, to leave evidence of their presence on Aconcagua. These signs of body, self, group, and nation

Figure 8.1. The Hotel Refugio Plaza de Mulas is a short trek from the main base camp. Climbers coming from Confluencia often access the Hotel Refugio via the Cuesta Amarilla instead of the Cuesta Brava that leads to lower Plaza de Mulas. The Patrulla de Rescate (the rescue squad) maintains its Mulas headquarters next door to the Refugio.

are set in place spontaneously and freely by the mountaineers themselves, with no compliance to a guiding directive mandated by chronological history or traditional world area divisions. In this way, early expeditions are juxtaposed with later ones, national groups with individuals and with other national groups. In this space there is no systemized order of progress toward an idealized future in the way that traditional displays have been organized since the Western concept of the museum originated two centuries ago (Levin 2002, 63).

In the kind of nonprogressive and nonhierarchical scheme that the Refugio site represents, there is an underlying assumption that such cultural displays would be interpreted from "more egalitarian and arguably more authentic perspectives" (Levin 2002, 63). While one might argue that the displays are more "authentic" by reason of their being chosen and ordered by the subjects themselves, the egalitarian nature of the exhibits, while opening up the viewers' interpretative field, is still conditioned by what kinds of social, cultural, and political meanings and identities are evoked in the displays and the exclusionary ideologies that they represent. Some mountaineers choose to place or to write on their artifacts in response to previous displays and texts, and most artifacts have the name, nationality, and date of the expedition or summit. While the display order might seem haphazard at times, at others, it appears decidedly planned, not only to contest, but also to rearticulate hierarchies in mountaineering patterns, national conflicts, and gender tensions.

A predominant theme in the Refugio museum is Aconcagua as a realm of individual challenge and quest where the solitary romantic self is fused with national identity construction. Messages in differing languages, of celebratory and congratulatory tone, speak of physical and emotional struggle, sacrifice, and triumph. A sense of the internalized gratifications of mountaineering and the pride and satisfaction of accomplishment enjoyed by the climbers are externalized in these notes, signings, and artwork where there is a claiming of the mountain for one's own, or for one's nation (see fig. 5.1). These exhibits publicly elevate the status of the climbers and duplicate Aconcagua in a never-ending series of conquests.

The same kind of individual, regional, and national identity politics that played out in the Catalan TV show *El cim* are also held here in the exhibits, some of which carry inflammatory political commentaries that elicit protests from subsequent climbers with opposing views. For example, according to Eduardo Ibarra, the longtime Hotel Refugio manager, there have been French complaints about Corsican exhibits and Spanish criticisms of Basque separatist rhetoric.[6] Flags and banners have been removed and stolen in this game of national and regional one-upmanship. For the most part, these international representations of climbing Aconcagua are articulated via a modernist filter of mountaineering that reinforces and marks national differences. Although the modernist North-South hierarchies of mountaineering may dominate in the texts, images, and messages on the wall and in the hangings, their preeminence is markedly disrupted by their positions next to or across from remnants of other mountaineering projects from those nations traditionally marginalized by the Anglo-European mountaineering legacy, such as Peru, India, and Brazil.

The Refugio exhibits offer a postmodern view of Aconcagua in their destabilizing of the hegemony of the North-South dichotomy of mountaineering's imperialist paradigm and in their representational disruption of modernity's assumed order of progress from which the modern museum evolved. The Refugio's postmodern, collaboratively constructed museum is, of course, also a reading of the effects of economic globalization and the commodification of adventure in mountaineering. However, the exhibits do not present a globalized vision of mountaineering on Aconcagua in the sense of projecting a homogeneous transnational mountaineering body or subjectivity, at least not in terms of national identity. Although no longer seen as tied to institutional projects based on center-periphery relations, mountaineering is still taken to represent national difference according to a modernist mode.

The individual as the repository of national or regional characteristics is emphatically highlighted in the Refugio self-exhibits. Huyssen (2000) sees, since the 1970s, "a popular obsession with 'self-musealization' by video recorder, memoir writing, and confessional literature" (24), to which we can add blogging and YouTube uploads. The Hotel Refugio museum reflects a variant of this process as it symbolically inscribes the bodies and names of the exhibitors on Aconcagua in the modernist tradition of the earliest mountaineers whose names engraved the routes and sites of the mountain. Huyssen (2000) also tells us that "memory practices work against globalization" in that "they express the growing need for spatial and temporal anchoring in a world of increasing flux in ever denser networks of compressed time and space" (36). This push and pull between memory, which would maintain identity categories, and globalization, which would rupture or elide them, is played out in the Refugio museum.

Although there is an overriding postmodernist tone in the haphazard order and disconnected varieties of displays in the Refugio museum, these self-exhibits also paradoxically ground identities and memories in the Hotel Refugio, synecdoche of the mountain, to be memorialized by name, date, and time, in the moment of the expedition, for future consumption. Thus, they reinscribe and stabilize the modernist imperial order of mountaineering where nonlocal climbers' interpretations of nation, time, space, and memory hold sway. Within this order, although some Mendocino guides' affirmations are present on the t-shirts, posters, flags, and banners that expeditioners have brought along to leave behind, they are by no means the majority, and the arrieros and most signs of Mendocino administration on the mountain are dramatically absent.

What is present, however, is a sense of what Bayers (2003) calls an "imperial masculine ethos" that frames these national mountaineering bodies and that is evoked by the texts, art, and articles of clothing of the museum. This cult of national masculinities is exemplified by the long tenure that was held by a pair of Stars and Stripes boxer shorts in a most prominent location in the dining hall. The representation of manliness in this and several other drawings and sayings that focus on competitive masculine prowess conforms to Bayers's explanation of the mountaineering project whereby "the supposed virility of the imperial male body [comes] to dominate the natural environment" (2003, 5).

If male bodies compete to dominate the natural environment of the dining hall exhibits, and by extension the mountain, female bodies have historically been absent from the displays, or, when present, have been submissive to masculine authority. In 2006 the only overtly feminine exhibit to be allowed to remain in the dining hall was posted on a wall by the door: a black lace bra and panty set was attached to a cardboard drawing of a female figure, partnered beside an underwear-clad male figure already in residence for over six years. Tellingly, the female figure was drawn with two large hands claiming the figure's breasts, a claiming of the mountain and the female body as a sexualization of the mountaineering experience, a tendency that both cultural theorists and mountaineers have described

Figure 8.2. A Basque flag display at Hotel Refugio Plaza de Mulas.

Figure 8.3. At the Hotel Refugio Plaza de Mulas, pennants, flags, t-shirts, and other items of apparel document the history of nations and climbers on Aconcagua.

(Ortner 1999, 162). Women's names and signatures adorn several of the displays but, like women's corporeal presence on Aconcagua where feminine difference is subsumed by the masculinized nature of the traditions, practices, and gear of mountaineering, or is naturalized and hidden away in domestic spaces and roles, the feminine here is objectified for masculine desire and naturalized as subordinate to masculine action and agency. Aconcagua, as represented by the Refugio, still remains a man's world.

Diversity on Aconcagua

Although the displays in the Refugio museum carry no interpretative signage, Eduardo Ibarra, the Refugio manager and the unofficial curator, willingly interprets the history of Aconcagua for the climbers by pointing out the kind of events present, but not explicitly described for the public, that destabilize the hegemony of modernist mountaineering paradigms and national and masculine identity constructions in the archive: the first all-gay expeditions, personal and agency animosities, transnational cooperations, regional and national political tensions, record summits, accidents and deaths, and the subversive nature of feminine undergarments (the only pre-2006 display he felt compelled to remove),[7] Mendoza's significant history in Aconcagua mountaineering, and the history of the rescue squad.

In contrast to the overriding representation of the Refugio museum, as well as the case of Quintero Sylva, where Mendoza is erased or diminished on Aconcagua, the comings and goings of the Mendoza Patrulla de Rescate de Alta Montaña in the Hotel Refugio highlight Mendocino authority. The Patrulla's Plaza de Mulas camp is located next to the Refugio, and the rescue squad members frequently are in attendance there. The Patrulla's uniformed presence in the Refugio, playing Ping-Pong during their downtime, sharing mate with the Refugio workers, and chatting with the expeditioners and guides, reinserts Mendoza professionalism and governance back into the representation of adventure and achievement on Aconcagua that is exhibited in the climbers' museum. The Patrulla's daily presence counters the tendency of the displays to extract Aconcagua from its local social, political, and economic context, providing a corporeal grounding of Aconcagua to Mendoza.

The Patrulla's presence and associations with international climbers have strengthened Mendoza's relationship to Aconcagua on the mountain and beyond. The local nature of rescue is projected globally via the website (http://ar.groups.yahoo.com/group/Patrullarescate) that the Patrulla maintains and in its Internet forum. The website houses historical archives of Aconcagua rescues, the mission statement of the squad, mountain photos of Aconcagua and other international sites, and other related items dealing with courses, environmental issues, and local mountain news that are also sent out to the forum group of national and international members. Within Mendoza, the local and national media spotlights of the Patrulla's rescues throughout the climbing season and their favorable representation as one of the factors for the lower fatality rate in recent years create positive publicity for Mendocino governance of the park. This positive recognition of the Patrulla by the media has interpreted, at least until 2009, the local business of rescue as an expression of Mendocino professionalism and an understanding of mountain adventure as ennobling sacrifice in the service of others. The Patrulla, however, as part of the Mendocino police force, is also a problematic presence on Aconcagua. Mendoza's police force has the reputation among many Mendocinos of being one of the most repressive and corrupt in the nation (second to the Buenos Aires police, of course, they add). The stationing of the Patrulla on the mountain also invokes the negative connotations of this legacy for some Mendocinos who also work on Aconcagua.

Several park authorities have cited the need for all park services to be civilian and believe that the Mendoza police force has no business in the park unless there has been a crime committed. In other words, park authorities believe that a park rescue squad should be composed of civilian members and be under the jurisdiction of the park rangers. The 1990–91 civilian rescue squad is often mentioned in their arguments and pointed to as being the benchmark of skill and effectiveness (because it was a season that had no fatalities). This was a rescue squad made up of some of the leading mountain men of the Generation of the 80s. In contrast to this team that was composed of the highest-level professional mountaineers that Mendoza has ever had, the police team consists of trained "amateurs" whose full-time jobs, until recently, have been law enforcement in Mendoza. While I have heard from the Patrulla's critics that the off-season duties of the police team restricted their possibilities for training and practice, those same critics have also praised the personal dedication and sacrifice of the police rescue squad members. The questioning of the squad seems to be more about the vying for power and control within the park among the different institutions and less about the merits of the team.

However, the positive image of the rescue squad and, by extension, Aconcagua management, was heavily tarnished by the media scandal of 2009 when a clip of an unsuccessful rescue attempt was seen in international TV news reports and uploaded to YouTube, as I discussed in the introduction to this book. Unsuccessful is a relative term here, as three of the five people who were lost were eventually found and led to safety. The guide had mistaken their location when radioing for help and for nearly a day the rescuers searched on the wrong side of the mountain. Subsequently, after a helicopter eventually spotted the group, the rescue squad and the other volunteers had to reach the North summit and descend down the other side of the mountain to the stranded expedition and then resummit with the lost expeditioners to get them back down the North Route. Despite the massive show of solidarity and heroics during this operation, it was the death of the guide and the nearly three-minute image of him being pulled by a rope and seemingly bullied by his rescuers that brought an international outcry concerning the safety practices on Aconcagua. (It is rumored that a disgruntled faction of the Mendoza police, who believes that the rescue squad gets preferential treatment, leaked the video to discredit them.) While contemporary media coverage, websites, blogs, and YouTube internationalized Aconcagua by disseminating these tragic images across the ether, blog entries that discussed the event showed how firmly entrenched these old center-periphery stereotypes still are.

From many Mendocino-based websites the question of "what will they think of us?" was predominant. The question grew from accusations of substandard (read: Third World) practices, materials, and ethics that were put forth by national, international, and even Mendocino bloggers who most often commented on what they interpreted as the mistreatment of the victim by the rescuers and the lack of preparation, equipment, and training of the rescue squad. Mendocino andinistas countered by complaining that the most vociferous bloggers did not seem to know what led to or occurred during the 30-hour crisis, and the bloggers did not understand the cruel realities of working at high altitude for hours when you can't breathe and are exhibiting signs of frostbite and pulmonary edema. Andinistas also pointed out that the harshest critics of the Patrulla de Rescate did not appreciate that Aconcagua is the only mountain of this altitude to even have a full-time rescue squad. But their blogs defending the rescuers held very little weight compared to the power of the YouTube clip to generate meaning for Aconcagua mountaineering.

In a very definitive way, the YouTube video undoes folkloric Aconcagua, not just by debunking the notion of a glorious, noble, or uplifting mountaineering death by providing a very painful vision of death at altitude. It also illustrates how Aconcagua is no longer isolated or a mere reflection of nineteenth-century ideals. It is now a twenty-first-century mountain, a postmodern icon that is most often comprehended out of context, in fragmented ways, primarily through visual cues rather than narrative ones, via a clip rather than a story. And the repercussions of this YouTube video and a globalized notoriety are what the Aconcagua industry, according to bloggers, might have cause to worry about. (With two years of declining numbers, 2008–2010, and in light of the worldwide recession and fear about the H1N1 virus that could keep international clients away, the Aconcagua industry certainly did not need any added detractors.) The YouTube video strips away romantic notions of Aconcagua mountaineering, as well as questioning those other modern expectations held by an international public concerned with safety, ecological practices, modern equipment, and technology. And its fallout also jeopardizes the status and authority of the rescue squad on Aconcagua for the following seasons, not only with foreign expeditioners but also among other administrative and service groups on Aconcagua.

The jostling for authority among the rangers, the rescue squad, and experienced guides and base-camp workers has actually been characteristic of Mulas. Until 2002 there was no official training required for provincial rangers, and this lack of experience and knowledge often weakened the perception of the rangers' authority on Aconcagua. In the 2000–2001 season, there was an inside joke in Mulas where guides and agencies referred to the rangers as the "Teletubbies," based on their view of the representatives of provincial control as being physically unfit, unknowledgeable, and basically just there "for the fun of it." In addition, their authority was undermined when the rangers consistently suffered turnovers from year to year, which became especially acute after the 2001–2 season, when the next year park rangers lost one-third of their members. The national economic crisis in 2002 that made the promise of regular pay and benefits from provincial coffers doubtful, or made in *petrom*, the provincial scrip issued during the 2002 economic crisis, prompted many to seek other employment. Most who left found that they were able to make more money and depend on set pay periods by working on Aconcagua for service-providing agencies in cook tents or as porters or assistant guides. The eroding of the rangers' authority and their perception as "unqualified" was girded up by a new professionalization of the corps. In 2002 training courses, developed by Danielón Rodríguez, a Generation of the 80s member, later evolved in the following two years into a full-fledged course of studies in the Provincial Park Ranger Academy, similar in scope to EPGAMT, whose foundation he also spearheaded. In this way Rodríguez's belief in education and training to raise standards in the mountaineering industry have set the bar for both guides and rangers and decidedly given the institutions of Mendocino supervision of mountaineering practices on Aconcagua complementary outlooks and approaches. However, pay issues remain real problems for park rangers who, like the rescue squad, are paid by the provincial government and not by private agencies whose employees find work on Aconcagua much more lucrative.

Multiple Mulas

Plaza de Mulas es lo de siempre: una ciudadela de asedio. Hombres de todos lados, mercenarios de vanidades, locuras y sueños nos concentramos allí esperando nuestro momento. (Plaza de Mulas is just as it always is: a citadel of siege. Men from everywhere, mercenaries of vanities, madness, and dreams, we concentrate there waiting for our moment.)

—LUIS JAIT (2004, 88)

Plaza de Mulas, where international understandings of mountaineering prevail and local groups vie for authority, is a space where we could expect to see the working out of transcultural processes to produce a kind of global cultural identity, as well as the tensions inherent in globalization that problematize this kind of identity construction. According to Stuart Hall (2000), "what we call 'the global' is always composed of varieties of articulate particularities. I think the global is the self-presentation of the dominant particular. It is a way in which the dominant particular localizes and naturalises itself and associates with it a variety of other minorities" (67). The dominant particulars of mountaineering on Aconcagua that naturalize and link themselves to other histories on the mountain especially are traced back to Anglo-European traditions. The Refugio museum illustrates that there is a generalized acceptance that mountaineering is the high adventure of testing limits that reflects back on the worth of both the masculine self and nation. This is seen in both Anglo-European displays as well as those done by the traditionally peripheral or "Third-World" nations' exhibits that spotlight the same kind of individual and national identity constructions. However, those other "hidden in plain sight" representations of mountaineering, for example, those highlighting transnational initiatives, gay, or women's projects, undo this hegemony. As Ortner (1996) has explained, in this "high-altitude borderland" there are always other kinds of understandings and practices that compete with the dominant elements for meaning and that change power dynamics.

The most prevalent and dominant particular of mountaineering on Aconcagua is the exchange of tourism capital and the commodification of adventure with which earlier Anglo-European traditions have linked. It is capitalism that underlies the hegemony of masculine imperial ideologies and constructs them as the performance of an experience molded to the needs and desires of an adventure tourist market. The Seven Summits effect of mountaineering on Aconcagua reveals that the notions of national superiority and "manly virtues of the empire" (Bayer 2003) are really based on access to disposable income and leisure time. One local guide contends that what connects most mountaineering clients is a common dream of what they "believe" mountaineering to be, and it is that dream that corresponds to how Aconcagua is sold as a chance for heroic adventure, possible for all. Adventure seekers who have no high-altitude or even backpacking experience come to the highest peak outside of the Himalayas for the feasibility and affordability offered by what is bought and sold as a "trek." People who are not in good physical shape, or even in good general health, or who have never been much higher than sea level, flock to the mountain because they believe that it is a walk-up, an easy way to experience the thrill of mountaineering adventure. For them the performance of imagined adventure is translated into reality by simply writing a check, but its playing out sometimes conflicts with the very real dangers of the Aconcagua climate and altitude, as I discussed in chapter 7. Although they all may want to be "Indiana Jones," according to local perceptions, only about 20 percent of international clients coming to summit Aconcagua have any previous mountaineering experience when they arrive in Mendoza.

While Mendocino adventure tourism agencies sell Aconcagua's accessibility to novice mountaineers in an attempt to broaden the mountaineering market, official park regulatory and service-providing groups are placing more and more controls on how this accessibility should be structured. The presence of the helicopter for quicker evacuations, more stringent medical controls at base camp (blood pressure and oxygenation are checked on arrival and before ascent to the next camp), establishing a second campsite for the Patrulla at Nido, and requiring professional training for the park rangers have all been helpful for reducing fatalities. These measures also mark Mendoza's authority on the globalized mountain as a dominant and very visible presence.

While the visual reminders or traces of Mendoza are subordinate in number and hue to the trademark colors of the big gear companies whose tents adorn the base camp, they are also the ones that most clearly mark the modern social structure of Plaza de Mulas. Mendoza, in its official capacity of providing governance, security, health, communication, and food and transport services, is seen in the tented enclaves of the service-providing agencies, the permanent shelter of the park rangers, the medical tent, the official bathroom facilities, and, in the distance, the rescue squad shelter and the Hotel Refugio.

The very visible supervisory role of the park's governing bodies and the regulation of who can intervene in any situation and how such intervention can and should be done has caused some local enthusiasts to mourn the passing of the less organized model of early Aconcagua mountaineering. Today, Mulas as a global village sports clearly marked "streets"; has medical, sanitation, safety, and judiciary branches; an art gallery; a "pub"; its own holiday "Porters' Day"; and even an unofficial mayor, Chapu, the camp manager at Parra's Aconcagua Trek. Mulas as a community negates the vision of mountaineering as a wilderness activity and the sense of imperialist adventure that needs the illusion of empty space for conquest. Tellingly, to publicize Aconcagua adventure agencies do not offer many photos of crowded dining tents, lines at the toilet facilities, or streams of hundreds of climbers all going up to high camp at the same time. The solitary figure and desolate space still prevail in campaign ads.

In this same vein, there has been much criticism in local Mendoza circles and media about the crowded climbing conditions on the Normal Route and the entertainment atmosphere at Plaza de Mulas on Aconcagua. Many of those who have worked on Aconcagua, and especially those who have spent multiple seasons at base camp in Plaza de Mulas, have lamented the loss of its "folkloric" quality. The term "folkloric" is a recurring one, used by many "oldtimers" who have described to me how Plaza de Mulas functioned before the most recent climbing boom of the last two decades: there was a spirit of sharing, bartering, assessing of needs together without the restrictions of "civilization." In a way this longing for the "simpleness" of the lost past exemplifies the Mendocino mountaineers' distancing from modernity and their pointed rejection of the materiality of consumerism as a product of globalization. Their nostalgia for a Golden Age of climbing (which paradoxically is a modernist construct itself) is also based on a sense of loss of personal autonomy due to the imposition of rules, regulations, and authority. This translates to their idealization of a "folkloric" past and their disdain for what Aconcagua has become since the international climbing momentum on Aconcagua began to build in the late 1980s. Increased local regulation and control are by-products of capitalist development: the necessary results of selling Aconcagua, which has drawn rising numbers to the park and created environmental, safety, revenue, and cultural questions of concern for the Mendocino mountaineering industry to address. While globalization has allowed for the reinscription of traditional understandings of mountaineering that ignore Mendoza's presence and history on Aconcagua, it also has created the possibility and need for Mendoza to assert its presence and authority more stringently.

Routines of Identity

Me siento extranjero acá. (I feel like a foreigner here.)

—ANDINISTA FROM BUENOS AIRES ON ACONCAGUA EXPEDITION, PLAZA DE MULAS

If principal concerns about globalization query how to safeguard cultural autonomy and economic survival at the local and national level (Appadurai 2000, 2–3), the evolution of the mountaineering industry in Mendoza, then, provides a rich forum in which to consider its impact on these issues. Within this globalized adventure tourism community, what sense of

Argentine or Mendocino cultural identity is possible? The idea of cultural autonomy is, of course, problematic on any level. Cultural identities are always in process, negotiated, unstable, caught between the tendency to include and exclude, and constructed "in relation to one another, produced, represented and perceived through the ideologies and narratives of situated discourses" (Wolff 2000, 167). In Mulas the discourses of mountaineering, tourism, and globalization filter interpretations of self and nation.

If globalization is about the homogenizing tendencies of dominant particularities, then it is US culture that tends to set the daily routine standard in Mulas. Ulf Hannerz (2000) reminds us that the process of globalization does not create an egalitarian global village. There remains an asymmetry of center and periphery, where the periphery is still more the taker than the giver of meaning (107). North American dominance in the world economy and global cultural is repeated on Aconcagua.

In Mulas the lingua franca is English, and signs are often posted in both English and Spanish, or just in English. The US economy has set the standard until now, and prices are listed in both dollars and pesos. (Before the 2002 devaluation, only dollars were listed.) American clients are also physically present in the greatest numbers. This usually translates to white and male. One Mendocino guide who has worked for over ten years on Aconcagua, predominantly with Americans, has never had an African American client, and says women make up only about 15 percent of the total number of Americans in any given year.

Cultural, linguistic, and economic adjustments are made primarily by Argentines to accommodate clients, not so much the other way around. This has created a two-tiered cultural life, based on a tourist economy, that functions first to meet client needs and then allows base-camp workers and officials to segregate from foreign experiences in the base camp. Meals are scheduled according to American and northern European timelines, with an early dinner hour. This has taken its toll on the Argentine guides who have been obliged by their agencies to eat with the clients. Even so, they may eat with clients, and then eat again, or at least accompany, the porters and service workers who dine much later at the normal Argentine hour. Food provided for the expeditioners is fairly international: pastas, potatoes, meats, soups, US breakfast cereals, and eggs and bacon. The availability of fresh meats and vegetables, and pizzas and desserts hot from the oven, often surprise international clients. A packed lunch is provided to climbers who are absent from any of the camps during lunchtime and base-camp workers call this "un lunch," using the English term, while a sit-down lunch remains *almuerzo*.

While there is a generalized Americanization of the daily routine, the local Mendocinos still, however, persevere in cultivating the uniqueness of their culture in the interstices of structured camp life. Dulce de leche is often served alongside jams and jellies for breakfast or afternoon snacks, and mate is the Mendocinos' drink of choice. At times, Mendocinos even entice international climbers to try it. In the evening, after clients have gone to bed, there are often gatherings with camp workers, park officials, and guides, sometimes with guitar and folkloric music. Plazamuleros have also made concerted efforts to tie themselves to regional and national life and reflect the sociopolitical and cultural events in Mendoza and the nation by organizing their own *cacerolazos* of protest during the crisis of 2002 and a Vendimia celebration complete with princesses and a queen.

A regional take on Argentinidad is highlighted by the celebration of Mendocino holidays, the prominence of Mendoza's authority on Aconcagua, and even the Mendocino accent, which clearly differentiates its speakers from the Buenos Aires dialect. Perhaps it is not surprising that the porteño whose quote started out this section proclaimed that he did not feel at home in Mulas. The global nature of Mulas, the international majority of climbers, and the cultural, administrative, and linguistic regional dominance there diminish a sense of national Argentine identity, usually translated as those characteristics associated with Buenos Aires. The process of globalization that tends to fracture the nation-state and weaken national institutions' control of international interactions is reflected on Aconcagua in the dominance of the regional over the national, in the primacy of Mendoza's presence and connectivity in the global network of international mountaineering. Mendoza has usurped the role of the state, represented as Buenos Aires, which has traditionally been the "broker between the transnational and the local" (Hannerz 2000, 117). If Aconcagua is not Argentine territory, as another porteño remarked to me several years earlier, then it is a global zone with a decidedly Mendocino accent.

This globalized area of Mulas that is Americanized in terms of schedules, prices, and language, and Argentinized in Mendocino terms, is still a space where nationalities clearly mark their differences. According to camp workers and park officials, there are several categories that highlight national characteristics and allow them to easily differentiate national subjectivities: foodstuffs, music, bathing habits, voice and noise levels, willingness to follow the park rules, and sometimes gear (though this is the most unreliable trait due to the transnational aspect of the mountaineering gear industry). However, there is also a great amount of sharing and mixing of many of these items between clients and between clients and camp workers that blur the boundaries that they supposedly set up. After a Japanese actor's summit attempt was produced for a Japanese TV documentary, the generosity of the production crew when they left resulted in a widespread change in diet and equipment across Plaza de Mulas.

There are also other topics and practices that seem to transcend nationalities to create transnational moments. Soccer (except for North Americans), especially before and after World Cup years, personal experiences in the mountains, and international mountaineering heroes and narratives all seem to find resonance across nations and genders. Music and movies, generally North American and British productions, also function in the same way. The rest days in Mulas especially give time to the climbers on open expeditions who did not know each other before the expedition started to broaden their commonalities and form an incipient sense of *communitas* beyond the "peg" (Gordon 2006, 20), the desire to summit, that holds them together.

Obviously, though, the degree to which these kinds of issues connect mountaineers to each other and to the local workers and officials depends on their ability to communicate with each other. And that usually means speaking English, which is mandatory in the EPGAMT. Many guides have signaled the importance of language in group dynamics and in the overall experiencing of the expedition. While several Mendocino guides have told me that they "hate English," they recognize its hegemony on the mountain and most feel that it is absolutely essential. While there is room for individual and national identities to be articulated on Aconcagua, there is still an overriding need to accommodate North American expressions.

Debriefs

Aconcagua, illustrated by cybermedia representations, the Refugio climbers' informal museum, and the social makeup and practices of Mulas itself, reveals how international and local imaginations have converged and competed for dominance on the mountain. Attitudes and beliefs about mountaineering, flows of bodies and capital, media networking, and market and memory practices all form part of what defines Aconcagua and how the mountaineering industry functions there today. As Mendocino governmental and business entities engage and promote the hybrid and transnational nature of Aconcagua, they also relocate Mendoza within a global economy that repositions its traditional place within national identity politics. Ultimately, a study of global Aconcagua illustrates how the national has been subsumed to local and international constructions of peril, profit, and patrimony that in combination have invented mountaineering on America's highest peak as both global and regional.

Conclusion

Final Debriefs

Aconcagua as Global

La identitidad se define y redefine . . . en interacción con otras sociedades, . . . conviene . . . tener en cuenta cómo nos ven otros y cómo asimilamos nosotros esos modos de mirarnos. (Identity is defined and redefined . . . in interaction with other societies, . . . it's advisable . . . to keep in mind how others see us and how we assimilate those ways of seeing.)

—GARCÍA CANCLINI (2000, 85)

The globalization of Aconcagua has evolved out of the growth of the adventure tourism market, the commodification of adventure, and the influential nature of North America therein, all of which condition the way mountaineering is experienced and how cultures interact on the mountain. Mendocino presence and control of mountaineering practices counter the homogenizing impulse of the United States, at the same time that they resist national urges to define Aconcagua as Argentine in the traditional way that ignores its provincial identity. The globalizing confluence of capital, interests, radical improvements in gear, and a higher profile for mountain climbing would promote Aconcagua but also pose challenges for Mendoza.

While Mendoza mountaineering benefited from the currents of globalization, the globalizing forces of neoliberal economics and transnational financial workings debilitated the Argentine economy at the turn of the millennium. However, Mendoza was already positioned to fill the vacuum that the empty coffers of the national government left, in terms of its regional economy, by focusing ever more on the promotion of international tourism vis-à-vis the devaluation of the peso. Aconcagua mountaineering was already a major drawing card, and the province was able to capitalize on its recognition quotient. Although Aconcagua tourism plays a modest part in Mendoza's overall tourism industry, the celebrated peak is the province's best-known international attraction. Its role in provincial tourism became even more significant when at the turn of the millennium the Mendocino government decided to allow the Dirección de Recursos Naturales y Renovables to keep Aconcagua revenues to administer all the province's natural reserves. This move not only gave more administrative freedom to the Dirección, but it also assured monies for the natural reserves that were not tied to national or regional support but that instead were contingent on international economies and tourist markets. In a sense, following the tendencies of Menem's Argentina of the 1990s, Mendoza essentially privatized its Dirección to sink or swim in the waters of international tourism and free market capitalism. Aconcagua tourism, as a product of globalization in this sense, reflects Mendoza's increased dependence on direct connections with transnational financial situations and systems that are not filtered by or dependent on nationally driven directives or fully controlled by regional governing bodies.

While generally regarded in Mendoza as beneficial, reliance on Aconcagua's international tourism dollars to support the Dirección's budget has also been seen as prejudicial for the well-being of the park. Some Mendocino critics have complained that the park is driven to issue more entrance permits than its ecosystems and infrastructure can manage due to the Dirección's budgetary needs. The pressure to expand the Dirección's budget is also seen as the cause for allowing encroachment into areas of the park that are those wild and distant zones most marketable in adventure tourism markets but that have been designated by Mendoza as off-limits to tourism or mountaineering. In other words, using Aconcagua mountaineering as an example, we see that global capitalism not only fractures national-regional connections but it also undercuts local public control of its resources.

This conflict between needs for increased revenue and desires to ensure ecological preservation was highlighted again in late 2006 when plans were announced for a new tourist center to be built adjacent to Highway 7, the international highway to Chile, at the entrance to Aconcagua Provincial Park, and to pave the road that leads to the Horcones ranger station. This tourist center with its entrance fees and improved access into the park were explained to me by various park officials as an effort to capture more tourist bodies and monies with the least amount of ecological repercussions. This plan was not meant as a measure for bettering or increasing mountaineering numbers, but rather as a way to attract national and international travelers who might stop for an hour, on their way to or from Chile, to visit the Horcones lagoon, stroll through the area designated for touristic use, get a glimpse of Aconcagua, and take a few pictures. The idea for the tourist center had been in the works for several years, but neither the funds nor the plan were viable until 2006 when both federal and international agencies, such as SOPDE (Sociedad de Planificación y Desarrollo, Málaga, Spain), signed on to collaborate. This endeavor by the province marked the first time that changes to the park had coincided with an ecological study of sustainability. It also paralleled an announcement by the park administration that, starting in November 2007, but later postponed to the 2008–9 season (but as of 2011 not yet enacted), there would be a ceiling on mountaineering permits, although they did not specify what the limit would be, and they had not yet made a comprehensive ecological study to guide their decision. No one expects the Dirección to restrict entrance permits to numbers less than the park's highest entrance level in 2007–8, which has spurred criticism that such a restriction is still primarily driven by the budgetary needs of the Dirección and not by the needs of the park.

Ecological degradation of the park remains a major negative factor attributed to the increased volume of international adventure tourism and its power to destabilize local regulating bodies wanting for revenue. In this same vein, global capitalism undermines public institutions by inciting its competition with private industry. This is well illustrated by the case of the provincial park ranger unit, which has found it difficult to keep up with the wages and salary guarantees that private service providers could afford. For this reason it continues to struggle to keep its rank-and-file members from year to year.

The global nature of Aconcagua is complex, and it clearly encompasses much more than just the number of international climbers that come to try its summit. Yet those mountaineers do indeed contribute to the mountain as a global nexus. The narrations of memory and the practices of mountaineering of these climbers demonstrate that the idea of romantic exploration of transcendent magnitude, for the benefit of the masculine self and the nation, is still a master trope for narrating Aconcagua, regardless of the changes in style of travel or mode of narrativization. While these narratives illustrate the enduring legacy of Anglo-European hegemony in mountaineering, they also show, however, that the unanimity of this portrayal is being contested by other narrations emanating from diverse, previously marginalized subjectivities and locations that multiply Aconcagua and reterritorialize it in differing geographical imaginations.

Mendoza grapples with the history of mountaineering in terms of center-periphery relationships of power that invoke hierarchical understandings of self and nation as it seeks to create its own self-determined stamp on local mountaineering. For Mendoza this has meant contesting its subordinate position, especially through education and professionalization, while also recognizing the selling power of its subordination within Anglo-European adventure markets when its image is projected as exotic and premodern. It is this latter representation that allows Mendoza mountaineering to highlight its Amerindian heritage as Incan but one that also erases the contemporary indigenous movements in the province and the nation. The integration by Mendoza of this representation is not just driven by Northern desires for adventure, but it coincides with the traditional national understanding and valuing, or devaluing, of Argentina's indigenous peoples. The global forces of mountaineering may support the reifying of Mendoza's indigenous peoples in a long-lost Incan imperial past, but this tendency was already part and parcel of the Mendocino collective imaginary.

Traditional expectations and novel realities also come face to face in the relatively young Mendocino-based profession of mountain guiding. The presence and function of Mendocino guides on Aconcagua point to a breaking down of the naturalized selectiveness of mountaineering adventure that historically excluded participants on the basis of nation, class, race, and gender. The change in the Mendocino mind-set and the level of participation by Mendocinos in mountain adventure on Aconcagua have developed primarily through efforts based on education at the institutional level: at EPGAMT, in the polideportivos, and in local high schools. It has also been especially driven by the very lucrative business of guiding on Aconcagua. However, Mendoza's democratization of mountain adventure has not simply erased the historical elitism of mountaineering. Mendoza's mountain guides, as transculturative figures in local society, represent both change and continuity, especially in terms of Mendoza's struggle to articulate the traditional and elitist suppositions of where mountaineering subjects come from and what they do and look like, with new codes that evoke the commodification of adventure and the problematics of gender divisions on the mountain.

In sum, Aconcagua is characterized by images, movements, and the discourses of adventure that insert it into imagined geographies founded on tourist economies and by regional and national identity construction. Globalization on Aconcagua, then, has meant a constant reworking by Mendoza of its mountaineering identity, at once seen as modernized safety and romantic solitude, based on both technological advances and pre-Columbian heritage, and being both foreign and marginal as well as intrinsically Mendocino. It has also meant working out assumptions about gender roles and gender-based labor, as well as looking at suppositions about sexual orientation, age, and ethnicity as Mendocino mores and standards come into contact on Aconcagua with differing international values and beliefs. And ultimately, it has signified a reconsideration of how Mendocinos see themselves in conjunction with Aconcagua and the mountains. This, in some ways, signals a rupture of Mendoza's grounding itself in its past of agriculture and ties to Buenos Aires, to include a new focus on a present and future directed toward tourism and the global. For Mendoza, Aconcagua symbolizes an uncomfortable, yet inevitable, repositioning of the province within a globalized world.

The global nature of Aconcagua serves, in some ways, as the harbinger of the Mendoza that is to come or that, in actuality, already has been for several decades. It is characterized by dependence on the economic and cultural drives of international capital, the weakening of national claims to the region and national brokering of international connections, and Mendoza's striving to insert itself as an influential particular and important destination for tourism in a globalized world. Mendocino emphasis on education, training, authority, regulation, communication, and control on Aconcagua are models of initiatives that would steer the province through the fast-moving channels of transnational capitalism and the powerful homogenizing currents of globalized culture into a twenty-first century in which it would ideally participate fully but would still be able to recognize itself as Mendoza.

Notes

Introduction

1. All translations are my own.

2. According to Marcus Vinicius Gasques in *Montanha em fúria* (2002), experts believe that one of the fatal errors that the team made was to follow the Messner Ridge, which, in times of unstable weather and heavy snowfall, leaves climbers vulnerable to avalanches for about 600 meters. Most climbers concur, according to Gasques, that the French Route (opened in 1954) is safer in these conditions but is longer, tacking on an extra day or two.

3. See the 2001 BBC documentary *Mountain Men*, and Conefrey and Jordan, *Mountain Men* (2002).

4. Other accounts of the Everest tragedy in May 1996 appear in Boukreev, *The Climb* (1999); Dickinson, *The Other Side of Everest* (1999); Breashears, *High Exposure* (2000); Gammelgaard, *Climbing High* (2000); Weathers, *Left for Dead* (2001); and a 1997 made-for-TV movie titled *Into Thin Air: Death on Everest*. The Hollywood film about tragedy on K-2, *Vertical Limit* (2000), also obviously drew from the veiled and explicit accusations discussed in the Everest accounts that competition and commercialization caused the 1996 disaster.

5. This is as reported in the local and national newspapers *Uno*, *Los Andes*, and *Clarín* during the last two weeks of February and the first two weeks of March 2009, and also on websites and blogs such as www.mounteverest.net; www.youtube.com; www.aconcaguanow.com; and the Internet message board of the Mendocino Patrulla de Rescate, http://ar.groups.yahoo.com/group/Patrullarescate/.

Chapter 1. "They All Want to Be Indiana Jones"

1. In colonial times, Mendoza was founded on the site of a Huarpe settlement by Pedro del Castillo in 1561 and was named in honor of Chile's viceroyal governor at the time, Don García Hurtado de Mendoza, who had sent the expedition.

2. These are the dates of their expeditions. Their publications came later. Darwin's narrative was first published in 1839 as *Journal of Researches into the Geology and Natural History of the Various Countries Visited by H.M.S. Beagle*; Güssfeldt's geological studies were published in 1884; FitzGerald's *The Highest Andes: A record of the first ascent of Aconcagua and Tupungato in Argentina, and the exploration of the surrounding valleys*, which included Vines's narratives, was published in 1899; and in 1902 Sir Martin Conway published *Aconcagua and Tierra del Fuego*.

3. Güssfeldt explored the Aconcagua area during a five-month period spanning from November 1882 to March 1883.

4. Although it was Darwin's account that held most interest for the scientist-explorers of the 1880s and later, other earlier travel narratives of the area include H. M. Brackenridge, *Voyage to Buenos Ayres, performed in the years 1817 and 1818, by order of the American government, by H. M. Brackenridge, esq., secretary to the mission*; Robert Proctor (1825), *Narrative of a Journey across the Cordillera of the Andes and of a Residence in Lima* (1825); Charles Brand, *Journal of a voyage to Peru: A passage across the Cordillera of the Andes in the winter of 1827, performed on foot in the snow; and a journey across the pampas* (1828); Joseph Andrews, *Journey from Buenos Ayres, through the provinces of Cordova, Tucuman, and Salta, to Potosi, thence by the deserts of Caranja to Arica, and subsequently to Santiago de Chili and Coquimbo: Undertaken on behalf of the Chilian and Peruvian Mining Association, in the years 1825–1826* (1827).

5. This process of feminization is reminiscent of the orientalism of European representation of the Middle East, as theorized by Said (1978).

6. Irwin (1950, 317) explains that Vines is quoting here from the first edition (1839) of *The Voyage of the Beagle* and that in the second edition in 1845 this section was reduced to just one sentence with no mention of volcanic activity.

7. *The Highest Andes* was first published in London in 1899 by Methuen. I refer to the 1899 New York edition by Scribner located in the Mandeville Special Collections of the University of California at San Diego, Geisel Library, La Jolla, Calif.

8. Güssfeldt's narrative of Aconcagua dealt with descriptive geography, observations and hypotheses on the geological makeup and origin of the mountains, information on topographical names, altitude readings, descriptions of glacier snow, and the effects of altitude on humans.

9. Criollos were American-born descendants of the first Spanish colonists.

10. According to Domicelj, by 1862 in Britain there already was a widespread interest in detailing mountainous features and in the utilization of technology and instruments that could measure altitude and distance, as well as help in overcoming the difficulties of climbing (2003, 48).

11. Irwin describes FitzGerald as living a "life generally devoted to the occupations of a gentleman of means and to inconspicuous military service" who only emerged into the public eye when he led two mountaineering expeditions: the first was to the New Zealand Alps, and the second to Aconcagua (1950, 301). Conway, who wrote of his travels with FitzGerald in the European Alps in *The Alps from End to End* (1900), journeyed several times to the Andes.

12. For a more extensive analysis of the ideologies of adventure in terms of mountaineering, see Logan (2006) and Houston (2006).

13. "Andinismo" refers to mountaineering in general and is used interchangeably with *montañisimo* by Mendocinos. "Alpinismo" means alpine style for Argentines, when the expedition members carry all materials with them without establishing or leaving stocked camps along the route of the ascent.

14. All of these sentiments have been expressed to me during the four seasons (2000–2006) I spent doing field work at base camp on Aconcagua.

15. This statement was made to me by two Mendocino guides. See Logan (2006) for a discussion of gender-based labor divisions in Aconcagua mountaineering.

Chapter 2. No Longer the Lettered City

1. On Argentine national identity and sports, especially soccer, see Archetti, *Masculinities* (1999); Braceli, *De fútbol somos*: La condición (2001); Galeano, *El fútbol a sol y sombra* (1995); and Mason, *Passion of the People?* (1995).

2. See www.turismo.gov.ar/esp/menu.htm. Argentina saw a 15 percent increase in international arrivals via Buenos Aires' Ezeiza airport in 2007. However, tourist arrivals at Ezeiza do not reflect a comprehensive picture of Argentina's tourism growth. This is especially the case for Mendoza, which sees many international arrivals enter from Chile via highway or by a short 30-minute flight from Santiago.

3. The 2008-2009 season registered the first decline in entrance numbers since the devaluation of the peso. Entrance figures were taken from Di Bari (2008) and the Mendoza government's official Aconcagua website (www.aconcagua.mendoza.gov.ar).

4. For a discussion of the Argentine crisis, see Fiorucci and Klein, eds., *Argentine Crisis of the Millennium* (2005); Olarra, Olarra Jiménez, and Vinuesa, *El derrumbe argentino* (2003); and Cafiero and Llorens, *La Argentina robada* (2005).

5. These figures are based on numbers taken from the Mendoza government's official Aconcagua website and from Di Bari (2008). The park's entrance numbers for 2007-2008 were the highest ever, approaching 8,000. The three following seasons, including 2010–11, each registered around 7,000.

6. This evaluation won the first prize in the 2007 contest "100 Years of Tourism," organized by the Secretaría de Turismo (SECTUR) ("Fue presentado" 2007).

7. The monument, which was sculptured in 1914, depicts three historical moments: the preparation of arms by Fray Luis Beltrán, the donation of jewels by Mendocino families, and the departure of the troops to the mountains.

8. It was inaugurated on June 28, 2001. The expenses were reimbursed by the National Tourism Secretariat.

9. See Gallardo 2001.

10. See "El turista" (2007) and "Mendoza recibió" (2008).

11. For *TurPlan* (2000), adventure tourism offers opportunities to experience new emotions, participate in out-of-the-ordinary activities, and take advantage of the benefits of nature (190).

12. I am speaking only of the 8th Mountain Brigade and not the Argentine military in general.

13. See *Aconcagua: Techo de América* (1998).

14. See www.unwto.org/index.php.

Chapter 3. Indigenous Identities

1. A shortened version of this chapter was published as "Constructing Indigeneity in Argentina: At the Crossroads of Mountaineering, Tourism, and Re-ethnification," *Journal of Latin American and Caribbean Anthropology* 14, no. 2 (2009): 405–431.

2. "Pukios," a Quechua term, means a spring of pure and crystalline water (Masa 1978, 107). Aconcagua Trek maintains its staging facilities at Los Pukios. Aymará has facilities at Puente del Inca, where it also manages the Hostería Puente del Inca.

3. I am referring to the *campañas al desierto*: the Pampa-Patagonia expedition led by Julio Roca in 1879 and subsequent military interventions there through 1885, as well as the 1884 expedition to the Chaco by Benjamín Victorica.

4. This is an allusion to the national model imagined by Domingo F. Sarmiento's *Facundo*, first published in 1845.

5. Of the 950,000 Argentines who self-identify as indigenous, approximately 500,000 live in urban areas (Gorostiaga 2003, 18).

6. The Huarpes originally inhabited the region of Cuyo. The Milcayac had settlements in today's Mendoza, the Allentiac in the north, in the San Juan area, and the Puntanos in the east, San Luis.

7. Several agencies, like Aconcagua Expeditions and Aconcagua Trek, have sections of their websites dedicated specifically to the history and the discovery of the Incan mummy.

8. Ceruti participated in one of the most important finds of high-altitude sacrifices in 1999, in Salta, with the discovery of three of the best-preserved Incan mummies in existence on the Llullaillaco summit (6,736 meters) (www.nationalgeographic.com/emerging/constanzaCeruti.htm).

9. Schobinger prefers to see the pilgrimage and sacrifice as a purely religious, rather than a state, affair (2001e, 432).

10. Graburn explains that he is paraphrasing Mauss (1898) (1995, 28).

11. The archaeologists Julio Ferrari, Eduardo Guercio, and Víctor Durán also formed part of the expedition (Cabrera 2001, 23).

12. Based on my archival research in the Mendoza Secretariat de Turismo and the *Diario Los Andes* in Mendoza (for example, see Lilloy [1997], Masud [1997], Pincolini [1997], and Raía [1997]), and from my readings of the academic publications of archaeologist Juan Schobinger (1995, 2001f).

13. Schobinger stated that "this was not a sports or political issue, but rather one of science" (1997a).

14. Lafalla had participated in opening up the "Mendocino Guides Route" on Aconcagua in 1994 (www.aconcagua.com).

15. As reported in *Los Andes*, May 3, 1999.

16. Claudia Briones argues that the 1994 constitutional reform was less an indication of real transformation in Argentina's political economy of diversity and more an adjustment to changing international systems of capital exchange (2006, 50). For a discussion of indigenous rights movements in Argentina, see Escolar (2007), Briones (2006), Carrasco (2000) and *The Journal of Latin American Anthropology* 8, no. 3 (2003).

17. The constitution recognizes the cultural preexistence of indigenous peoples, the legal status of their communities and possession of traditionally occupied lands,

and their right to participate in actions concerning natural resources therein (Gorostiaga 2003, 18).

18. Dr. Teodora Zamudia (2008) reports that there are 996 indigenous communities in Argentina. According to the National Institute of Indigenous Affairs, thirty-one different native peoples in twenty-three provinces have received juridical recognition. See www.fondoindigena.org/apc-aa-files/documentos/items/Informe_argentina.pdf.

19. Escolar, focusing on groups in San Juan, cites the use of the media, public performances, school presentations, and judicial and legislative actions as characterizing Huarpe social mobilizations of the 1990s (2007, 187–188).

20. Michielli concludes that the territory of the Huarpes should be seen as having extended to the principal or frontal range of the Andes, and not just to the pre-Cordillera (low range) as has been commonly theorized (1983, 69–70).

21. Candito explains that the cooperative is the organizational form closest to that of the area's originary peoples (La Quebrada del Sauce 2007).

22. Jonathan W. Warren sees a trend of "Indianizing" in Latin America since the 1990s in which individuals who previously did not self-identify as indigenous are now doing so (2004, 225–226).

23. See "Nuevo atropello" 2006.

24. See http://argentina.indymedia.org/news/2006/09/443184.php, post of January 17, 2007.

25. See Agüero (2003) and Ramos (2003).

26. The Mercado has been supportive in exhibiting and selling artisan work by groups and individuals of the Huarpes in Lavalle.

Chapter 4. Fashioning Adventure

1. See www.marmillod.info/Interview/DorlyInterviewEnglish.htm

2. Dick Bass had oil holdings in Texas, coal in Alaska, and the Snowbird Ski Resort in Utah.

3. The villain of the 2000 mountaineering movie *Vertical Limit*, who sets into motion the events that lead to tragedy, is patterned after this archetype of the businessman athlete who buys and, in the movie, bullies his way up the mountain.

4. Johnston and Edwards (1994) and Beedie (2003) have discussed the impacts of technological improvements in gear and equipment on mountaineering in the late twentieth century, especially citing as consequences the improvements in convenience, comfort, and safety, as well as an increase in the number of practitioners.

5. Although Columbia was founded earlier, in 1938, its business exploded in the 1970s and now boasts of selling its outdoor, ski, and mountain clothing in more than fifty countries with 12,000 retailers worldwide (www.columbia.com/who/overview.aspx). Black Diamond is the re-organized Chouinard Equipment, which was initiated as an employee-owned company in 1989. Mountain Hardware began in 1993.

6. See www.patagonia.com/web/us/contribution/patagonia.go?assetid=3351.

7. Napier does not mention Chouinard by name in his text, but it is obvious that the French-American selling mountaineering tools from his garage that he references is indeed Chouinard (Napier 2006, 85).

8. See www.patagonia.com/web/us/contribution/patagonia.go?assetid=3351.

9. Ibid.

10. See www.thenorthface.com/na/our-story.html.

11. Beedie (2003) discusses the power that catalogs and adventure magazines have had in conditioning the behavior of mountain adventure participants.

12. Bayers believes that postmodernity problematizes the construction of masculinity via the notion of imperial adventure that modernity instilled in mountaineering (2003, 129).

13. See http://marmot.com/service/about/index.php.

14. Ibid.

15. Among Messner's publications are *Reinhold Messner, Free Spirit: A Climber's Life* (1991) and *Everest: Expedition to the Ultimate* (1979), which recounts the first summit of Everest without the use of supplemental oxygen that he had achieved with his climbing partner, Peter Habeler, in 1978. Messner also wrote *The Crystal Horizon: Everest—The First Solo Ascent* (1989), the story of his solo summit of Everest in 1980.

16. Johnston and Edwards cite Messner in their discussion of mountaineering as ecotourism and the desire to "restore integrity to mountaineering" (1994, 471).

17. See www.marmillod.info/Interview/DorlyInterviewEnglish.htm.

Chapter 5. Local Heroics

1. As reported in *Los Andes* in March 1934 (*Los Andes* archives, Mendoza). The members of the Polish team were Victor Otrowski, Konstanty Narkiewicz-Jodko, Jan Dorwaski, and Stefan Osiecki.

2. See the Brigade's official website, www.cbrimon8.ejercito.mil.ar.

3. Perón's first presidency included two terms from 1946 until 1955 when he was ousted by a military coup.

4. The first summit of Everest was completed by Edmund Hillary and Tenzing Norgay in 1953.

5. While some websites cite Neate (1994) as the source of this description, others simply repeat it as common knowledge and do not attribute it to any one source.

6. See www.marmillod.info/Interview/DorlyInterviewEnglish.htm.

7. The facts and dates of Argentine mountaineering expeditions in the Himalayas are from a website (www.alborde.com.ar) that cites *Historia del montañismo* by Jorge González as a primary source.

8. Magnani also published *Argentinos al Himalaya* (1955).

9. Although Grajales died in 2004, his son continues to run the agency under his father's name.

10. This was his second attempt at an 8,000-meter peak. His first was at Annapurna in 1988.

11. The presence of Mendocino climbers in the Himalayas continued through the 1990s and into the twenty-first century.

12. Membership is restricted by the Chamber of Commerce of Service Providers. Not all Mendocino agencies can participate in the chamber or get access to the park to set up camp facilities in Confluencia, Plaza de Mulas, or Plaza Argentina.

13. The difficulty of the Guide School and its high dropout rate, however, maintain the professional exclusivity of mountain guides, while its entrance and tuition policies do just the opposite by being very inclusive.

Chapter 6. Matters of Life and Death

1. See Lanata (2003).
2. See www.pizarroexpediciones.com.ar.
3. During climbing season arrieros set out on their own, or in pairs, to make the trip to base camp and back with a herd of loaded mules. While they routinely follow the trail every day, depending on the weather, the mules, and climbers on the trail, there may be some unforeseen changes to their route.
4. Carolina Codó was the first Argentine woman to summit the South Face via Messner's route in 1989 with her brother.
5. No one was able to summit in the 2005 expeditions (www.argentinosahimalaya.com.ar/g1g2/presentacion.htm). As of early 2011 Silvestrini remains the only Mendocino woman to have summited an 8,000-meter peak. However, in 2009, Mercedes Sahores, from Neuquén, reached the summit of Everest and she became the first Argentine woman to do so.
6. Both trekking guides and high-altitude guides must pass all course work in the Mendocino guide school, EPGAMT. In addition, experience outside the classroom is also required before earning the guiding credential. To become a high-altitude guide requires at least four summits on mountains over 6,000 meters, two following the Normal Route and two on routes of medium difficulty; twelve summits of mountains over 5,000 meters, divided between normal and more technical routes; and experience in leading climbs on both rock and ice (www.epgamt.com.ar/altamont.htm). A trekking guide is legally permitted to guide to 4,300 meters, or Plaza de Mulas, on Aconcagua.
7. As of 2011 there was no capacity limit set for Aconcagua climbers.
8. This is according to Danielón Rodríguez and has been substantiated by many graduates of the school.
9. Gordon (2006) has written on the importance of the camera in the development of adventure travel.
10. The 2010–11 entrance fee for Argentines in high season with permission to summit was set at 720 pesos, and for international climbers at 3,000 pesos.
11. The Circle of Sportswriters and MÁS Sports named Orona the outstanding Mendoza athlete in 2000 from among other regional standouts in soccer, rugby, volleyball, swimming, cycling, boxing, basketball, and race-car driving.

Chapter 7. The Dream Weaver

1. On a seven-day permit, trekkers have permission to go no higher than Plaza de Mulas, 4,300 meters. Short-term permits for three days, as well as for one day, are also offered.

2. From 2002 to 2009, 83.89 percent of the summit permits issued were to international climbers (www.aconcagua.mendoza.gov.ar/estadisticas.pdf).

3. The vegetation ends at about 3,500–4,000 meters on Aconcagua, but it continues to 5,000 meters in the Himalayas (Kikstra 2005, 54).

4. This is also a problem for higher camps like Nido de Cóndores and Berlin. The park has recently initiated a more stringent policy of human waste removal.

5. I am alluding to both the book (1989) and the film (2004) of the same name, *Touching the Void*, which documents the ordeal in Peru of a British climber, Joe Simpson, who disappeared into a crevasse and later crawled his way back to base camp.

6. The very technical South Face routes are accessed via Confluencia.

7. See www.aconcagua-express.com/eng/guanacos_route.shtml.

8. Tupungato was first summited by Stuart Vines and Matthias Zürbriggen, members of the FitzGerald Aconcagua expedition of 1896–97. Paul Güssfeldt was the first European to summit Maipo, before his aborted attempt on Aconcagua in 1883.

9. While Berlin has been the traditional last high camp from which expeditions on the Normal Route leave for the summit, several agencies have started to avoid Berlin due to the crowded and unhygienic conditions there. Camp Cólera is one of the new campsites at relatively the same altitude.

10. Porteño (from the port) is the Spanish term used to refer to the inhabitants of the capital city, Buenos Aires.

11. See www.thenorthface.com/na/our-story.html.

12. See www.patagonia.com/web/us/contribution/patagonia.go?assetid=3351.

Chapter 8. Plaza de Mulas

1. This is according to the *Aconcagua Instructional Guide*, which the Mendocino government provides to trekkers and mountaineers entering the Aconcagua Provincial Park.

2. The forum participants asked for whom *El cim* was directed and if it was simply a narcissistic lovefest for Catalunya because TV-3 only broadcasts in Catalunya, not to mention that the show, web reports, and the online forum were in Catalan.

3. As reported in *Los Andes* by Nicolás García (2003a).

4. Its services are not those of a hotel but rather are those of a mountain lodge. It provides a different atmosphere and choice for climbers who choose to stay there rather than in a tent in lower Mulas. Although there is a fixed menu and serving schedule, café services are available throughout the day. There is a large dorm room for climbers on the third floor, as well as private accommodations on the second. The shared bathroom and shower facilities are located on the basement level.

5. See Logan (2006).

6. For a discussion of the Basque polemic in detail, see Logan (2006).

7. See Logan (2006).

Works Cited

Aconcagua: Techo de América. 1998. Mendoza: Internacional Video.

Aconcagua Instructional Guide. n.d. Mendoza: Gobierno de Mendoza, Ministerio de Ambiente y Obras Públicas.

Agüero, Pupi. 2003. "Cultura, patrimonio, y turismo." *Los Andes*, December 3. Accessed December 14, 2003. www.losandes.com.ar/nrc=161536.

Anderson, Benedict. 1983. *Imagined Communities: Reflections on the Origins and Spread of Nationalism*. London: Verso.

Appadurai, Arjun. 2000. "Grassroots Globalization and the Research Imagination." *Public Culture* 12:1–10.

Archetti, Eduardo P. 1999. *Masculinities: Football, Polo and the Tango in Argentina*. Oxford: Berg.

Ayassa, Eduardo Luis. 1997. "Aconcagua a 100 años de la primera cumbre." *Los Andes*, January 11, p. 9.

Balf, Todd. 1992. "Aconcagua-A-Go-Go: It Isn't Easy Being the World's Most Vogue Mountain." *Outside* (May): 27–28.

Bárcena, J. Roberto. 2001. "La infraestructura arquitéctonica incaica en relación con el sitio ceremonial de altura del Cerro Aconcagua: El caso de las estructuras de pirca del Cerro Penitentes y de Confluencia." In *El santuario incaico del cerro Aconcagua*, ed. Juan Schobinger, 361–375. Mendoza: EDIUNC.

Bass, Dick, Frank Wells, and Rick Ridgeway. 1986. *Seven Summits*. New York: Warner.

Bayers, Peter L. 2003. *Imperial Ascent: Mountaineering, Masculinity, and Empire*. Boulder: University Press of Colorado.

Beedie, Paul. 2003. "Adventure Tourism." In *Sport and Adventure Tourism*, ed. Simon Hudson, 203–236. Binghamton: Haworth.

Beedie, Paul, and Graham Bourne. 2005. "Media Constructions of Risk: A Case Study of the Stanforth Beck Incident." *Journal of Risk Research* 8, no. 3:331–339.

Bernstein, Richard J. 1983. *Beyond Objectivism and Relativism: Science, Hermeneutics and Praxis*. Philadelphia: University of Pennsylvania Press.

Beverley, John. 1999. *Subalternity and Representation: Arguments in Cultural Theory*. Durham, N.C.: Duke University Press.
Bhabha, Homi K. 1994. *The Location of Culture*. London: Routledge.
Bossi, Jesica. 2003. "De identidades y luchas: Entrevista: Ana María Spadafora." *Segundo enfoque: Periodismo por vocación*, March 2003. Accessed September 3, 2004. www.segundoenfoque.com.ar/spadafora.htm.
Boukreev, Anatoli. 1999. *The Climb*. New York: St. Martin's Griffin.
Braceli, Rodolfo. 2001. *De fútbol somos: La condición argentina*. Buenos Aires: Sudamericana.
Breashears, David. 2000. *High Exposure: An Enduring Passion for Everest and Unforgiving Places*. New York: Simon and Schuster.
Briones, Claudia. 2006. "Questioning State Geographies of Inclusion in Argentina: The Cultural Politics of Organizations with Mapuche Leadership and Philosophy." In *Cultural Agency in the Americas*, ed. Doris Sommer, 248–278. Durham, N.C.: Duke University Press.
Burnett, D. Graham. 2002. "'It Is Impossible to Make a Step without the Indians': Nineteenth-Century Geographical Exploration and the Amerindians of British Guiana." *Ethnohistory* 49, no. 1: 3–40.
Cabrera, Gabriel A. 2001. "El descubrimiento." In *El santuario incaico del cerro Aconcagua*, ed. Juan Schobinger, 20–25. Mendoza: EDIUNC.
Cafiero, Mario, and Javier Llorens. 2005. *La Argentina robada: El corralito, los bancos y el vaciamiento del sistema*. Buenos Aires: Macchi Grupo.
Campana, Carlos, and Jorge Omar Campana. 2004. "Los suizos y el primer ascenso al Aconcagua." *Los Andes*, February 2. Accessed June 7, 2007. www.losandes.com.ar/2004/0208/Especiales/Hechosypersonajesmendocinos/nota167327_1.htm.
Campana, Carlos, Jorge Campana, and Analía Boggia. 2004. *Memoria de los Mendocinos*, ed. Lorenzo Sartori. v.1–12: 1–127. Mendoza: *Los Andes*.
Candito, Claudia, director. n.d. *El sueño del Millcayac*. Mendoza: Realizaciones Sur.
Canessa, Andrew, ed. 2005. *Natives Making Nation: Gender, Indigeneity, and the State in the Andes*. Tucson: University of Arizona Press.
Carrasco, Morita. 2000. *De los derechos de los pueblos indígenas en Argentina*. Buenos Aires: Asociación de Communidades Aborigenes LHAKA HONHAT, IWGIA (International Work Group for Indigenous Affairs).
Castro-Gómez, Santiago. 2002. "No Longer Broad but Still Alien Is the World: The End of Modernity and the Transformation of Culture in the Times of Globalization." Trans. Mario Sáenz. In *Latin American Perspectives on Globalization: Ethics, Politics and Alternative Visions*, ed. Mario Sáenz, 25–39. Oxford: Rowman & Littlefield.
Centro de Documentación Mapuche. 2001. "Algunos viven del negocio de ser indio." March 19. Accessed September 18, 2006. www.mapuche.info/news02/metro010119.html.
Ceruti, María Constanza. 2001a. "La sacralidad de las montañas en el mundo andino: Ensayo de análisis simbólico." In *El santuario incaico del cerro Aconcagua*, ed. Juan Schobinger, 370–394. Mendoza: EDIUNC.
———. 2001b. "Apéndice II: Nuevo intento de ascensión del hallazgo." In *El santuario incaico del cerro Aconcagua*, ed. Juan Schobinger, 438. Mendoza: EDIUNC.

Clifford, James. 1997. *Routes: Travel and Translation in the Late Twentieth Century*. Cambridge: Harvard University Press.

Cloutier, Paul. 2003. "The Business of Adventure Tourism." In *Sport and Adventure Tourism*, ed. Simon Hudson, 241–272. Binghamton: Haworth.

Conway, Sir William Martin. 1899. "Aconcagua and the Volcanic Andes." In *Harper's New Monthly Magazine*, 109–124. New York: Harper and Brothers.

———. 1900. *The Alps from End to End*. Westminster, U.K.: Archibald Constable and Co.

———. 1902. *Aconcagua and Tierra del Fuego*. London: Cassel and Co.

Conefrey, Mike, and Tim Jordan. 2002. *Mountain Men: A History of the Remarkable Climbers and Determined Eccentrics Who First Scaled the World's Most Famous Peaks*. Cambridge, Mass.: Da Capo.

Corte, Arturo E. 2001. "Los emplazamientos rituales incas en el permafrost de los Andes (Observaciones paleoclimáticas)." In *El santuario incaico del cerro Aconcagua*, ed. Juan Schobinger, 61–76. Mendoza: EDIUNC.

Crouch, Gregory. 2002. *Enduring Patagonia*. New York: Random House.

Cruz, Juan Carlos. 2001. "Estudio en imagenología (radiología y tomografía computarizada)." In *El santuario incaico del cerro Aconcagua*, ed. Juan Schobinger, 89–93. Mendoza: EDIUNC.

Darwin, Charles. [1839] 2004. *The Voyage of the Beagle*. Washington, D.C.: National Geographic Adventure Series.

Davidson, Lee. 2008. "Tragedy in the Adventure Playground: Media Representations of Mountaineering Accidents in New Zealand." *Leisure Studies* 27, no.1: 3–19.

Davison, Guillermo, and Andrés Cuyul. 2007. *La organizacíon de los Pueblos Indígenas en Argentina: El caso de la ONPIA*. Buenos Aires: Los Gatos.

Deberle, Alfred Joseph. 1878. *Historia de la América del Sur desde su descubrimiento hasta nuestros días*. Barcelona: Jané Hermanos.

de la Cadena, Marisol. 2000. *Indigenous Mestizos: The Politics of Race and Culture in Cuzco, Peru*, 1919–1991. Durham, N.C.: Duke University Press.

Di Bari, Virginia. 2008. "Aconcagua: Temporada con más visitas y menos víctimas." *Los Andes*, May 5. Accessed June 30, 2008. www.losandes.com.ar/includes/modulos/imprimir.asp?id=357186&tipo=noticia.

Dickinson, Matt. 1999. *The Other Side of Everest: Climbing the North Face through the Killer Storm*. New York: Three Rivers Press.

Domicelj, Serge. 2003. "Mountain Motivations—The High Andes and Other Endeavors." Paper presented at the meeting for *Celebrating Mountains—An International Year of Mountains*, Jindayne, New South Wales, Australia.

Escolar, Diego. 2006. "Los Huarpes: De la invisibilidad a la visibilidad." CRICYT/CONICET. Accessed January 26, 2007. www.cricyt.edu.ar/imprimir.php?idnoticiaprint=36.

———. 2007. *Los dones étnicos de la Nación: Identidades huarpe y modos de producción de soberanía en Argentina*. Buenos Aires: Prometeo.

Fioquetta, Gladys. 1998. "La 'comunidad huarpe' bajo la lupa legislativa." *Uno*, July 21. Secretaria de Ayuda a Personas Afectadas por Sectas Destructivas. Accessed September 18, 2006. www.geocities.com/elause/diarios10.htm.

Fiore, Mario. 2000. "Bajo lluvia, Aconcagua 2000 abrió sus puertas." *Los Andes*, November 30. Accessed December 15, 2000. www.losandes.com.ar/notas/2000/11/30/economía-1507.asp.

Fiorucci, Flavia, and Marcus Klein, eds. 2005. *Argentine Crisis of the Millennium: Causes, Consequences and Explanations (CEDLA)*. Amsterdam: Aksant.

Fischer, Michael J. J. 1999. "Worlding Cyberspace: Toward a Critical Ethnography in Time, Space, and Theory." In *Critical Anthropology Now: Unexpected Contexts, Shifting Constituencies, Changing Agendas*, ed. George Marcus, 245–304. Santa Fe: School of American Research Press.

FitzGerald, Edward A. 1899. *The Highest Andes: A record of the first ascent of Aconcagua and Tupungato in Argentina, and the exploration of the surrounding valleys*. New York: Charles Scribner's Sons.

Franco, Jean. 1999. *Critical Passions: Selected Essays*. Durham, N.C.: Duke University Press.

"Fue presentado el documento final del TURPLAN II 2007–2011." 2007. *Diario online de la industria del turismo y la hospitalidad*. December 3. Accessed July 1, 2008. www.hostnews.com.ar/2007/ev/071339.htm.

Galdi, Fabián. 2003. "Experiencia en el Aconcagua: Honrar la vida." *Los Andes*, February 28. Accessed March 9, 2003. www.losandes.com.ar/imprimir.asp?nrc=112084.

Galeano, Eduardo. 1995. *El fútbol a sol y sombra*. Madrid: Siglo XXI.

Gallardo, Dario. 2001. "Inauguran obras en sitios históricos." *Los Andes*, August 8. Accessed August 31, 2001. www.losandes.com.ar/imprimir.asp?nrc=36592.

Gammelgaard, Lene. 2000. *Climbing High: A Woman's Account of Surviving the Everest Tragedy*. New York: Perennial.

García, María Elena, and José Antonio Lucero. 2004. "Un país sin indígenas? Rethinking Indigenous Politics in Peru." In *The Struggle for Indigenous Rights in Latin America*, ed. Nancy Grey Postero and Leon Zamosc, 158–188. Brighton, U.K.: Sussex.

García, Nicolás. 2003a. "Grajales: Es parte de nuestra cultura." *Los Andes*, January 25. Accessed March 12, 2003. www.losandes.com.ar/imprimir.asp?nrc=.

———. 2003b. "120 años de exploración en el Aconcagua." *Los Andes*, December 13. Accessed February 21, 2004. www.losandes.com.ar/imprimir.asp?nrc=112323.

———. 2004. "El volcán Tupungato, cerca de convertirse en parque nacional." *Los Andes*, June 27, 15A.

———. 2007. "Alfred Magnani, el Aconcagua al mundo." *Los Andes*, June 27. Accessed November 1, 2007. www.losandes.com.ar/imprimir.asp?nrc=384045.

García Canclini, Néstor. 2000. *La globalización imaginada*. Buenos Aires: Paidós.

Gasques, Marcus Vinicius. 2002. *Montanha em fúria: Aventura e drama no cerro Aconcágua, o maior pico das Américas*. São Paulo: Globo.

"Geographical Progress." 1902. In *Appleton's Annual Cyclopædia and Register of Important Events of the Year 1901*, 260–261. New York: D. Appleton & Company.

"Geography and Travels." 1885. In *The American Naturalist* 19, no. 2: 158–162.

Gil, Mariana. 2001. "Señalizan las Rutas Sanmartinianas." *Uno*, June 28, 10.

Gilardone, Liliana. 1990. *Aconcagua: Una Manera de Vivir*. Buenos Aires: Ediciones Gizeh, S.A.

Gordillo, Gastón, and Silvia Hirsch. 2003. "Indigenous Struggles and Contested Identities in Argentina: Histories of Invisibilization and Reemergence." *The Journal of Latin American Anthropology* 8, no.3: 4–30.

Gordon, Robert J. 2006. "Introduction." In *Tarzan Was an Eco-tourist and Other Tales in the Anthropology of Adventure*, ed. Luis A. Vivanco and Robert J. Gordon, 1–23. New York: Berghahn Books.

Gorostiaga, Sergio. 2003. "Los olvidados de siempre." *Rumbos* 15:18–26.

Graburn, Nelson H. H. 1995. "Tourism: The Sacred Journey." In *Hosts and Guests: The Anthropology of Tourism*, ed. Valene L. Smith, 21–36. Philadelphia: University of Pennsylvania Press.

"La gran aventura del Glaciar Horcones." 2005. *Los Andes*, January 12. Accessed January 15, 2005. www.losandes.com.ar/imprimir.asp?nrc=22821.

Güssfeldt, Paul. 1884. "Dr. Güssfeldt's Work in the Andes." *Proceedings of the Royal Geographical Society and Monthly Record of Geography New Monthly Series* 6(11): 658–661.

Hall, Stuart. 2000. "Old and New Identities." In *Culture, Globalization and the World System: Contemporary Conditions for the Representation of Identity*, ed. Anthony D. King, 40–68. Minneapolis: University of Minnesota Press.

Hannerz, Ulf. 2000. "Scenarios for Peripheral Cultures." In *Culture, Globalization and the World System: Contemporary Conditions for the Representation of Identity*, ed. Anthony D. King, 107–128. Minneapolis: University of Minnesota Press.

Hidalgo, Liliana. 2001. "Las rutas sanmartinianas estarán identificadas en toda Mendoza." *Los Andes*, June 28, 20.

Houston, David L. R. 2006. "Five Miles Out: Communion and Commodification among the Mountaineers." In *Tarzan Was an Eco-tourist and Other Tales in the Anthropology of Adventure*, ed. Luis A. Vivanco and Robert J. Gordon, 147–160. New York: Berghahn Books.

Huyssen, Andreas. 2000. "Present Pasts: Media, Politics, Amnesia." *Public Culture* 12, no. 1: 21–38.

Irwin, William Robert, ed. 1950. "Introduction to Tupungato Ascended." In *Challenge: An Anthology of the Literature of Mountaineering*, ed. Robert William Irving, 301. New York: Columbia University Press.

Jait, Luis. 2004. *Elogio de la desmesura: Una aventura de autosuperación en el Aconcagua*. Mendoza: Zeta.

Johnston, Barbara R., and Ted Edwards. 1994. "The Commodification of Mountaineering." *Annals of Tourism Research* 21, no.3: 459–478.

Kaplan, Caren. 1998. *Questions of Travel: Postmodern Discourses of Displacement*. Durham, N.C.: Duke University Press.

Kikstra, Harry. 2005. *Aconcagua: Summit of South America*. Landrick Lodge, U.K.: Rucksack Readers.

Kirschenblatt-Gimblett, Barbara. 1998. *Destination Culture: Tourism, Museums, and Heritage*. Berkeley: University of California Press.

Krakauer, Jon. 1998. *Into Thin Air: A Personal Account of the Mt. Everest Disaster*. New York: Anchor.

Lacoste, Pablo. 2000. *El Ferrocarril Trasandino 1872–1984: Un siglo de ideas, política y transporte en el sur de América*. Santiago, Chile: Editorial Universitaria.

——. 2002. "El Ferrocarril Trasandino y la construcción de la cordillera como espacio social (1893–1947)." Paper presented at VI Seminario Argentino Chileno de Ambiente, Humanidades y Relaciones Internacionales, Mendoza, May 27–29, 2002.

——. 2003. "Mendoza, provincia inteligente." *Los Andes*, February 17. Accessed June 15, 2003. www.losandes.com.ar/asp?nrc=.

Lanata, Jorge. 2003. *Argentinos II*. Buenos Aires: Ediciones B.

Langer, Erick D. 2003. "Introduction." In *Contemporary Indigenous Movements in Latin America*, ed. Erick Langer and Elena Muñoz, xi–xxix. Wilmington, Del.: Scholarly Resources.

Larson, Brooke. 2004. *Trials of Nation Making: Liberalism, Race, and Ethnicity in the Andes, 1810–1910*. Cambridge: Cambridge University Press.

Levin, Miriam. 2002. "Museums and the Democratic Order." *Wilson Quarterly*, Winter 2002:50–65.

Lilloy, Raúl. 1997. "La maldicón de la momia." Letter to the editor. *Los Andes*, January 21, 8.

Lledo, Pablo. 2001. "Nuevos productos y servicios reposicionan el sector turístico de Mendoza." *Los Andes*, June 18. Accessed July 8, 2001. www.losandes.com.ar/asp?nrc=27428.

Logan, Joy. 2006. "Crampons and Cookpots: The Democratization and Feminizations of Adventure on Aconcagua." In *Tarzan Was an Eco-tourist and Other Tales in the Anthropology of Adventure*, ed. Luis Vivanco and Robert Gordon, 161–178. New York: Berghahn Books.

Luna Rangel, Raymundo. 1996. *La ascención al Aconcagua*. México: Ediciones Gráficas Zeta.

Magnani, Alfredo. 1955. *Argentinos al Himalaya*. Buenos Aires: Fluixa.

Magnani, Alfredo, and Luis A. Parra. 1981. *Aconcagua, Argentina*. Mendoza: Ediciones Dhaulagiri.

Manitta, Sebastián. 2004. "El cuidado del patrimonio debería enseñarse en la escuela." *Los Andes*, March 18. Accessed March 18, 2004. www.losandes.com.ar/nrc=177294.

Manoni, Gisela. 2004. "El MERCOSUR impulsa el Camino del Inca como destino turístico." *Los Andes*, March 15. Accessed March 15, 2004. www.losandes.com.ar/nrc=176834.

Mariño, Viviana. 2001. "Beatriz Sarlo: 'Somos un país sin proyecto.'" *Los Andes*, May 6. Accessed October 21, 2002. www.losandes.co.ar/imprimir.asp?nrc=46478.

Martín Alcoff, Linda. 2002. "Foreword." In *Latin American Perspectives on Globalization: Ethics, Politics and Alternative Visions*, ed. Mario Sáenz, vii–xi. Oxford: Rowman & Littlefield.

Masa, Juan Isidro. 1978. *Toponimia, tradiciones y leyendas mendocinas*. Mendoza: Rotary Club Mendoza Sur.

Mason, Tony. 1995. *Passion of the People? Football in South America*. London and New York: Verso.

Masud, A. Rez. 1997. "Letter to the Editor." *Uno*, January 21.

Mathers, Kathryn, and Laura Hubbard. 2006. "Doing Africa: Travelers, Adventurers, and American Conquest of Africa." In *Tarzan Was an Eco-tourist and Other Tales in the Anthropology of Adventure*, ed. Luis Vivanco and Robert Gordon, 197–216. New York: Berghahn Books.

Mauss, Marcel, and Henri Hubert. 1898. "Essai sur la nature et la fonction du sacrifice." *L'Année sociologique* 2:29–138.

"Mendoza recibió más de 50 mil turistas durante los primeros días de enero." 2008. *Los Andes*, January 14. Accessed January 25, 2008. www.losandes.com.ar.imprimir.asp?nrc+419159.

Messner, Reinhold. 1999. *All Fourteen 8000ers*. Seattle, Wash.: The Mountaineers.

Michielli, Catalina Teresa. 1983. *Los huarpes protohistóricos*. San Juan: Universidad Nacional de San Juan.

Mignolo, Walter. 2002. "Globalization and the Borders of Latinity." In *Latin American Perspectives on Globalization: Ethics, Politics and Alternative Visions*, ed. Mario Sáenz, 77–101. Oxford: Rowman & Littlefield.

Mitchell, Richard G., Jr. 1983. *Mountain Experience: The Psychology and Sociology of Adventure*. Chicago: University of Chicago Press.

Mowforth, Martin, and Ian Munt. 2003. *Tourism and Sustainability: Development and New Tourism in the Third World*. London: Routledge.

Napier, A. David. 2006. "Avant-garde or Savant-garde: The Eco-tourist as Tarzan." In *Tarzan Was an Eco-tourist and Other Tales in the Anthropology of Adventure*, ed. Luis Vivanco and Robert Gordon, 73–90. New York: Berghahn Books.

Neate, Jill. 1994. *Mountaineering in the Andes: A Sourcebook for Climbers*. London: Royal Geographical Society.

Norman, Geoffrey. 2000. *Two for the Summit: My Daughter, the Mountains, and Me*. New York: Plume.

"Nuevo atropello a la espiritualidad e identidad de los Pueblos Originarios." 2006. Accessed March 14, 2007. http://argentina.indymedia.org/news/2006/09/443184.php.

Nunn, Paul. 1987. "Alpine Climbing." In *The Climbers Handbook*, ed. Audrey Salkeld, 134–199. San Francisco: Sierra Club Books.

Occhipinti, Laurie. 2003. "Claiming a Place: Land and Identity in Two Communities in Northwestern Argentina." *The Journal of Latin American Anthropology* 8, no.3: 155–174.

Olarra, G., Rafael Olarra Jiménez, and Raúl Vinuesa. 2002. *El derrumbe argentino: De la convertibilidad al "corralito."* Madrid: Planeta.

Ortiz, Fernando. [1947] 2003. *Cuban Counterpoint: Tobacco and Sugar*. New York: Knopf.

Ortner, Sherry B. 1996. *Making Gender: The Politics and Erotics of Culture*. Boston: Beacon Press.

———. 1999. *Life and Death on Mt. Everest: Sherpas and Himalayan Mountaineering*. Princeton: Princeton University Press.

Oviedo, Jorge Enrique. 1997. "Editorial." *Los Andes*, January 16, 8.

Palmer, Catherine. 2002. "'Shit Happens': The Selling of Risk in Extreme Sports." *The Australian Journal of Anthropology* 13, no.3: 323–336.

Pastor, Gabriel C., Laura M. Torres, Elma C. Montaña, and Elena M. Abraham. 2006. "Artesanías y desierto: Una aproximación a los fenómenos de desrerritorialización [*sic*] del patrimonio cultural huarpe." *Revista THEOMAI: Estudios sobre Sociedad, Naturaleza, y Desarrollo*, 13. Accessed July 1, 2008. http://revista-theomai.unq.edu.ar/NUMERO13/artpastor.htm.

Perón, Juan. 1953. "Prólogo." In *Historia del Aconcagua* by Mayor Orlando Mario Punzi, Mayor Valentín J. Ugarte, and Mario L. De Biasey, 8–9. n.p.

Pigna, Felipe. 2004. *Los mitos de la historia argentina: La construcción de un pasado como justificación del presente*. Buenos Aires: Grupo Norma.

Pimentel, Luz Aurora. 2004. "The Representation of Nature in Nineteenth-Century Narrative and Iconography." In *Literary Cultures of Latin America: A Comparative*

History, ed. Mario J. Valdés and Djelal Kadir, 156–172. Oxford: Oxford University Press.

Pincolini, Carlos Diego. 1997. "¿A quién pertenece la momia? ¿Debe restituirse?" Letter to the editor. *Los Andes*, January 25, 10.

Polidori, Celeste. 2001. "Las rutas del Libertador están listas para ser recorridas el 17." *Los Andes*, August 9. Accessed August 31, 2001. www.losandes.com.ar/imprimir.asp?nrc=93445.

Ponte, Jorge Ricardo. 1987. *Mendoza, aquella ciudad de barro. Historia de una ciudad andina desde el siglo XVI hasta nuestros días*. Mendoza: Municipalidad de la Ciudad de Mendoza.

Postero, Nancy Grey, and Leon Zamosc. 2004. "Indigenous Movements and the Indian Question in Latin America." In *The Struggle for Indigenous Rights in Latin America*, ed. Nancy Grey Postero and Leon Zamosc, 1–31. Brighton, U.K.: Sussex.

Pratt, Mary Louise. 1991. "Arts of the Contact Zone." *Profession* 91:33–40.

——. 2008. *Imperial Eyes: Travel Writing and Transculturation*. London: Routledge.

Punzi, Orlando Mario. 1978. *San Martín: El primer montañés de América*. Mendoza: Ediciones Culturales de Mendoza.

Quammen, David. 2004. "Introduction." In *The Voyage of the Beagle* by Charles Darwin, xv–xxii. Washington, D.C.: National Geographic Adventure Series.

La Quebrada del Sauce. 2007. "Pueblos Originarios Huarpes 'Comunidad Huaytamari.'" Accessed August 5, 2008. http://laquebradadelsauce.blogspot.com/2007/10/pueblos-originarios-huarpes-comunidad.html.

Quesada, María Sáenz. 2001. *La Argentina: Historia del país y de su gente*. Buenos Aires: Sudamericana.

Quijada, Mónica. 2004. "De mitos nacionales, definiciones cívicas y clasificaciones grupales. Los indígenas en la construcción nacional argentina, siglos XIX a XXI." In *Calidoscopio latinoamericano: Imágenes históricas para un debate vigente*, ed. Waldo Ansaldi. 425–450. Buenos Aires: Ariel.

Raía, Rubén Carlos. 1997. "Letter to the Editor." *Los Andes*, January 22, 8.

Rama, Angel. 1982. *Transculturación narrativa en América Latina*. México: Siglo Veintiuno.

Ramos, Carmen María. 2003. "Entre el deseo y la realidad." *Los Andes*, December 13. Accessed December 14, 2003. www.losandes.com.ar/nrc=161535.

Randis, Alejandro. 1991. *El Aconcagua: El Centinela de Piedra*. Mendoza: Zeta Editores.

"Recent Mountaineering." 1901. In *Quarterly Review* 194: 126–148.

"El regreso de Julián Weich." 2008. *Los Andes*, May 6. Accessed June 3, 2008. www.losandes.com.ar/notas/2008/6/5/estilo-362458.asp.

Rodowick, D. N. 2002. "Introduction: Mobile Citizens, Media States." *PMLA* 117, no.1: 13–23.

Ryan, Jim. 2004. *Aconcagua: Highest Trek in the World*. Milnthorpe, U.K.: Cicerone.

Sáenz, Mario. 2002. "Introduction: Periphery at the Core." In *Latin American Perspectives on Globalization: Ethics, Politics and Alternative Visions*, ed. Mario Sáenz, 1–24. Oxford: Rowman & Littlefield.

Sahalie Catalogue. 2006. Portland, Ore.

Said, Edward W. 1978. *Orientalism*. New York: Random House.

Sala, Germán. 2003. "Qué sectores mueve el turismo." *Los Andes*, July 20. Accessed July 28, 2003. www.losandes.com.ar/notas/2003/7/20/económico-78694.asp.

Salvatore, Ricardo D. 1999. "Re-discovering Spanish America: Uses of Travel Literature about South America in Britain." *Journal of Latin American Cultural Studies* 8, no.2: 199–217.

Sarmiento, Domingo Faustino. [1845] 2005. *Facundo. Civilización y barbarie*. Madrid: Cátedra.

Schobinger, Juan. 1995. *Aconcagua: Un enterratorio incaico a 5.300 metros de altura*. Mendoza: Author.

——. 1997a. "Letter to the Editor." *Los Andes*, January 14, 7.

——. 1997b."La momia del Aconcagua: Una falsa maldición." Letter to the editor. *Los Andes*, February 25, 6.

——. 2001a. "Apéndice I: "Diario de la expedición de investigación y rescate." In *El santuario incaico del cerro Aconcagua*, ed. Juan Schobinger, 436–437. Mendoza: EDIUNC.

——. 2001b. "La expedición de investigación y rescate. Descripción del yacimiento. Trabajos de laboratorio." In *El santuario incaico del cerro Aconcagua*, ed. Juan Schobinger, 26–48. Mendoza: EDIUNC.

——. 2001c. "Indicios arqueológicos en Confluencia (sector central de la quebrada de Horcones)." In *El santuario incaico del cerro Aconcagua*, ed. Juan Schobinger, 355–359. Mendoza: EDIUNC.

——. 2001d. "Introducción. La arqueología de la alta montaña. Exploraciones previas en la zona del Aconcagua." In *El santuario incaico del cerro Aconcagua*, ed. Juan Schobinger, 13–19. Mendoza: EDIUNC.

——. 2001e. "Los santuarios de altura y el Aconcagua: Aspectos generales e interpretativos." In *El santuario incaico del cerro Aconcagua*, ed. Juan Schobinger, 415–435. Mendoza: EDIUNC.

——, ed. 2001f. *El santuario incaico del cerro Aconcagua*. Mendoza: EDIUNC.

Secor, R. J. 1999. *Aconcagua: A Climbing Guide*. Seattle, Wash.: The Mountaineers.

Simmel, Georg. 1972. "The Adventurer." In *On Individuality and Social Forms*, 187–198. Chicago: University of Chicago Press.

Soriano, Fernando. 2009. "Con dolor y bronca, los andinistas defienden la 'ley de la montaña.'" *Clarín*, February 22. Accessed March 9, 2009. www.clarin.com/suplementos/zona/2009/02/22/z-01863781.htm.

Suttles, Gerald. 1983. "Foreword." In *Mountain Experience: The Psychology and Sociology of Adventure*, ed. Richard G. Mitchell Jr., vii–xii. Chicago: University of Chicago Press.

Swarbrooke, John, and Colin Beard, Suzanne Leckie, and Gill Pomfret. 2003. *Adventure Tourism: The New Frontier*. Oxford: Butterworth-Heinemann.

Tapia, Gonzalo. 2006. "Mendoza aprendió a vivir del turismo." *Los Andes*, September 28. Accessed June 15, 2007. www.losandes.com.ar/notas/2006/9/28/sociedad-208871.asp.

Taplin, Thomas E. 1992. *Aconcagua: The Stone Sentinel, Perspectives of an Expedition*. Santa Monica, Calif.: Eli Ely.

Taranto, Pablo. 2002. "Turismo: Comer y beber." *La voz del interior*. Accessed June 10, 2003. www.intervoz.com/2002/0414/suplementos/turismo/nota91882_1.htm.

Taylor, Diana. 1997. *Disappearing Acts: Spectacles of Gender and Nationalism in Argentina's "Dirty War."* Durham, N.C.: Duke University Press.

Triviño, Luis. 2004. "Mendocino, montañés?" *Los Andes*, July 11, 15A.

"El turismo es hoy en la Argentina, política de Estado." Accessed July 20, 2008. www.turismo.gov.ar/esp/menu.htm.

"El turista de enero gastó más que en 2006." 2007. *Uno*, February 1. Accessed February 15, 2007. http://diariouno.net.ar/imprimir.php?id=137402.

Turner, Victor. 1969. *The Ritual Process: Structure and Anti-structure*. Chicago: Aldine.

——. 1979. *Process, Performance, and Pilgrimage: A Study in Comparative Symbology*. New Delhi: Concept.

TurPlan. 2000. *Plan Estratégico de Desarrollo Turístico de Mendoza*. Subsecretaría de Turismo de la Provincia.

Urry, John. 1997. *The Tourist Gaze: Leisure and Travel in Contemporary Societies*. London: SAGE.

van Vuuren, Chris. 2000. "Why We Climb, Trek, and Backpack: Notions of Pilgrimage and Ritual and the Quest for the Other." *Journal of the Mountain Club of South Africa* 103:8–13.

Videla, María A., and Jorge A. Suárez. 2001. "El Aconcagua: Primeras ascenciones." In *El santuario incaico del cerro Aconcagua*, ed. Juan Schobinger, 51–53. Mendoza: EDIUNC.

Villafañe, Lorena. 2006. "Las mujeres mandan en Confluencia." *Los Andes*, February 5. Accessed February 15, 2006. www.losandes.com.ar/notas/2006/2/5/sociedad-182823.asp.

Vines, Stuart. 1950. "Tupungato Ascended." In *Challenge: An Anthology of the Literature of Mountaineering*, ed. William Robert Irwin, 301–321. New York: Columbia University Press.

Walker, Marina. 2003. "Las mujeres pisan fuerte en el Aconcagua." *Los Andes*, February 3. Accessed February 10, 2003. www.losandes.com.ar/asp?nrc=.

Warren, Jonathan. 2001. *Racial Revolutions, Antiracism and Indian Resurgence in Brazil*. Durham, N.C.: Duke University Press.

——. 2004. "Socialist *Saudades*: Lula's Victory, Indigenous Movements, and the Latin American Left." In *The Struggle for Indigenous Rights in Latin America*, ed. Nancy Grey Postero and Leon Zamosc, 217–231. Brighton, U.K.: Sussex.

Weathers, Beck. 2001. *Left for Dead: My Journey Home from Everest*. New York: Villard.

Whymper, Edward. 1893. *Scrambles amongst the Alps*. London: John Murray.

Wolff, Janet. 2000. "The Global and the Specific: Reconciling Theories of Culture." In *Culture, Globalization and the World System: Contemporary Conditions for the Representation of Identity*, ed. Anthony D. King, 161–173. Minneapolis: University of Minnesota Press.

Zamudia, Teodora. 2008. "Derecho de los pueblos indígenas." Accessed February 6, 2011. www.indigenas.bioetica.org/base-d.htm#N%C2%B0.

Zorrilla, Juan José. 1997. "El centenario del Centinela de Piedra." *Desnivel, Revista de Montaña* 126:28–43.

Index

About the Author

Joy Logan is a member of the Division of Spanish and Latin American and Iberian Studies and an affiliate faculty member of the International Cultural Studies Graduate Certificate program at the University of Hawai'i at Mānoa. Her research and publications have focused on issues of gender and ethnic identity construction, especially with respect to redemocratization, postmodernism, and creative and narrative expression in the Southern Cone. Most recently, her interests in tourism studies have taken her to west-central Argentina where she has conducted field research on adventure and high-altitude mountaineering.